the VERMONT FARM TABLE COOKBOOK

150 Home-Grown Recipes from

the Green Mountain State

the VERMONT FARM TABLE COOKBOOK

150 Home-Grown Recipes from the Green Mountain State

TRACEY MEDEIROS

Author of **Dishing Up Vermont**

Photographs by **Oliver Parini**

THE COUNTRYMAN PRESS · WOODSTOCK, VT.

CIP data are available.

The Vermont Farm Table Cookbook
978-1-58157-166-0

Published by The Countryman Press, P.O. Box 748, Woodstock, VT 05091

Distributed by W. W. Norton & Company, Inc., 500 Fifth Avenue, New York, NY 10110

Printed in the United States of America

10 9 8 7 6 5 4 3 2 1

The Countryman Press

Woodstock, Vermont

www.countrymanpress.com

I dedicate this book to my beautiful son, Peter, my nephews, Mason and Maxwell, and my niece, Lillian.

You inspire my passion for a healthier planet.

ACKNOWLEDGMENTS

My hope is that the profiles, recipes, and photographs in this book have put a face on the hardworking people who so very generously helped to make *The Vermont Farm Table Cookbook* an appetizing reality. A heartfelt thank you to all of the farmers, chefs, and food producers who work endlessly toward the common goal of building and maintaining healthy soil, which produces wholesome, sustainable foods that feed and promote wellness for communities. This book would not have been possible without you.

Thank you to the entire team at The Countryman Press, particularly Kermit Hummel, who gave me the opportunity to bring this book to life. Oliver Parini, my very talented photographer, for his beautiful images and helping to create a stunning book. To my recipes testers, Pamela Cohan and Justin Molson, for generously offering your feedback and for making sure that each contributor's recipe delivers. Finally, I must thank my caring husband, Peter, mother, Sheridan, and sister, Kelley, who make me believe that all things are possible. I am grateful for your undying support. Thank you.

A portion of the proceeds from the sale of this book will be donated to the Vermont Foodbank.

Contents

Vegetables 71

Sandwiches, Pizza, and Savory Pies 95

From Our Farms to Your Table

Vermont has long been considered the epicenter of all foods good and wholesome. This picturesque state of rolling farmlands and breathtaking mountain vistas offers a wonderful diversity of agriculture on its sprawling, earthy canvas. Farmers' markets and community-supported farms provide direct access to fresh, locally grown products while supporting the state's agricultural philosophy to bring the food to the people, know the source of your food, and support the local food chain.

The Vermont Farm Table Cookbook is a culinary tribute to Vermont's farmers, food producers, and chefs, and to the inestimable benefits of buying local. Vermonters' support of sustainable food systems not only enriches the landscape but promotes overall wellness for their communities.

Vermont farmers are at the top of the food chain, demonstrating the importance of mobilizing community support and commitment to buying and eating locally grown foods. This direct consumer connection to local food sources means that farmers and community tables have effectively forged an alliance, one in which consumers are proud to invest in local farms by willingly paying a fair market value for their food. By spending local dollars for local products, consumers are ensuring the economic health of the agricultural system and the preservation of their neighbors' farms for future generations. The Vermont farmers, chefs, and food producers who contributed the delectable recipes in this book strongly believe that what they do is more than a livelihood—it is a way of life that they hold dear.

Each recipe in this book is an edible story. Some are culinary heirlooms, handed down from generation to generation; contributors have skillfully created others. Patriotic Potato Salad, Leftover Roast Leg of Lamb Tacos, Apple-Stuffed Chicken Breasts, Maple Crème Brûlée—these are just a few of the delectable offerings waiting for you. Some dishes showcase specialty products; all are made with the highest quality ingredients to assure great taste in every bite. From robust and substantial comfort foods to luscious and delicate entrées, these mouthwatering creations will hasten your family to the table.

It is my hope that the variety of recipes and profiles in *The Vermont Farm Table Cookbook* will capture your interest and whet your appetite for more as you embark on a culinary exploration of the Green Mountain State. We offer you this appetizing collection of versatile, nutritious recipes from our farms to your forks!

BREAKFAST

CLEARY FAMILY FARM

John and Lauren Cleary began their farming careers leasing land in Burlington's Intervale. The two were eager to expand their operation and spent a number of years looking for their own farm. It was in Plainfield, under the shadow of Spruce Mountain, that they found a farmstead dating back to 1860, with deep loam soils, 35 acres of pasture, and a brand new barn, which was perfect for housing chickens and the rest of their livestock throughout the winter months. They revived the old farm and brought its fields back into production, and today the Cleary farm is a certified organic grazing operation that produces organic eggs, chickens, beef, pork and fresh milk.

Dutch Baby

SERVES 3 TO 4

This is a beautiful puffed pancake that is light and airy with golden hues. You can top it simply with maple syrup, lemon juice and confectioners' sugar, or add sautéed vegetables, crumbled bacon, or sausage gravy for a heartier breakfast.

4 tablespoons (2 ounces) unsalted butter
6 large eggs, lightly beaten
1/2 cup whole milk, room temperature
1/2 cup all-purpose flour

1. Preheat the oven to 425 degrees. Melt the butter in a 12-inch cast-iron skillet over medium-low heat.

2. With an electric mixer, beat the eggs and milk. Gradually add the flour until well combined.

3. Scrape the batter into the prepared skillet, using a rubber spatula, and distribute evenly. Bake until the edges are puffed and golden brown, 15 to 20 minutes. Serve immediately.

Cleary Family Farm

TYLER PLACE FAMILY RESORT

Located on a mile of private lakeshore on Lake Champlain, the Tyler Place Family Resort is surrounded by natural beauty. Since 1933, this Vermont country inn has been offering all-inclusive family vacations and is rated among the top 10 family-friendly destination resorts in the United States.

Local foods are the key to their menu. The Tyler Place is committed to supporting local purveyors of fresh products. The chef, kitchen staff, and food manager seek out the best the area has to offer, from local dairies to vegetable growers, creameries to smokehouses.

Crème Brûlée French Toast

SERVES 6 TO 8

4 cups half-and-half
1 cup pure Vermont maple syrup
3 large eggs, lightly beaten
1 1/2 teaspoons vanilla extract
2 loaves challah bread, sliced 3/4 to 1 inch thick, slices cut in half
8 tablespoons (4 ounces) unsalted butter
1 cup packed light brown sugar
Confectioners' sugar

1. Lightly grease two 9 x 13-inch baking pans. In a large bowl, whisk together the half-and-half, maple syrup, eggs, and vanilla. Place the bread slices in a single layer in the prepared pans. Divide the custard mixture between the two pans, pouring it evenly over the bread, and press on the bread to allow it to absorb the liquid. Cover with plastic wrap and refrigerate overnight.

2. Preheat the oven to 350 degrees. Cover the pans with foil and bake until the custard is set, 25 to 30 minutes. Remove from the oven and let cool slightly.

3. Meanwhile, combine the butter and brown sugar in a small saucepan over medium-low heat and cook, whisking occasionally, until the butter is melted and the sugar is dissolved.

4. Drizzle the French toast with the brown sugar mixture, dust with confectioners' sugar, if desired, and serve.

Tyler Place Family Resort

Pecan and Caramel French Toast Soufflé

SERVES 6

Chefs at the Stowe Mountain Lodge use dinner rolls from Red Hen Baking Company, eggs from Maple Meadow Farms, and maple sugar from the Green Mountain Maple Sugar Refining Company in this rich, creamy, aromatic custard.

4 large eggs, lightly beaten
1 1/2 cups whole milk
1 cup heavy cream
3/4 cup granulated sugar
1 teaspoon grated nutmeg
1/2 tablespoon ground cinnamon
1 teaspoon vanilla extract
8 (3-inch) day-old dinner rolls
8 tablespoons (4 ounces) unsalted butter, room temperature
1/3 cup packed light brown sugar
6 tablespoons maple sugar, crumbled
1/2 cup pecans, toasted and coarsely chopped
Pure Vermont maple syrup
Confectioners' sugar

1. In a large bowl, whisk together the eggs, milk, cream, granulated sugar, nutmeg, cinnamon, and vanilla.

2. Lightly grease a 9-inch square baking pan. Cut each roll in half horizontally, and place cut side down in the prepared pan (the rolls should fit snugly in the dish). Pour the custard mixture over the rolls and press on the rolls to allow them to absorb the liquid. Cover with plastic wrap and refrigerate overnight.

3. Preheat the oven to 400 degrees. With an electric mixer, cream together the butter, brown sugar, and maple sugar. Fold in the pecans.

4. Turn the rolls cut side up and spoon about 1 tablespoon of the butter mixture onto each roll. Bake until the custard is set, about 40 minutes. Let cool slightly. Drizzle with maple syrup, dust with confectioners' sugar, if desired, and serve.

The Stowe Mountain Lodge

FROM THE GROUND UP

When Abby Knapp and Matt Tucker became sensitive to gluten, they decided to adopt a gluten-free diet based on their doctor's recommendation. The two wanted to continue to enjoy eating baked goods, but finding whole foods that were delicious and gluten-free was a challenge. They began experimenting with whole grains in order to create their own recipes. Making their own flour from whole sorghum, rice, buckwheat, and millet, the couple created gluten-free flours and flour mixes.

Abby and Matt enjoyed this creative process so much that they decided to open From the Ground Up Bakery so they could share their wholesome treats and milled flours with others. All their products were made with whole grains and no starches, in a dedicated, gluten-free kitchen. The business was committed to building partnerships with local farmers by purchasing eggs, vegetables, fruits, and gluten-free grains from them whenever possible.

Before they closed the bakery in 2012 they published a cookbook featuring all the recipes from the bakery, *Gluten-Free Baking with From the Ground Up*. Through their book, blog, and cooking classes, Knapp and Tucker continue to promote and support local growers, educate eaters about gluten-free grain processing, and suggest ways to grow gluten-free grains at home.

Whole-Grain Waffles

MAKES 4 (8-INCH) BELGIAN WAFFLES

These hearty, healthy waffles are delicious served for breakfast or with ice cream as dessert.

1 1/4 cups sorghum flour
1/2 cup buckwheat flour
1/4 cup millet flour
1 teaspoon baking soda
1/2 teaspoon ground cinnamon
1/4 teaspoon salt
1 1/2 cups milk
2 large eggs
1 tablespoon Vermont honey
1 tablespoon vegetable oil
1/2 teaspoon vanilla extract
Pure Vermont maple syrup (optional)
Blueberries, blackberries and/or raspberries
    (optional)
Butter (optional)

1. In a medium bowl, sift together the sorghum, buckwheat, and millet flours, baking soda, cinnamon, and salt.

2. In a second medium bowl, whisk together the milk, eggs, honey, oil, and vanilla. Add the wet ingredients to the dry and stir until just combined (the batter will be slightly runny). Do not overmix. Let the batter rest for at least 10 minutes or up to overnight.

3. Preheat the waffle iron according to the manufacturer's directions, then lightly spray with nonstick cooking spray. Ladle or spoon the batter onto the prepared iron, making sure not to overfill it. Cook until the waffles are golden brown and crispy. Repeat with the remaining batter. Serve with maple syrup, berries, and butter, if desired.

From the Ground Up

Variation: For a vegan alternative, substitute 2 tablespoons of ground flaxseeds mixed with 6 tablespoons warm water for the eggs.

Variation: For pancakes, lightly grease a griddle or skillet. Using a 1/4-cup measure, spoon the batter onto the prepared griddle and cook until bubbles begin to form, about 3 minutes. Flip the pancakes and cook until golden brown, about 2 minutes.

THE WARREN STORE

The Warren Store was built in 1839, as a midway stagecoach stop between Boston and Montreal. It is nestled in picturesque Warren, in the Mad River Valley. Fun and always funky, the Warren Store wears many different hats. First and foremost, the store is the social hub of the community and a favorite meeting place of locals and visitors alike. The store has a wonderful deli and bakery where all of the products are made from scratch, using local ingredients whenever possible. There is also an award-winning wine shop and a boutique that showcase an array of men's and women's clothing (both fashionable and functional), accessories, jewelry, toys, and housewares.

Harvest Hash

SERVES 8 TO 10

This recipe is sweet and smoky with big, bold, earthy flavors. The cooks at the Warren Store use Green Mountain Smokehouse bacon. Serve the hash as a hearty side dish for breakfast or dinner.

1 pound Brussels sprouts, trimmed and halved
3 pounds butternut squash (1 large), peeled, seeded, and diced
1 large sweet potato (about 1 pound), peeled and diced
2 medium red potatoes (about 1 pound), peeled and diced
3 tablespoons olive oil

12 ounces (about 12 slices) maple-cured bacon, chopped into 1/2-inch strips
3 McIntosh apples, peeled, cored, and diced
1 shallot, diced
2 garlic cloves, minced
1 tablespoon chopped fresh thyme
1 cup Vermont apple cider
4 ounces Vermont cheddar cheese, shredded (about 1 cup)

1. Preheat the oven to 350 degrees. Lightly grease a baking sheet and set aside.

2. Place the Brussels sprouts, squash, sweet potato, red potatoes and olive oil in a large bowl and toss to coat. Spread the vegetables in a single layer on the prepared baking sheet. Season generously with salt and pepper. Roast the vegetables, stirring occasionally, until fork-tender, about 50 minutes.

3. Cook the bacon in a large skillet over medium-high heat until crisp, about 7 minutes. Reduce the heat to medium, add the apples, shallot, garlic, and thyme, and sauté until soft and translucent, about 3 minutes. Add the vegetables and cider, bring to a simmer and cook until the liquid is absorbed, about 1 minute. Season with salt and pepper to taste. Spoon the hash onto plates, sprinkle the cheddar over the top, and serve.

The Warren Store

NEW LEAF ORGANICS

New Leaf Organics is located in the Champlain Valley, on the town line between Bristol and Monkton. In 2001, Jill Kopel began transforming what had been a small dairy farm for many years into an organic vegetable and flower farm. Of the 90-acre farm, 4 acres of land are in production and mostly devoted to vegetables. The flower gardens are beautiful and give inspiration to visitors. Every "flattish" piece of ground is planted during the growing season. The rest of the farm sits high above the road offering great views of Hogback Ridge. People who live within a 20-mile radius of the farm enjoy most of the food they produce. New Leaf Organics offers CSA shares, participates in two farmers' markets, and has wholesale accounts in Middlebury and Burlington. Their farmstand offers mostly vegetable, herb, and flower plants in the spring and then produce when it becomes available. Their flowers show up at events throughout Chittenden and Addison counties. New Leaf is a labor of love for Kopel, her husband, Skimmer Hellier, and their children, Ruby and Ada.

Spring Frittata

SERVES 6

This is one of the Kopel family's favorite breakfast recipes. It is delicate and creamy, with subtle layers of flavor. Any slightly tangy, full-bodied raw-milk cheese can be used in place of the Orb Weaver cheese here.

3 medium yellow potatoes, quartered
    and thinly sliced

Kosher salt and freshly ground black pepper

7 large eggs, lightly beaten

1/2 teaspoon chopped fresh rosemary,
    plus extra for garnish

1/2 teaspoon chopped fresh sage,
    plus extra for garnish

2 tablespoons (1 ounce) unsalted butter

1 small zucchini, finely diced

1 large shallot, minced (about 3 tablespoons)

3 garlic cloves, minced

8 ounces baby spinach leaves, rinsed,
    dried, and coarsely chopped

3 ounces Orb Weaver Farmhouse cheese,
    crumbled (3/4 cup)

1 1/2 ounces Grana Padano cheese,
    grated (3/4 cup)

1. Combine the potatoes and 1/2 teaspoon salt in a medium saucepan, cover with cold water, and bring to a boil over medium-high heat. Cook until the potatoes are just tender, about 10 minutes. Drain in a colander and set aside.

2. In a medium bowl, whisk together the eggs, rosemary, sage, and salt and pepper to taste.

3. Adjust an oven rack to the top position and heat the broiler. Melt the butter in a 12-inch broiler-proof nonstick skillet over medium heat. Add the zucchini and cook until tender, about 5 minutes. Add the shallots and garlic and cook until soft and translucent, about 3 minutes. Add the spinach and cook until just wilted, about 2 minutes. Add the potatoes and cook for 2 minutes more.

4. Spread the vegetables evenly over the bottom of the pan. Pour the egg mixture over the vegetables. Using a spatula, gently lift up the vegetable mixture along the sides of the skillet to allow the egg mixture to flow underneath. Sprinkle with the Orb Weaver cheese. Reduce the heat to medium-low and cook until the frittata is almost set but still slightly runny.

5. Place the skillet under the broiler and broil until the frittata is puffed and golden brown, about 3 minutes. Let rest for 5 minutes, then, using a rubber spatula, loosen the frittata from the skillet and carefully slide onto a platter. Top with the Grana Padano cheese. Cut into wedges, sprinkle with rosemary and sage, and serve.

New Leaf Organics

BREADS

KING ARTHUR FLOUR

Founded in 1790, King Arthur Flour is the oldest flour company in America. The bakery, baking education center, café, and store are located in Norwich. King Arthur Flour's fundamental mission is to support and seek to expand all aspects of baking by being the highest quality product, information, and education resource for, and inspiration to, bakers worldwide. The company has been employee-owned since 1996.

INGREDIENTS	WEIGHT	BAKER'S PERCENTAGE
Sifted whole-wheat pastry flour	.545 kg	100%
Sugar	.136 kg	25%
Baking powder	.032 kg	6%
Salt	.003 kg	.5%
Butter, cold	.136 kg	25%
Currants	.109 kg	20%
Heavy cream	290 kg	53.1%
Buttermilk	205 kg	37.5%
Eggs, large	1 (.06 kg)	11%

Currant Scones

MAKES 12 TO 14 SCONES

These scones are in the Irish style—moist, rich, and light. They are made daily at the King Arthur Flour Bakery. Cranberries can substitute nicely for the currants, or the dried fruit can be omitted entirely.

4 1/3 cups sifted whole-wheat pastry flour
1/2 cup plus 1 tablespoon granulated sugar
3 tablespoons baking powder
1/2 teaspoon salt
8 tablespoons (4 ounces) unsalted butter, cut into small pieces
1 cup dried currants or cranberries
1 cup plus 3 tablespoons heavy cream
1 cup buttermilk
1 large egg

1. Preheat the oven to 425 degrees. Spray a baking sheet with nonstick cooking spray and set aside.

2. Using a stand mixer fitted with the paddle attachment, mix together the flour, sugar, baking powder, and salt. Add the butter and beat on low speed until the mixture forms pea-sized lumps. Add the currants and mix just until combined.

3. In a small bowl, whisk together the cream, buttermilk, and egg. Add to the dry mixture and stir by hand just until combined.

4. Using a 1/2-cup scoop, portion the dough onto the prepared baking sheet. Bake until the tops are slightly springy, 15 to 18 minutes. Serve warm.

Note: If desired, in step 4 whisk 1 large egg with 2 tablespoons milk or water and brush over the tops of the scones before baking them.

King Arthur Flour

Rory's Irish Scones

MAKES 54 SMALL SCONES

The Pearces' friends Darina and Tim Allen own and operate the esteemed Ballymaloe Cookery School in Shanagarry, Ireland; this quick and easy recipe is from Darina's brother, chef Rory O'Connell. At Simon Pearce's restaurant, they make these scones using King Arthur unbleached bread flour. Serve these scones with soups, salads, or main courses; they are perfect any time.

4 cups bread flour, plus extra for rolling
1/2 heaping teaspoon baking soda
1 teaspoon salt
1/2 heaping teaspoon granulated sugar
2 cups buttermilk

1. Preheat the oven to 400 degrees. Lightly flour a baking sheet and set aside.

2. Sift the flour, baking soda, salt, and sugar into a large mixing bowl. Make a well in the center of the dry mixture and add the buttermilk. Mix together by hand until thoroughly combined. (Be careful not to overwork the dough; it should be light and springy to the touch).

3. Turn the dough out onto a well-floured surface and form into a large rectangle. Using a rolling pin and extra flour as needed, roll the dough into a 9 x 6-inch rectangle about 3/4 inch thick.

   Cut the dough into 9 strips about 1 inch wide, then cut each of the strips into six 1-inch squares.

4. Arrange the dough squares on the prepared baking sheet in nine rows of six, so they are just barely touching. (As they rise in the oven, the scones will merge together.) Bake until the scones are golden brown, 17 to 20 minutes, rotating the baking sheet halfway through the baking time. Let the scones cool on the baking sheet for 5 minutes, then remove them from the sheet and gently separate them before serving.

Simon Pearce

Organic Milk Biscuits

MAKES 12 BISCUITS

These biscuits are light and airy with a hint of creaminess, which emanates from within. Dropping the biscuits onto the baking sheet avoids overworking the dough, which could lead to toughness. To give the biscuits a nice, savory twist, incorporate some fresh herbs into the dough. At Kimball Brook Farm, they use their own organic butter and milk, along with organic flour from King Arthur Flour.

2 cups all-purpose flour
1 tablespoon baking powder
1/2 teaspoon salt
6 tablespoons (3 ounces) unsalted butter,
    cut into pieces and chilled
1 cup whole milk, cold

1. Preheat the oven to 425 degrees.

2. In a large bowl, sift together the flour, baking powder and salt. Using a fork or your fingertips, cut in the butter until the flour mixture resembles crumbs.

3. Make a well in the center of the flour mixture and slowly pour in the milk. Stir until the dough just starts to come together. Do not overmix.

4. Spoon or scoop about 1/4 cup of dough for each biscuit onto an ungreased baking sheet. Press down gently on each biscuit. Bake until golden brown, about 15 minutes.

Kimball Brook Farm

Nana's Caraway Seed Biscuits

MAKES ABOUT 18 BISCUITS

These biscuits come from Mary Moran, owner of High Ridge Meadows Farm in East Randolph. Moran's grandmother taught her how to make caraway seed biscuits many years ago. Her grandmother would make them for the extended family every week, never measuring the ingredients; just a handful of this and a pinch of that. You can use between 2 and 3 tablespoons of caraway seeds, depending on how "seedy" you like your biscuits. They are delicious and easy to make; serve them alongside a hearty meal or on their own, with butter and a drizzle of honey, if desired.

1/4 cup shortening, lard, or unsalted butter
2 1/2 cups whole milk
1 tablespoon granulated sugar
2 tablespoons active dry yeast
5 cups all-purpose flour, or as needed
2–3 tablespoons caraway seeds
2 teaspoons salt

1. Melt the shortening in a medium saucepan over medium heat. Add the milk and sugar and heat until very warm, about 110 degrees. Remove from the heat and add the yeast. Let stand for 2 minutes or until bubbles begin to form.

2. Combine the flour, caraway seeds, and salt in a large bowl. Stir in the yeast mixture until a soft dough forms. Cover with a damp dishcloth and let rise in a warm place until the dough doubles in volume, about 45 minutes.

3. Preheat the oven to 375 degrees. Lightly grease a baking sheet. Roll the dough out and cut with a 2-inch biscuit cutter, or simply tear pieces off with your fingers and form biscuits.

Place the biscuits on the prepared baking sheet. Cover with a damp dishcloth and let rise in a warm place until the dough doubles in volume, about 45 minutes. Bake until golden brown, about 20 minutes. Serve.

High Ridge Meadows Farm

Hush Puppies

MAKES ABOUT 20 HUSH PUPPIES

New Mexico chile powder is a mildly hot chile powder made from grinding whole, dried New Mexico chiles, seeds, and pods. Serve these hush puppies with Spicy Mayo (page 181).

8 cups peanut oil

2 large eggs, lightly beaten

1 cup buttermilk

1 small onion, grated

1/2 cup chopped pickled jalapeños

1 2/3 cups cornmeal

1/3 cup all-purpose flour

2 teaspoons baking powder

1 1/2 teaspoons New Mexico chile powder

1 teaspoon granulated sugar

1 teaspoon kosher salt

1/2 teaspoon baking soda

1. Heat the oil in a large, heavy-bottomed saucepan over medium-high heat to 350 degrees. (The oil should measure about 3 inches deep.)

2. In a medium bowl whisk together the eggs and buttermilk. Stir in the onion and pickled jalapeños. In a large bowl, stir together the cornmeal, flour, baking powder, chile powder, sugar, salt, and baking soda. Add the buttermilk mixture and stir until just combined.

3. Using a small scoop or two spoons, drop the batter, one scoop at a time, into the prepared oil. (Cooking the hush puppies in batches of four works well). Fry until golden brown, turning occasionally with a spoon to brown on all sides, 1 to 2 minutes. Remove the hush puppies with a slotted spoon and drain on paper towels. Serve immediately.

The Pitcher Inn

BUTTERWORKS FARM

Butterworks Farm, located in Westfield, is known as one of New England's most successful organic dairy farms. Starting off with 60 acres, back in 1976, the farm now spans 300 acres and produces 7,000 quarts of yogurt each week. This whole process is done within a three-day timespan—Monday, Tuesday, and Wednesday for processing the milk, and Thursday for delivery. The freshness is undeniable!

The owners, Jack and Anne Lazor, believe in taking care of the soil. They have always tried to put more back into their land than they take from it. The couple believes in "nourishing the soil so that it can nourish us."

Butterworks Farm has grown from solely producing yogurt to now offering kefir, heavy cream, buttermilk, cornmeal, wheat berries, whole-wheat flour, spelt flour, and rye flour, as well as a variety of beans. The Lazors have learned that each year that they are farming brings a different set of circumstances, giving them a chance to vary the way they do things. The Lazors daughter Christine and her husband, Collin Mahoney, along with their two daughters, Ginny and Ursala, live in a second house on the property. They have become partners in the business and are learning the ropes with a view toward carrying Butterworks Farm into the future.

Maple Cornbread

SERVES 8 TO 10

This slightly sweet, dense, sturdy cornbread showcases Butterworks Farm's Early Riser cornmeal. Early Riser is made from open-pollinated corn grown on the farm from seed that is selected from the highest quality ears. Only heavy, hard-textured, deep orange kernels make the cut. The careful selection produces fresh-tasting cornmeal with a natural sweetness not found in industrially produced versions. Maple syrup reinforces the natural sweetness of the corn.

1 cup coarse cornmeal
1 cup whole-wheat pastry flour
1 tablespoon baking powder
1 teaspoon salt
4 tablespoons (2 ounces) unsalted butter
1 cup buttermilk
1/2 cup pure Vermont maple syrup
2 large eggs, lightly beaten
Vermont honey, for drizzling

1. Preheat the oven to 400 degrees. Spray an 8-inch square baking pan with nonstick cooking spray and set aside.

2. In a large bowl, combine the cornmeal, flour, baking powder, and salt. Melt the butter in a medium saucepan and set aside to cool slightly then whisk in the buttermilk, maple syrup, and eggs. Make a well in the center of the dry ingredients and pour in the wet mixture. Stir just to combine.

3. Pour the batter into the prepared pan and smooth with a spatula. Bake until golden brown and a toothpick inserted in the center comes out clean, about 25 minutes. Let cool for 10 minutes. Serve drizzled with honey, if desired.

Pamela Cohan

TWO BLACK SHEEP FARM

Two Black Sheep Farm, located in South Hero, Vermont, is a little slice of agricultural paradise. When farm owners Kurt Sherman and Erik Van Hauer, decided to start a CSA business back in 1992, they originally called it Swallow Farm. In 2011, it was renamed Two Black Sheep Farm, after two black Romney Marsh sheep. The farm is located on 3 acres overlooking Lake Champlain, just before the Grand Isle Ferry. The owners have a little more than half an acre of tilled land, where they grow as many different vegetables and fruits as can be squeezed in. These are grown in an organic and sustainable manner. For many CSA members, the connection to the farm is as valuable as the produce they receive. When members pick up their share at the farm, they have the opportunity to connect with the source of their food and to learn more about sustainable agriculture. Members also enjoy receiving the weekly Two Black Sheep Newsletter, which contains photos and reports from the field, news, events, recipes, and more.

Zucchini Bread

MAKES 2 LOAVES

The zucchini bread recipe came from Kurt Sherman's grandmother, Hetty Sherman. When he first made this bread, Kurt didn't know the difference between "dice," "chop," and "purée" so he wound up puréeing the zucchini instead of shredding it. The accidental result produced a loaf of bread that the entire family found appealing. Sherman has baked these zucchini loaves on many special occasions and once made 120 loaves in a single day, as favors to be given to guests attending his daughter and son-in-law's wedding. (Fortunately, he had some help from the groom-to-be.)

3 large eggs, lightly beaten
1 cup canola or vegetable oil
1 tablespoon vanilla extract
3 cups all-purpose flour
2 cups granulated sugar
1 tablespoon ground cinnamon
1 teaspoon grated nutmeg
1 teaspoon sea salt
1 teaspoon baking soda
1/2 teaspoon baking powder
2 cups puréed unpeeled zucchini
1 cup raisins, chopped walnuts, or chocolate chips (optional)

1. Preheat the oven to 350 degrees. Spray two 9 x 5-inch loaf pans with nonstick cooking spray and lightly dust with flour. Set aside.

2. Whisk together the eggs, oil, and vanilla.

3. Sift together the flour, sugar, cinnamon, nutmeg, sea salt, baking soda, and baking powder. Add the flour mixture to the wet ingredients and stir until smooth. Stir in the zucchini and raisins, nuts, or chocolate chips, if using. Pour into the prepared loaf pans and bake until a toothpick inserted into the center of the bread comes out clean, about 1 hour.

4. Let the bread cool in the pans for about 15 minutes, then turn the loaves out onto a cooling rack. Let cool completely before serving.

Two Black Sheep Farm

Buttermilk Doughnuts

MAKES ABOUT 30 DOUGHNUTS

These tender buttermilk doughnuts appear on the Reluctant Panther's dessert list in the fall, accompanied by Spiced Cider Semifreddo (page 225), Autumn Spice Crème Anglaise (page 183), and Apple Cider Caramel Sauce (page 185). The dessert trio is a play on traditional apple orchard offerings using fresh, local cider in the semidfreddo and with doughnuts made in-house, as you would get them at the apple orchard.

3 1/2 cups all-purpose flour
1 1/2 tablespoons baking powder
1/4 teaspoon baking soda
1 teaspoon salt
3 large eggs plus 1 large egg yolk
1 1/4 cups granulated sugar
1 cup buttermilk
1 1/2 tablespoons vanilla extract
8 cups canola oil

1. Whisk together the flour, baking powder, baking soda, and salt in a large bowl. In a separate bowl, whisk together the eggs, yolk, and sugar until light and fluffy. Whisk in the buttermilk and vanilla. Fold the wet ingredients into the dry ingredients until a soft batter forms. Refrigerate the batter for at least 6 hours, or preferably overnight.

2. Heat the oil in a large, heavy-bottomed saucepan over medium-high heat to 275 degrees. (The oil should measure about 3 inches deep.) Using a 2-inch scoop, drop the batter in small batches into the hot oil and fry until golden brown, turning occasionally to brown on all sides, 4 to 5 minutes. (Do not crowd the pot.) Using a slotted spoon, remove the doughnuts and drain on paper towels. Serve.

The Reluctant Panther Inn and Restaurant

Hungarian Nokedli (Dumplings)

SERVES 4

Pitchfork Farm is a 16-acre organic vegetable farm located at the Intervale in Burlington, Vermont. The co-owners, Eric Seitz and Rob Rock, grow over 30 varieties of crops, which can be found in local restaurants and grocery stores. The partners are committed to growing only the highest quality fresh produce to sustain themselves, the land and the Vermont community. These little dumplings, a recipe from Seitz's grandmother, are a superb complement to Chicken Paprika (page 127).

Kosher salt
2 cups all-purpose flour
2 large eggs, lightly beaten
1/2 cup water, plus extra as needed
1 tablespoon unsalted butter
Grated Parmesan cheese
Chopped fresh parsley

1. Bring 3 quarts water and 1 tablespoon salt to a boil in a large saucepan. In a medium bowl, stir together the flour and 1/2 teaspoon salt. Make a well, add the eggs and water, and stir until a wet and sticky dough begins to form. (If necessary, add more water so that the dough is soft enough to press through a spaetzle maker.)

2. Working in batches, press the dough through a spaetzle maker and add the dumplings to the boiling water. Cook until the dumplings have floated to the surface, about 2 minutes per batch. Scoop out with a small sieve or slotted spoon and transfer to a large bowl.

3. Toss the spaetzle with the butter and Parmesan and season with salt to taste. Sprinkle with parsley and serve.

Pitchfork Farm

Note: If you don't have a spaetzle maker, you can push the dough through the largest holes in a box grater.

Caribbean Cornbread

MAKES 15 TO 18 PIECES

Conant's uses Early Riser Cornmeal from Butterworks Farm in this cornbread. If you can't find it, use any good whole-grain cornmeal.

1 cup all-purpose flour

1 cup cornmeal

2 tablespoons baking soda

3/4 cup granulated sugar

1 teaspoon kosher salt

16 tablespoons (8 ounces) unsalted butter, melted

4 large eggs, lightly beaten

1 1/2 cups fresh corn kernels and juice (cut from about 2 ears corn)

1/2 cup crushed pineapple, drained well

4 ounces mild or sharp cheddar cheese, shredded (1 cup)

1. Preheat the oven to 350 degrees. Spray a 9 x 13-inch baking pan with nonstick cooking spray and set aside.

2. In a large bowl, combine the flour, cornmeal, baking soda, sugar, and salt. In a medium bowl, whisk together the butter and eggs. Fold in the corn with its juice, pineapple, and 3/4 cup of the cheddar cheese. Make a well in the center of the dry ingredients and pour in the wet mixture. Stir until just combined.

3. Pour the batter into the prepared pan and smooth with a spatula. Sprinkle the remaining 1/4 cup cheese over the top. Bake until golden brown and a toothpick inserted into the center comes out clean, 35 to 40 minutes.

Conant's Riverside Farm/Riverside Produce

SOUPS AND SALADS

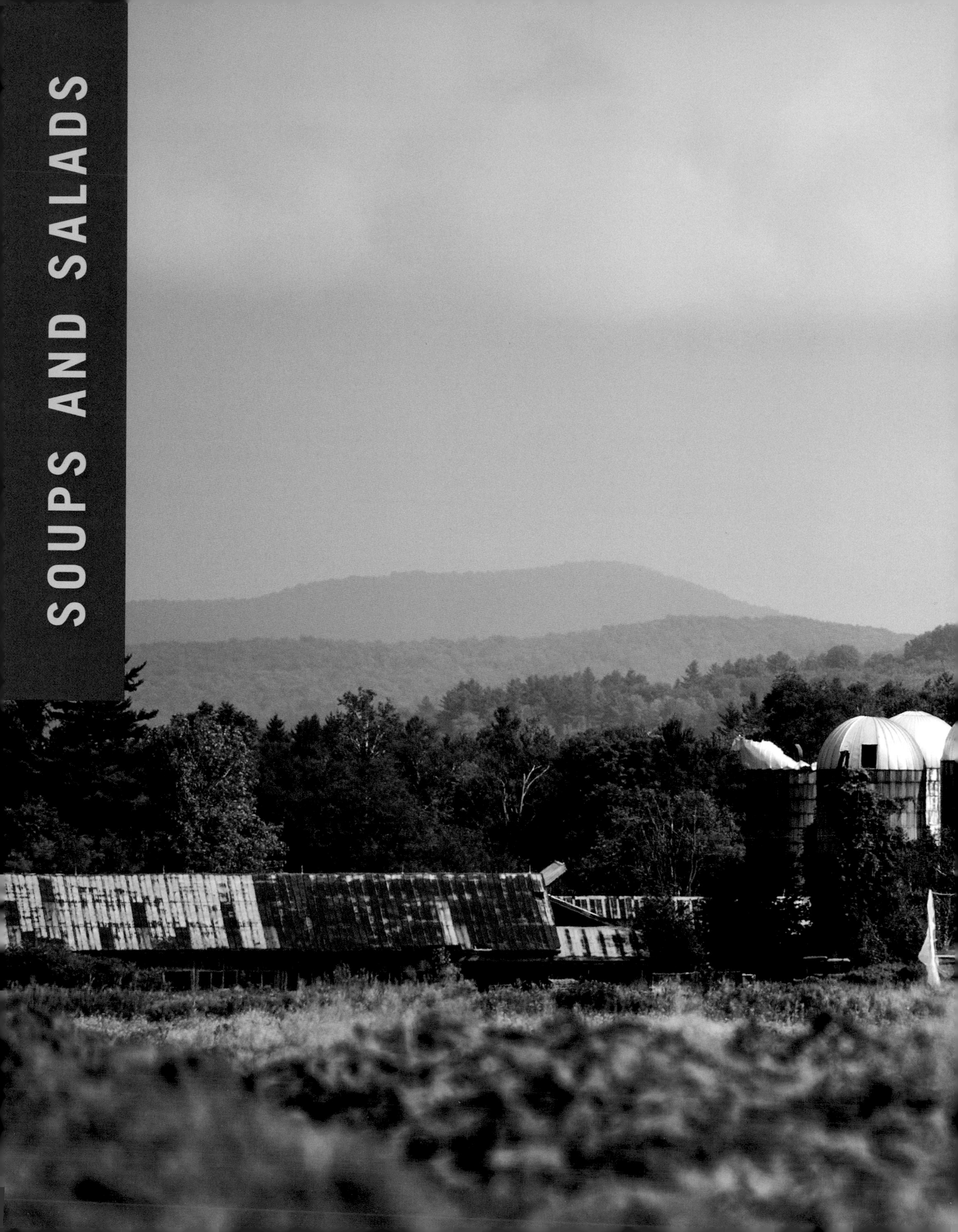

BELTED COW BISTRO

The Belted Cow Bistro, in Essex Junction, is an American bistro owned and operated by Chef John Delpha and his wife, Caitlin Bilodeau. The restaurant's unusual name refers to a rare Scottish breed of cattle called Belted Galloways, which have black bodies and a thick white belt around their midsection. The couple chose the name because they wanted to make a connection to the local agricultural landscape. Belted Galloways are one of the oldest improved breeds of beef cattle. They were first discovered in the mountainous areas of Southwestern Scotland in the province of Galloway, which, except for the lack of woods, mirrors the hilly Vermont terrain. Delpha and Bilodeau partner with Vermont distributors and farms to create seasonal menus that offer the highest-quality locally grown products.

Butternut Squash Soup with Smoky Bacon and Maple Syrup

SERVES 6 TO 8

John Delpha likes to use Vermont Smoke and Cure bacon and Red Hen Baking Company bread in this recipe. Serve this hearty soup with a tossed green salad.

4 ounces (about 4 slices) smoked bacon, chopped
8 tablespoons (4 ounces) unsalted butter
1 large Vidalia onion, chopped
3 pounds butternut squash (1 large), peeled, seeded and cut into 1-inch pieces
1/2 cup pure Vermont maple syrup
2 tablespoons fresh lemon juice, plus extra as needed
1 teaspoon ground cinnamon
1 teaspoon grated nutmeg
4 cups low-sodium chicken stock, plus extra as needed
Kosher salt and freshly ground black pepper
6–8 slices baguette, toasted and buttered
Chopped fresh chives

1. Cook the bacon in a large stockpot over medium-high heat until crisp, about 5 minutes. Using a slotted spoon, transfer to paper towels to drain. Drain all but 2 tablespoons of the bacon drippings from the pot, add 4 tablespoons butter, and melt over medium heat. Add the onion and sauté, stirring occasionally, until the onion is soft and translucent, about 5 minutes.

2. Add the squash, maple syrup, lemon juice, cinnamon, nutmeg, and chicken stock and bring to a boil over medium-high heat. Reduce the heat to a simmer and cook until the

squash is fork-tender, about 20 minutes. Working in batches, purée the soup and the remaining 4 tablespoons butter in a blender or food processor until smooth. Return the soup to the pot and add stock if necessary to achieve the desired consistency. Bring to a simmer and continue cooking until heated through. Season with additional lemon juice and salt and pepper to taste.

3. Place 1 baguette slice in the bottom of each bowl and top with the reserved bacon. Ladle the soup into the bowls and garnish with chives.

Belted Cow Bistro

ARCANA GARDENS AND GREENHOUSES

Arcana Gardens and Greenhouses is a 140-acre certified organic farm with retail greenhouses, located east of Burlington, in Jericho. Most of the plants sold at Arcana are grown on-site from seed, a practice that allows them to offer rare and unusual plants you can't find at a typical garden center or nursery. Arcana has the largest, most diverse, certified organic herbaceous perennial selection in Vermont. They also sell a wide variety of annual flowers, herbs, and vegetable seedlings, as well as growing produce for their CSA and farmers' market customers.

Celeriac, Fennel, and Leek Chowder Baked in Winter Squash

SERVES 8

When roasted, the soft, slightly sweet squash "meat" is delicious scooped into the chowder for additional flavor and texture. The reserved fennel fronds make a beautiful, edible garnish for this dish.

4 tablespoons (2 ounces) unsalted butter
2 leeks, white part only, halved lengthwise, cleaned and julienned
1 fennel bulb, fronds removed, chopped, and reserved; bulb quartered and julienned
4 cups vegetable stock, plus extra as needed
1/4 cup light cream
1 teaspoon chopped fresh thyme
1/4 teaspoon liquid smoke
Kosher salt and freshly ground black pepper
1 celeriac root (about 1 pound) peeled and diced
4 (2- to 3-pound) kabocha squash, cut in half horizontally

1. Preheat the oven to 350 degrees. Line a baking sheet with aluminum foil and set aside.

2. Heat 3 tablespoons of the butter in a large stockpot over medium heat. Add the leeks and fennel and sauté until the leeks are translucent and tender, about 8 minutes. Whisk in the stock and bring to a boil. Reduce the heat to medium-low and simmer for 10 minutes. Remove from the heat and let cool slightly. Working in batches, purée half of the soup in

a blender or food processor until smooth. Return the purée to the stockpot with the remaining soup and stir in the cream, thyme and liquid smoke. Season with salt and pepper to taste. If the soup is too thick, thin with additional vegetable stock.

3. Meanwhile, heat the remaining tablespoon butter in a medium skillet over medium heat. Add the celeriac and sauté, stirring often, until light golden brown, about 8 minutes.

4. Scrape the seeds and pulp from the squash halves with a melon baller or spoon. (Reserve the seeds for toasting, if desired.) Sprinkle the inside of each squash bowl with salt and pepper and arrange them on the prepared baking sheet. Divide the celeriac among the squash bowls, and ladle the soup evenly into each bowl. Bake until the squash is tender when tested with a fork, 60 to 65 minutes. Garnish with the reserved chopped fennel fronds and serve.

Arcana Gardens and Greenhouses

Roasted Squash Seeds

Pumpkins are not the only winter squash that have great seeds for roasting. Acorn, kabocha, and butternut squash seeds are just as delicious roasted. You can eat the roasted seeds by themselves as a healthy snack or use them in salads, soups, and risotto dishes.

Preheat the oven to 325 degrees. Rinse the squash seeds to remove any pulp and drain them well. Place them in a large bowl and toss with just enough olive oil to coat. Spread the seeds in an even layer on an ungreased baking sheet and season with fine sea salt to taste. Bake, stirring occasionally, until the seeds are dry and crunchy, about 15 minuts. Let cool. The seeds can be stored in an airtight container at room temperature.

Vermont Cheddar Soup

SERVES 6 AS A FIRST COURSE

One of the all-time favorite recipes at Simon Pearce, this creamy soup, created by former Simon Pearce chef Paul Langhans, is deliciously addictive. The soup is best the day after it is made; the flavors develop over time. It has a creamy, velvet-like texture with a slight acidic bite from the cheddar cheese. Be sure to use your favorite Vermont-made extra-sharp cheddar cheese. Serve alongside Rory's Irish Scones (page 27) and enjoy two of Simon Pearce's most popular flavors.

1/2 cup grated carrots
1/2 cup minced celery
8 tablespoons (4 ounces) unsalted butter
1 small onion, finely chopped
1 teaspoon chopped fresh thyme
1 bay leaf
1/2 cup all-purpose flour
4 cups chicken or vegetable stock, hot
12 ounces extra-sharp Vermont cheddar cheese, shredded (3 cups)
1 cup half-and-half, plus extra as needed
Kosher salt and freshly ground pepper
Chopped fresh parsley
Worcestershire sauce

1. Bring a medium saucepan of water to a boil, add the carrots and celery, and cook for 30 seconds. Drain well and set aside.

2. Melt the butter in a large saucepan over low heat. Add the onion, thyme, and bay leaf, increase the heat to medium-high, and cook until the onion is translucent.

3. Reduce the heat to low, add the flour, and cook, stirring, for 2 minutes. Turn the heat to medium-high and cook until the roux bubbles.

Add the stock 1 cup at a time, making sure the liquid is at a boil the entire time, and whisk until smooth.

4. Add the cheddar cheese to the soup in two batches and stir until the cheese has melted. Add the half-and-half, carrots, and celery; if necessary, add extra half-and-half to thin the soup to the desired consistency. Remove the bay leaves and season with salt and pepper to taste. Garnish with parsley and a drizzle of Worcestershire sauce, if desired, and serve.

Simon Pearce

Tomato Coconut Soup

SERVES 4

Cedar Circle Farm served this soup garnished with purple basil, fresh coconut cream, and lime sugar at their 2011 Tomato Tasting. It was a huge hit! The success of the soup depends upon the quality of the ingredients. Use ripe, flavorful tomatoes to make the paste, good quality coconut milk like Natural Value (or another brand that doesn't contain any guar gum or preservatives) and homemade chicken stock—ideally from pastured or certified organic poultry. This soup is best served barely warmed on a hot summer's day, accompanied by a piece of crusty bread or a salad.

2 tablespoons extra-virgin olive oil
1 large sweet onion, finely chopped
1 1/2 cups Homemade Tomato Paste
   (recipe follows)
2–2 1/2 cups chicken stock
1 1/2 cups coconut milk
Salt and freshly ground pepper
4 fresh basil leaves, thinly sliced
Fresh lime juice
Lime Sugar (recipe follows)

1. Heat the oil in a large saucepan over low heat. Add the onion and cook, stirring occasionally, until soft and just faintly colored, 15 to 20 minutes. Increase the heat to medium, add the tomato paste and stir, browning the tomato paste. Add 2 cups of the stock and the coconut milk and bring the soup just to a boil. Lower the heat and simmer gently for 5 minutes to allow the flavors to merge.

2. Working in batches, transfer the soup to a blender and purée until smooth. Return it to the pot and season with salt and pepper

to taste. If the soup is too thick, add more chicken stock as needed. Serve warm with fresh basil, a splash of lime juice and a sprinkle of lime sugar, if desired.

Alison Baker and Cedar Circle Farm

Lime Sugar

MAKES ABOUT 1 1/2 CUPS

Lime sugar is great to have on hand for baking or for making limeade.

Remove the zest from 3 limes in strips with a vegetable peeler. Trim away any white pith from the zest (pith imparts a bitter flavor), and then chop the zest. Process the zest and 1 cup granulated sugar in a food processor until the mixture is pale green and bits of zest are still visible. Store in the refrigerator for up to 3 days.

Homemade Tomato Paste

MAKES ABOUT 1 1/2 CUPS

6 pounds plum tomatoes (about 36 tomatoes)
Olive oil
Salt

1. Preheat the oven to 200 degrees. Line two large baking sheets with parchment paper.

2. Score each tomato by cutting an "X" on the underside. Set aside. Bring just enough water to cover the tomatoes to a boil in a large pot. Fill a large bowl halfway with ice water. Working in batches if necessary, with a slotted spoon, carefully place the tomatoes in the boiling water and blanch until the skins begin to crack, about 20 seconds. Carefully remove the tomatoes and place them in the ice water for 1 to 2 minutes. Remove the tomatoes from the water and peel off the skins.

3. Slice the tomatoes in half, remove the seeds, and place them on the prepared baking sheets cut side up. Sprinkle with oil and salt to taste, and bake until most of the liquid has evaporated and the tomatoes are sweet, 6 to 7 hours.

4. Let the tomatoes cool and then, working in batches, transfer them to a blender or food processor and process to make a light, loose tomato paste. Use immediately or freeze in zipper-lock plastic bags.

Alison Baker and Cedar Circle Farm

Vegan Chili

SERVES 6 TO 8

This chili is so popular at the City Market, Onion River Co-op that it is served in the deli every day of the week. Many farms in Vermont grow dried beans, which you can easily substitute for the canned beans in this recipe; you will need 1 1/2 cups cooked kidney beans and 2 1/2 cups cooked black beans. Vary the amount of jalapeños you add to suit your taste.

1 tablespoon sunflower oil

1 medium yellow onion, diced

1 cup shredded carrots

1–2 jalapeño peppers, stemmed, seeded, and minced

3 garlic cloves, minced

1/2 cup bulgur, rinsed

2 tablespoons chili powder

1 tablespoon ground cumin

2 cups diced fresh tomatoes (about 2 medium or 6 plum tomatoes)

1 1/2 cups tomato sauce

1 (15-ounce) can kidney beans, drained and rinsed

1 1/2 (15-ounce) cans black beans, drained and rinsed

1 1/2 teaspoons kosher salt, or to taste

Plain yogurt

Chopped fresh cilantro

1. Heat the oil in a Dutch oven or large heavy pot over medium-high heat. Add the onion, carrots, and jalapeño and sauté, stirring often, until the onion is soft and translucent, about 5 minutes. Add the garlic and sauté for 1 minute. Add the bulgur, chili powder, and cumin and stir until well combined.

2. Stir in the tomatoes, tomato sauce, and beans. Bring to a boil, then reduce the heat, cover, and simmer, stirring occasionally, until the beans are tender, about 1 hour. Season with salt to taste. Serve with a dollop of yogurt and a sprinkling of cilantro, if desired.

City Market, Onion River Co-op

ARIEL'S RESTAURANT

For a year Lee Duberman and Richard Fink searched for the perfect spot to open their dream restaurant. They found it tucked away in the quiet, idyllic hamlet of Brookfield. Ariel's is an early-19th-century farmhouse situated on a small, picturesque lake, which is next to the only floating bridge in the Northeast. One has to drive for 5 miles along a dirt road to get to Ariel's, but it's worth it. Since opening the restaurant in 1997, Duberman has been searching out the best ingredients from the many small farms around Brookfield. In 2010, Ariel's was instrumental in starting the Floating Bridge Food and Farms' Co-op, a collective of local farms and food crafters who work together to promote small-farm viability, sustainability, and delicious local food.

Duberman and Fink travel whenever possible, incorporating into Ariel's menu the intense flavors of Mexican street food, the spices of the Middle East and the fresh herbal savor of Southeast Asia, as well as creative versions of regional American specialties. Duberman's cooking not only brings the flavors of the world to her corner of Vermont, but also teases the ultimate flavor from local meats and produce. Fink seeks out the best wines, offering a well-curated wine list. He uses ingredients that he forages from the fields and woods near the restaurant to create unusual cocktails with wild ginger syrups, pickled fiddlehead garnishes, and other seasonal flavors and infusions.

Ramp and Potato Soup with Ramp Dumplings and Pea Shoots

SERVES 8 AS AN APPETIZER

In the spring, Duberman and Fink love to forage for ramps (wild leeks) in the nearby cool woods. Ramps are plentiful, and Duberman uses them in many recipes, always starting the spring season with this simple soup. The dumplings are a great garnish, but you can enjoy the soup without them. They can also be served on their own, or with a little sour cream.

2 bunches ramps (about 24)
2 tablespoons olive oil
1/2 cup finely sliced shallots (about 3)
1 large garlic clove, minced
6 cups low-sodium chicken stock or broth
1 pound yellow potatoes, peeled and thinly sliced
1 1/2 teaspoons chopped fresh tarragon
Kosher salt and freshly ground black pepper
1/4 cup light cream or half-and-half
1 teaspoon grated lemon zest
16 Ramp Dumplings (recipe follows)
1–2 ounces pea shoots

1. Wash the ramp leaves and bulbs under cold running water and dry thoroughly with paper towels. Cut the root ends from the bulbs, then separate the white parts of the ramps from their leafy greens. Roughly chop the leafy greens and set aside. Roughly chop the white bulbs and stalks and set aside.

2. Heat the oil in a stockpot over medium-high heat. Add the ramp bulbs and stalks and sauté until soft, about 5 minutes. Add the shallots and garlic, stirring often, and cook until the

shallots are translucent, about 2 minutes. Add the stock and potatoes and bring to a boil. Reduce the heat to a simmer and cook until the potatoes are fork-tender, about 20 minutes. Stir in the ramp greens, tarragon, 1 1/2 teaspoons salt, and 1/8 teaspoon pepper. Let the soup cool slightly.

3. Working in batches, transfer the soup to a blender and purée until smooth. Return the soup to the stockpot over low heat. Slowly whisk in the cream and cook until heated through. Stir in the lemon zest and season with salt and pepper to taste. Ladle the soup into warm bowls and top each serving with two dumplings and a few pea shoots.

Ariel's Restaurant

Ramp Dumplings

MAKES 16 DUMPLINGS

In addition to complementing the ramp and potato soup, these dumplings make a great brunch dish or hors d'oevre. Because ramps are such a spring delicacy and at their best when fresh, these dumplings should be made right before serving.

1 medium yellow potato (about 8 ounces),
    peeled and quartered
Kosher salt and freshly ground black pepper
4 ramps, cleaned and patted dry
2 tablespoons olive oil
16 gyoza (dumpling) or wonton wrappers

1. Preheat the oven to 375 degrees.

2. Place the potato in a medium saucepan and cover with cold water; add 1/2 teaspoon salt. Bring to a boil over medium-high heat and cook until pieces are fork-tender. Drain in a colander, transfer to a medium bowl,

and mash with potato masher or fork until slightly lumpy.

3. Meanwhile, place the ramps on a baking sheet and toss with 1 tablespoon olive oil. Season with salt and pepper to taste. Bake until they are soft and slightly browned and leaves are wilted, about 10 minutes. Let cool slightly then, chop into fine pieces. Stir the ramps and 1 1/2 teaspoons of the oil into the potatoes. Season with salt and pepper to taste.

4. Lay the dumpling skins on a clean work surface and brush the edges with water. Place about 1 1/2 teaspoons potato-ramp filling in the center of each skin. Fold the skins over and crimp to close.

5. Bring a large pot of salted water to a boil and add the dumplings. Cook for about 1 minute. Remove dumplings from water with a slotted spoon and let cool on a baking sheet.

6. Heat a 10-inch cast-iron or stainless steel skillet over medium heat. Add the remaining 1 1/2 teaspoons oil to the skillet. Place 8 dumplings in the skillet and cook until lightly browned and crispy on one side. Turn the dumplings over and brown lightly, about 45 seconds. Serve.

Ariel's Restaurant

Nettle Soup with Brioche Croutons

SERVES 6

When cleaning stinging nettles, wear rubber gloves to protect your hands. Remove and discard the woody stems and wash the leaves three times under cold running water.

4 tablespoons (2 ounces) unsalted butter
1 onion, minced
1 leek, white part only, finely diced
1/2 fennel bulb, minced
2 celery ribs, minced
1 shallot, minced
4 cups vegetable stock
8 ounces nettles, stemmed and cleaned
1 tablespoon sherry vinegar
Kosher salt and freshly ground pepper
1 ounce trout roe
1 teaspoon fresh lemon juice, or to taste
6 wood sorrel sprigs
Brioche Croutons (recipe follows)

1. In a large stockpot melt 2 tablespoons of the butter over medium heat. Add the onion, leek, fennel, celery and shallot and sauté, stirring occasionally, until the onion is soft and translucent, 6 to 7 minutes.

2. Add the vegetable stock and bring to a boil over medium-high heat. Add the nettles and cook until soft and tender, about 2 minutes. Working in batches, purée the soup in a blender or food processor until smooth. Return the soup to the pot and add the vinegar and 1 tablespoon butter. Bring to a simmer and continue cooking until heated through. Season with salt and pepper to taste.

3. Place the remaining 1 tablespoon butter in small skillet over medium heat and cook until light brown. Add the trout roe and lemon juice and cook until heated through.

4. Ladle the soup into bowls and garnish with the trout roe, sorrel sprigs, and croutons. Serve.

Misery Loves Co.

Brioche Croutons

1 (12-ounce) loaf brioche or challah bread, cut into 3/4-inch cubes (6 to 8 cups)
2 1/2 tablespoons extra-virgin olive oil or 3 1/2 tablespoons unsalted butter, melted
Kosher salt and freshly ground black pepper

Preheat the oven to 350 degrees. In a large bowl, toss the bread cubes with the olive oil and season with salt and pepper to taste. Spread the bread out in a single layer on a baking sheet and bake, tossing occasionally, until golden brown, 10 to 15 minutes. Let cool to room temperature. Store in an airtight container.

Misery Loves Co.

HIGH RIDGE MEADOWS FARM

High Ridge Meadows Farm is a small family-run, certified organic farm located in the hills of East Randolph. The goal of the owners, Mary and Jim Moran, is to raise the best grass-fed beef, lamb, and poultry possible for their family and the community. All of the farm's animals are raised using organic standards, and are given ample pasture to graze and pure spring water to drink.

The Morans are thrilled to be farming in Vermont, and they enjoy all the state has to offer. They feel it's important to preserve the beautiful mix of mountains, forests, and fields that are so unique to this state, and they're honored to continue its history of farming.

Musquée de Provence Pumpkin Bisque

MAKES 12 CUPS

Musquée de Provence is a French heirloom pumpkin variety, also known as the Fairytale Pumpkin. It is large and deeply ridged, with sweet flesh. You could substitute Hubbard squash or a sweet pie pumpkin. You will need 5 to 6 pounds of pumpkin for the purée. If possible, use organic coconut milk in this recipe.

1 tablespoon unsalted butter
1 large yellow onion, chopped
4 large garlic cloves, chopped
4 cups low-sodium chicken broth
3 1/4 cups fresh Musquée de Provence pumpkin purée (recipe follows), or 2 (15- ounce) cans pumpkin purée
2 large Granny Smith apples, peeled, cored, and chopped
1 jalapeño pepper, stemmed, seeded, and finely chopped
2 tablespoons pure Vermont maple syrup
2 teaspoons ground coriander
1/2 teaspoon ground cumin
Kosher salt and freshly ground black pepper
1 (14-ounce) can unsweetened coconut milk
Chopped fresh thyme (optional)

1. Melt the butter in a large stockpot over medium heat. Add the onion and cook, stirring occasionally, until soft and translucent, about 5 minutes. Add the garlic, stirring frequently, and cook for 1 minute.

2. Add the broth, pumpkin purée, apples, jalapeño, maple syrup, coriander, cumin, and 1 1/2 teaspoons salt and bring to a boil over medium-high heat. Reduce the heat to

a simmer and cook, stirring occasionally, for 30 minutes. Let cool for 10 minutes.

3. Working in batches, purée the soup in a blender or food processor, adding the coconut milk a little bit at a time, until smooth. Return the soup to the stockpot and cook until heated through. Season with salt and pepper to taste. Ladle the soup into cups and garnish with thyme, if desired.

High Ridge Meadows Farm

Fresh Pumpkin Purée

Preheat the oven to 375 degrees. Halve a 5- to 6-pound Musquée de Provence pumpkin and remove the seeds and strings. Rub the inside of the pumpkin with 1 tablespoon butter. Place, skin side down, in a large roasting pan and add enough water to generously cover the bottom of the pan. Roast until the flesh is fork-tender, about 45 minutes. Remove from the oven and let cool. Remove and discard the skin, place the pumpkin in a blender or food processor, and purée until smooth.

KIMBALL BROOK FARM

Tucked into the Champlain Valley, Kimball Brook Farm is a certified organic dairy farm. Their cows fertilize the land on which their feed is grown and walk to their pastures throughout the seven-month growing season. The farm's 955 acres are tended with respect, affection, and a careful eye toward conservation. Owners J. D. and Cheryl DeVos believe that stewardship of the land and care for the environment make for a product that's good for the planet, good for the herd, and simply good for consumers.

J. D.'s grandfather helped his father run a 20-cow dairy farm in Holland in the early 20th century. Together, the family milked all the cows and delivered their cream, milk, and butter to nearby towns, keeping a close connection to the land and its people.

When the family moved to upstate New York in 1948, starting a dairy business was the next logical step. The family business grew and stayed here for nearly 20 years, until the need for expansion ushered them north. In 1968, the DeVos family purchased the farmhouse in North Ferrisburgh, Vermont, that became the nucleus of Kimball Brook Farm.

J. D. and Cheryl bought the farm and set about improving its facilities and expanding the herd in 1999. Realizing the immensely positive impact organic farming could have on both their business and land, they embarked on a three-year-long journey of transitioning their operation to organic.

Today, Kimball Brook Farm is a thriving organic dairy with a herd of more than 200 cows. The family's latest venture is the opening of Green Mountain Organic Creamery. They are working to become a primary source of healthful, local, organic milk and dairy products, while also continuing their family tradition of good stewardship and responsible farming.

Corn Chowder

SERVES 6 TO 8

The DeVos family uses Vermont Smoke and Cure bacon and their own milk and butter in this hearty chowder. Serve with Milk Biscuits (page 28).

1 tablespoon olive oil

4 slices thick-cut bacon, chopped

1 tablespoon unsalted butter

1 medium sweet onion, diced

1 cup diced celery

1 garlic clove, minced

1/3 cup all-purpose flour

1/2 teaspoon celery salt

Kosher salt

1 teaspoon white pepper

5 cups low-sodium chicken stock, plus extra as needed

3 medium red potatoes, scrubbed and cut into 1/4-inch cubes

1 bay leaf

6 cups fresh corn kernels (cut from 6 to 7 ears corn)

4 cups whole milk

2 teaspoons fresh chopped basil, plus extra for garnish

1/4 teaspoon fresh chopped dill, plus extra for garnish

1. Heat the oil in a large stockpot over medium-high heat. Add the bacon and cook until crisp, about 5 minutes. Using a slotted spoon, transfer to paper towels to drain. Leave the bacon drippings in the pot. Reduce the heat to medium and add the butter, onion, and celery; cook until the onion is soft and translucent, about 10 minutes. Add the garlic and cook for 1 minute.

2. Reduce the heat to medium-low and sprinkle the flour, celery salt, 1 teaspoon salt, and white pepper over the vegetables. Cook, stirring frequently, for 3 minutes. Slowly whisk in the chicken stock. Increase the heat to medium-high, add the potatoes and bay leaf, and bring to a boil. Reduce the heat to a simmer and cook until the potatoes are almost tender, about 8 minutes.

3. Add the corn kernels, milk, basil, and dill and return to a simmer. Continue cooking until the corn is just tender, about 5 minutes. Discard the bay leaf and season with salt and pepper to taste. Sprinkle with the diced bacon, and extra basil or dill, if desired, and serve.

Kimball Brook Farm

MT. MANSFIELD CREAMERY

The folks at Mt Mansfield Creamery milk their own Holstein and Brown Swiss cows to produce several raw-milk cheeses using recipes with European origins. Their cheeses are aged a minimum of 60 days in their own cheese cave.

Creamy Camembert Cheese and Potato Soup with Black Pepper Croutons

SERVES 8 TO 10

This creamy, rich soup is not only delicious but also easy to make. Keith Smith, a student from the New England Culinary Institute, created the soup using only local ingredients, which he found at the Capital City Farmers' Market. Looking for inspiration, Keith walked through the market gathering ideas and ingredients. He then prepared the soup right at the market and handed out samples for folks to try. It was a big hit! The croutons can be made ahead and stored in an airtight container for up to two days. All-purpose potatoes are moderately starchy white potatoes.

Croutons

1/2 baguette, cubed
1/4 cup olive oil
Kosher salt and freshly ground black pepper

Soup

3 tablespoons unsalted butter
2 sweet onions, such as Vidalia or Walla Walla, thinly sliced

1 small garlic clove, minced
1/8 teaspoon celery salt
3 medium all-purpose potatoes, peeled and cut into 1-inch chucks
2 1/2 cups vegetable stock, plus extra as needed
1 cup milk
1/2 cup heavy cream
5 ounces Camembert cheese, cut into small pieces
1/4 teaspoon chopped fresh thyme or sage
Salt and freshly ground white pepper

1. To make the croutons: Preheat the oven to 350 degrees. Toss the bread cubes with the oil, salt, and pepper to taste. Transfer to a baking sheet and toast, tossing occasionally, until golden brown for about 15 minutes. Let cool.

2. To make the soup. Melt the butter in a large, heavy saucepan over medium-high heat. Add the onions, garlic, and celery salt and cook until the onions are soft but not brown. Add the potatoes, stirring to coat with butter, and cook for 5 minutes.

3. Add the stock and bring to a boil. Reduce the heat to medium-low, cover, and simmer until the potatoes are fork-tender, about 30 minutes. Let the soup cool slightly, then whisk in the milk and cream in a slow, steady stream. Reheat the soup over low heat. Stir in the cheese until melted.

4. Transfer the soup to a blender and purée in batches until smooth. Return soup to the saucepan and add the thyme and season with salt and pepper to taste. Thin with additional stock if necessary. Serve immediately, garnished with croutons, or refrigerate and serve cold.

Mt. Mansfield Creamery and the Capital City Farmers' Market

Ski Vermont Farmhouse Potato Chowder

SERVES 4 TO 6

Sugarbush Resort is a four-season resort located in the heart of Vermont, in the farm-rich Mad River Valley. The culinary team at Sugarbush takes full advantage of the produce, cheese, and livestock that thrive in the surrounding area. With several restaurants and a spectacular natural setting, Sugarbush offers an array of locally inspired dining choices that appeal to almost any palate. The resort's executive chef, Gerry Nooney, was named Vermont Chef of the Year in 2009, thanks, in part, to his commitment to cooking with local foods. When the Vermont Department of Agriculture asked Nooney to assist them in finding a way to help Vermont farmers sell more potatoes, he created this hearty chowder. It was inspired by both New England clam chowder and traditional leek and potato soup.

1 1/4 pounds potatoes, peeled and diced
4 cups chicken stock
3/4 cup Vermont apple cider
1 (4-ounce) link hot Italian sausage
2 tablespoons vegetable oil
1 small Spanish onion, diced
1 large celery rib, finely chopped
1 teaspoon smoked paprika
1/2 cup heavy cream
2 teaspoons chopped fresh marjoram
2 teaspoons chopped fresh basil
Kosher salt and freshly ground black pepper

1. Place 12 ounces of the potatoes in a large stockpot and cover with the chicken stock and cider. Bring to a simmer over medium-high heat and cook until the potatoes are very tender, about 10 minutes. Transfer potatoes and liquid to a blender and purée until smooth. Return the soup to the stockpot.

2. Meanwhile, place the sausage in a small skillet, add 1 cup water, and bring to a simmer over medium heat. Cook, turning the sausage occasionally, until the sausage is plump. Let the sausage cool, then coarsely chop and add to the soup.

3. Discard the water from the skillet, wipe it clean, and place over medium heat. Add the oil, onion, and celery and cook, stirring frequently, until the onion is translucent. Add the paprika and cook 3 minutes, stirring often. Add the vegetables to the soup. Slowly whisk in the cream.

4. Meanwhile, place the remaining 8 ounces of potatoes in a medium saucepan, cover with salted water, and bring to a simmer over medium-high heat. Cook the potatoes until fork-tender, about 10 minutes. Drain and rinse under cold water. Add to the soup mixture and return the soup to a simmer. Add the marjoram and basil and season with salt and pepper to taste. Serve.

Sugarbush Resort/Timbers Restaurant

SCREAMIN' RIDGE FARM

Screamin' Ridge Farm produces sustainably grown vegetables and a growing selection of flavorfully crafted foods such as soups, pesto, salsa, and tomato sauce. The farm is run by Joe Buley Jr. and his staff, who follow organic practices to run the farm year-round. They rely on unheated passive-solar greenhouses, interior row covers, raised beds, and sunny days for winter production.

Buley registered Screamin' Ridge Farm with the state of Vermont in 2004, but he hatched the ideas behind the farm, and began researching how to make his dream a reality several years before that. He called the concept behind the farm, culinary-supported agriculture. Buley started his career as a chef, his experience working with fine agricultural products began at the L'Ecole Supérieure de Cuisine Française—Centre Jean Ferrandi, a prestigious culinary school in Paris where he was the only American student at the time. There he learned the subtleties of flavor balance and the importance of starting with fresh, high quality ingredients.

For the next 20-plus years, Buley built a career as a chef in restaurants in Brooklyn, San Francisco, San Diego, Laguna Niguel, CA, and Austin. During that time, Buley spent most vacations on the East Coast, always with a visit to Vermont. Both of his parents were raised in Vermont and he spent a lot of time there as a child, visiting his grandparents in the summer and skiing with his family in the winter.

In 1999, plans came together to move the family to Montpelier, Vermont. Buley worked as a chef-instructor at the New England Culinary Institute, bought a house with 7 1/2 acres of land in East Montpelier, and began learning how to farm. For a few years, he pretty much worked two full-time jobs as he juggled his chef-instructor position and worked at getting a farm up and running. Finally, in July 2009, Buley was able to devote all of his time to the farm.

With three big double-wall greenhouses, a few employees, and just enough chickens to supply the family with eggs, Buley sells most of his produce at the summer and winter Montpelier Farmers' Markets and his collaborative CSA—the Central Vermont Food Hub. He also uses his produce, and that from other local farmers, to make soups and sauces for sale at the Capitol City Farmers' Market and Hunger Mountain Coop in Montpelier. Buley's vision of sustainable, culinary-supported agriculture is really starting to come together. His work augments that of other small farms, representing a viable, sustainable model that promotes business diversity, local community, and a hyper local economy. Screamin' Ridge Farm is proud to be a part of this movement—one really tasty bowl of soup at a time.

Lemon Ginger Roast Chicken with Brown Rice Soup

SERVES 6 TO 8

The inspiration for Buley's soups comes from his grandmother's kitchen in East Randolph. With equal regard for flavor and economy, his grandmother used whatever was on hand—from leftover roasted chicken to potatoes, onions, and vegetables picked from the garden, all of which were pulled together to create a great-tasting soup. This is a time- and labor-intensive soup to make, but well worth the effort. It offers an Asian twist on traditional chicken and rice soup.

1 (5-pound) whole chicken, preferably free-range, giblets removed

2 tablespoons olive oil

Kosher salt and freshly ground black pepper

4 ounces short- or medium-grain brown rice, rinsed

8 ounces onions, chopped

8 ounces carrots, chopped

8 ounces celery, chopped

2 cups dry white wine

Grated zest and juice from 3 lemons

2 tablespoons grated fresh ginger

2 garlic cloves, minced

1 teaspoon red pepper flakes

1/3 cup minced fresh parsley

Rice wine vinegar (optional)

1. Preheat the oven to 375 degrees. Rinse the chicken and pat dry with paper towels. Rub with 1 tablespoon oil and season generously inside and out with salt and pepper. Place breast side up in a roasting pan. Roast the chicken, basting every 15 minutes, until the skin is golden brown, juices run clear, and the chicken reaches an internal temperature of 160 degrees, about 1 1/4 hours.

2. When the chicken is cool enough to handle, remove the skin and set aside for the stock. Using two forks or your fingertips, shred or pull the meat from the bones and set aside.

3. Place the chicken carcass, skin, and 8 cups water in a stockpot. Bring to a boil over medium-high heat. Reduce the heat and simmer for 30 minutes. Strain the stock through a fine-mesh strainer into a medium bowl.

4. Place 1 gallon of water in a pot and bring to a boil over medium-high heat. Add the rice, cover tightly, and cook until tender, about 15 minutes. Strain and set aside.

5. Heat the remaining 1 tablespoon oil in a stockpot over medium heat. Add the onions, carrots, and celery and cook, stirring occasionally, until the onions are soft and translucent, about 10 minutes. Stir in the reserved chicken stock.

6. Purée the wine, lemon zest and juice, ginger, garlic, and red pepper flakes in a blender or food processor until smooth. Add to the stockpot with vegetables and bring to a boil over medium-high heat. Reduce the heat to a simmer, add the chicken, brown rice, and parsley, and continue cooking until heated through. Season with salt and pepper to taste; if the soup is too thick, add water as needed. Ladle into soup bowls, drizzle with rice wine vinegar, if desired, and serve.

Screamin' Ridge Farm

STERLING COLLEGE

Sterling College is a progressive liberal arts college located in the heart of the Northeast Kingdom. Sterling is distinguished by its small size, environmental focus, commitment to grassroots sustainability, and year-round schedule. The dining hall at Sterling practices a live-what-you-teach philosophy, focusing on food that is sustainable, local, nutritious and delicious. Over the course of a year students in the sustainable agriculture program grow 12 percent of the food served in the dining hall. A total of 52 percent of the food served is produced in Vermont. The school's cooking focuses on creative and delicious ways of using everything that's abundant in their part of the world—be it beets, cabbages, beef or cheese.

Roasted Beet Salad with Cilantro and Lime

SERVES 6

From late spring through the winter, some version of this beet salad is almost a constant in the Sterling dining hall. It's a great dish for non-beet lovers because the citrus juice, or vinegar, tempers the earthy taste of this root. To make the salad even milder, experiment with the many pink, yellow and white beets that are available at Vermont farmers' markets in the summer and fall. The lighter the color, the milder you'll find the flavor of the beet. Don't dry the beets after scrubbing them; the moisture helps them cook. Serve this salad alone or over a bed of mesclun and top with soft Vermont goat cheese, if desired.

8 medium red beets, tops removed, scrubbed
1 teaspoon cumin seeds
1/2 cup chopped fresh cilantro
4 scallions, thinly sliced
1/2 cup fresh lime or lemon juice (from 4 limes or 3 lemons)
2 tablespoons extra-virgin olive oil
Kosher salt and freshly ground black pepper

1. Preheat the oven to 400 degrees.

2. Place a large sheet of aluminum foil on a baking sheet. Put the beets (still wet from being scrubbed) in the center and carefully wrap them in the foil, making an airtight packet. Roast until fork-tender, 1 to 1 1/4 hours. Set aside to cool.

3. Toast the cumin seeds in a small nonstick skillet over medium-high heat, stirring frequently, until the seeds are dry and fragrant, about 30 seconds. Crush the seeds with a mortar and pestle, or on a cutting board with the bottom of a frying pan. Set aside.

4. When the beets are cool enough to handle, usee a paper towel to gently rub off their skins. Chop the beets into wedges and place in a large bowl. Add the cilantro, scallions, citrus juice, oil, cumin, and salt and pepper to taste. Toss to coat and set aside to marinate for 30 minutes. Serve. (The salad will keep, refrigerated, for up to 3 days.)

Sterling College

Variations: This salad is delicious with other types of vinegars such as sherry, champagne, red wine or apple cider. Try it with diced sweet white onions, scallions or garlic. You can also add different herbs, such as chopped mint or dill.

CLEAR BROOK FARM

Clear Brook Farm is located along historic Route 7A, in Shaftsbury. In 1994, Andrew Knafel started Clear Brook Farm with one greenhouse and an acre of organic vegetables. Today, Knafel continues to grow certified organic vegetables and berries on about 25 acres, as well as offering close to 225 varieties of vegetable starts for the home gardener. Developing and maintaining soil health is of utmost importance to him. Most of the farm's produce is sold at the on-site farmstand, but Knafel also operates a CSA in both winter and summer.

Arugula, Fig, and Goat Cheese Salad with Orange Vinaigrette

SERVES 4

The orange vinaigrette is light, with subtle citrus undertones, which allow all the layers of flavor in the salad to emerge.

3 tablespoons fresh orange juice
1 1/2 tablespoons white wine vinegar or Vermont apple cider vinegar
1 teaspoon sherry
1/4 cup extra-virgin olive oil, plus extra for the goat cheese
Kosher salt and freshly ground black pepper
4-ounce fresh goat cheese log, cut into 4 disks
2 bunches arugula, torn into bite-sized pieces
8 fresh ripe black Mission figs, quartered
1/2 cup toasted walnuts, chopped

1. Preheat the oven to 375 degrees. Spray a baking sheet with nonstick cooking spray.

2. In a small bowl, whisk together the orange juice, vinegar, sherry and oil. Season with salt and pepper to taste. Brush the goat cheese rounds with oil and place on the prepared baking sheet. Bake until just warmed through, about 5 minutes.

3. Combine the arugula, figs, and walnuts in a large bowl. Add the vinaigrette and toss to combine. Divide the salad among four plates and place one cheese round in the center of each salad; serve.

Clear Brook Farm

PEBBLE BROOK FARM

Pebble Brook Farm is a small certified organic farm in the village of West Brookfield, in the center of Vermont. The farm, owned and operated by Chip and Sarah Natvig, is known for its salad greens and heirloom tomatoes. They grow a variety of produce and storage crops, which they sell through a small member CSA, as well as to Food Works at the Two Rivers Center in Montpelier. In addition to farming, Sarah Natvig also co-owns the Black Krim Tavern with her business partner, Emily Wilkins. Much of the produce featured on the tavern's menu comes from Pebble Brook Farm and the chefs try to serve all local food.

Turnip Greens and Red Leaf Lettuce with Roasted Onions, Toasted Corn Kernels and Basil Vinaigrette

SERVES 4 TO 6

This salad is all about textures and depth of favor. Each component contributes a different texture, from the crisp turnip greens and crunchy croutons to the soft, sweet onion and starchy, caramelized corn. The sweet, earthy aroma of the basil pesto collaborates with the fresh lemon to give an extra punch of brightness.

Vinaigrette

1/3 cup chopped fresh basil
1/3 cup fresh lemon juice (2 to 3 lemons)
2 tablespoons shaved Parmesan cheese
1 teaspoon whole-grain mustard
1 garlic clove, minced
Pinch red pepper flakes
2 tablespoons extra-virgin olive oil
2 tablespoons vegetable oil
Kosher salt and freshly ground black pepper

Croutons and Salad

12 ounces baguette, cut into 1-inch cubes
    (about 3 cups)
1/2 cup extra-virgin olive oil
Kosher salt and freshly ground black pepper
1 medium red or sweet onion, thinly sliced
2 ears corn, kernels cut from cobs
3 garlic cloves, minced
1 bunch baby turnip greens,
    torn into bite-sized pieces
1 head red leaf lettuce, torn into bite-sized pieces

1. Preheat the oven to 350 degrees.

2. To make the vinaigrette: In a small bowl whisk together the basil, lemon juice, Parmesan, mustard, garlic, and pepper flakes. Whisking vigorously, add the olive oil and vegetable oil in a slow, steady stream. Season with salt and pepper to taste and set aside.

3. To make the croutons and salad: In a medium bowl, toss the bread cubes with 1/4 cup oil and salt and pepper to taste. Transfer to a baking sheet and toast, tossing occasionally, until golden brown, about 15 minutes. Remove from the oven and let cool. Increase the oven temperature to 400 degrees.

4. Place the onion slices on a baking sheet and toss with 1 tablespoon olive oil. Roast for 20 to 25 minutes and set aside.

5. While the onion is roasting, heat 1 tablespoon olive oil in a medium skillet over medium-high heat. Add the corn kernels and cook until light golden brown, 8 to 10 minutes. Remove from the heat and set aside.

6. Heat the remaining 2 tablespoons oil over in a small saucepan over medium heat. Add the garlic and cook until fragrant but not browned, 2 to 3 minutes. Let the oil cool, then combine with the corn.

7. In a large bowl, combine the turnip greens and red leaf lettuce and toss with the vinaigrette to taste. Top with the onion, corn, and croutons and serve.

Pebble Brook Farm and Black Krim Tavern

CITY MARKET, ONION RIVER CO-OP

City Market, Onion River Co-op is a food cooperative located in downtown Burlington. Owned by over 7,500 members, the co-op provides a large selection of local, organic and conventional products, as well as a variety of direct member benefits. City Market is dedicated to supporting the local economy and strengthening the local food system by working with community partners and thousands of local farmers and producers.

Massaged Kale Salad with Asian Peanut Dressing

SERVES 4

All of the massaged kale salad recipes that Meg Klepack, the outreach and local food manager of City Market, found used a simple olive oil and sea salt dressing. Bored with olive oil–coated kale, Klepack had an epiphany—she could use any of the more interesting dressings that were made for green salads for the massaged kale salad. She adapted an Asian-style peanut dressing from another recipe, and the result was pure kale bliss. If peaches are not in season, you can easily substitute apples in this salad. Feel free to use walnuts or sunflower seeds in place of pepitas. The flavor of the kale mellows as you massage it with the dressing; you can add more dressing to suit your taste.

1/3 cup pepitas
1 teaspoon extra-virgin olive oil
1/4 teaspoon kosher salt
1 bunch curly green kale, stemmed and cut into bite-sized pieces
1/2 cup Asian Peanut Dressing (recipe follows), plus extra to taste
2 small peaches, pitted and diced
2 ounces feta cheese, crumbled (1/2 cup)

1. Place the pepitas, oil, and salt in a medium skillet and toss to coat. Toast over medium heat until the pepitas turn light brown and start to pop, 2 to 3 minutes. Remove from the pan and set aside on paper towels.

2. In a large bowl, combine the kale and 1/2 of the dressing. Using your hands, massage the kale until it is bright green and slightly softened, 2 to 3 minutes, adding more dressing to taste. Top with the pepitas, peaches, and feta. Serve at once.

City Market, Onion River Co-op

Asian Peanut Dressing

MAKES 1 1/3 CUPS

This dressing can be stored in the refrigerator for up to one month.

1/4 cup rice vinegar
1/4 cup soy sauce
3 tablespoons plain yogurt
4 teaspoons grated ginger
4 teaspoons sesame oil
4 garlic cloves, minced
1 tablespoon peanut butter
2 teaspoons chili garlic sauce
1 1/2 teaspoons brown sugar

Whisk together all the ingredients until combined.

City Market, Onion River Co-op

Amee Farm Lemon Lavender Dressing

MAKES 3 1/2 CUPS

Situated just north of Killington Resort in central Vermont, Amee Farm is a year-round farming operation that produces salad greens, hothouse tomatoes, basil, and garlic, as well as free-range organic pork, beef, chicken, eggs, and honey. The vegetable gardens are planted and maintained by local gardening enthusiasts who work under the watchful eye of farmer Elizabeth Roma. Together, they bring the community a colorful array of fresh produce, all grown without the use of chemicals.

2 tablespoons coarsely chopped garlic
    (3 to 4 large cloves)
3 large eggs, lightly beaten
1/4 cup fresh lemon juice
2 tablespoons fresh lavender
2 tablespoons chopped fresh lemon thyme
2 tablespoons granulated sugar
2 tablespoons rice vinegar
2 1/2 cups extra-virgin olive oil
Kosher salt and freshly ground black pepper

Pulse the garlic in a food processor until minced. Add the eggs, lemon juice, lavender, thyme, sugar, and vinegar and pulse until well combined. With the processor running, gradually add the oil and process until a creamy dressing forms. Season with salt and pepper to taste. Transfer to a glass jar and refrigerate. (The dressing will keep for several days.)

Amee Farm

FARMER SUE'S FARM

Farmer Sue's Farm is on 4 acres in Bakersfield, not far from the Canadian border. Sue Wells and her son Ben grow vegetables using organic standards and grain to feed their pigs and a flock of more than a hundred chickens. The pigs include unusual heritage breeds—Red Wattle (named for both its color and its distinctive wattles) and American Mulefoot—both considered critically endangered by the American Livestock Breeds Conservancy.

Pickled Cucumber and Sweet Onion Salad

SERVES 4 TO 6

It's best to use English cucumbers or pickling cucumbers in this salad, because their skins are not waxed.

1/2 cup water
1/4 cup Vermont apple cider vinegar
2 tablespoons granulated sugar
2 tablespoons extra-virgin olive oil
1 teaspoon finely chopped fresh basil
1 teaspoon celery seeds
1 teaspoon coriander seeds
Kosher salt and freshly ground black pepper
1 large English cucumber or 1 to 1 1/4 pounds pickling cucumbers
1 small sweet onion, such as Vidalia or Walla Walla, thinly sliced
Fresh chopped dill for garnish

1. In a small bowl, whisk together the water, vinegar, sugar, oil, basil, celery seeds, coriander seeds, and salt and pepper to taste.

2. Remove the peel from the cucumber in long strips, leaving narrow, decorative stripes of peel attached. Thinly slice the cucumber into rounds. Place the cucumber and onion in a large, shallow dish, pour the marinade over the vegetables, and toss to coat. Cover with plastic wrap and refrigerate, turning occasionally, for at least 12 hours or overnight. Garnish with dill and serve, using a slotted spoon.

Sue Wells for the Burlington Farmers' Market

Patriotic Potato Salad

SERVES 6 TO 8

Try to buy small potatoes of a uniform size so they will cook at the same rate. Good varieties to try include Red Rosa, German Butterball, and Adirondack Blue. Vary the amount of dill, basil, and celery salt to suit your taste.

1 pound small red-skinned potatoes

1 pound small white-skinned, waxy-style potatoes

1 pound small purple or blue potatoes

4 slices thick-cut bacon

Salt and freshly ground black pepper

1 cup Simple Mayonnaise, plus extra as needed (recipe follows)

1 cup chopped celery

1 small onion, finely chopped

1 tablespoon Vermont apple cider vinegar

1 tablespoon Dijon mustard

1 tablespoon fresh chopped dill

1 tablespoon fresh chopped basil

1/8 teaspoon celery salt

3 large hard-boiled eggs, peeled and chopped

1. Combine the potatoes and 1/2 teaspoon salt in a large pot, cover with water, and boil over medium-high heat. Reduce heat and cook until fork-tender, 10 to 15 minutes. Drain the potatoes in a colander and set aside to cool. When cool enough to handle, cut into 1/2-inch-thick slices.

2. While the potatoes simmer, cook the bacon in a medium skillet over medium-high heat until crisp, 5 to 7 minutes. Drain on paper towels, then crumble.

3. Stir together the mayonnaise, celery, onion, vinegar, mustard, dill, basil, and celery salt in a bowl large enough to hold the potatoes.

MANCHESTER FARMERS' MARKET

Since 2001, the Manchester Farmers' Market has provided consumers with an array of farm fresh produce, cheeses, eggs and meats, locally prepared foods, as well as quality crafts and artisan wares. The outside marketplace also offers live music every week and projects for the children when school is out of session for the summer—all free of charge.

Fold in the potatoes and eggs and season with salt and pepper to taste. Sprinkle with the crumbled bacon and serve.

Simple Mayonnaise

When using raw eggs, use only fresh, clean, properly refrigerated eggs with intact shells. Makes 1 cup.

1 large egg yolk

1–2 tablespoons fresh lemon juice

1/2 teaspoon freshly ground black pepper

1/4 teaspoon kosher salt

3/4 cup canola or safflower oil, plus extra as needed

Process the egg yolk, 1 tablespoon lemon juice, pepper, and salt in a food processor to combine. With the motor running, slowly add the oil in a steady stream until well blended and the mixture has thickened; if necessary, add more oil for a thick, creamy consistency. Transfer to a bowl and add lemon juice to taste. Use immediately or cover and refrigerate for up to 2 days.

Manchesterr Farmers' Market

Late Summer Quinoa Salad

MAKES 4 CUPS

Quinoa is a versatile whole grain that was once a staple of the ancient Incas. Unlike other grains, quinoa contains a good balance of the nine essential amino acids, making it a complete protein. It cooks quickly, and doesn't have as strong a flavor as other whole grains. It's about the same size as couscous, and is a great choice when you want more fiber, protein and nutrients without the extra time or work.

Feel free to substitute other vegetables and flavorings for the ones in this recipe. Quinoa salad is great with roasted butternut squash cubes and walnuts instead of tomatoes and corn. In the winter, try sun-dried tomatoes and black olives with red wine vinegar instead of apple cider vinegar. Quinoa is a great backdrop to highlight whatever is local and in season. This salad is best eaten the day it's made.

1 cup quinoa, rinsed and drained
2 cups water
3 tablespoons extra-virgin olive oil
4 ears corn, kernels cut from cobs
1 cup cherry tomatoes cut into quarters
4 scallions, thinly sliced
1/2 cup chopped fresh parsley
1/2 cup Vermont apple cider vinegar
Kosher salt and freshly ground black pepper

1. Combine the quinoa and water in a small saucepan and bring to a boil over high heat. Cover, reduce the heat, and simmer until the quinoa is tender and the water is absorbed, 10 to 15 minutes. Let cool.

2. Heat 2 tablespoons of the oil in a medium cast-iron skillet over medium-high heat until very hot. Add the corn kernels and cook,

stirring constantly, until slightly blackened on the outside and barely cooked inside, about 30 seconds. Spread the corn on a plate in a single layer to cool.

3. Transfer the corn to a large bowl and add the quinoa, tomatoes, scallions, and parsley. Stir in the vinegar and remaining 1 tablespoon oil and season with salt and pepper to taste. Set aside to marinate at least 30 minutes or up to 3 hours. Serve.

Sterling College

KINGSBURY FARM

The 22-acre Kingsbury Farm was bought and conserved by the Vermont Land Trust in November of 2007. The property was subsequently sold to the Vermont Foodbank during the following year. The conditions of the sale were that the owners would grant public access along the property to the Mad River Path, they would protect permanent riparian buffers through no-till practice, and the remaining acreage would be used to produce food in an ecologically responsible manner. In the fall of 2009, the Vermont Foodbank put out a call to farmers to submit proposals for the use of the farm. In late December, they chose Aaron Locker and Suzanne Slomin.

Under its current structure, Kingsbury Farm offers about seven tillable acres upon which to grow food. Each year, a portion of this acreage is dedicated to growing storage crops for the Foodbank. The farm also works directly with 10 regional food shelves to meet their ongoing needs for fresh produce throughout the growing season. Locker and Slomin's lease requires them to provide the Foodbank with 30,000 pounds of produce annually in exchange for the use of the farm land and the infrastructure. Once these terms have been met, they can use the remaining acreage to grow food to be sold "for profit" out of their farm store and to other clients, such as local schools and/ or restaurants.

The Kingsbury Market Garden is managed naturally; that is, without the use of synthetic inputs. Locker and Slomin employ crop rotation, green manures, compost application, beneficial insect attraction and close observation to keep the land healthy and productive. They have constructed four movable unheated hoophouses, which enable them to significantly extend the northern Vermont growing season. They offer early spring strawberries and tomatoes, as well as late autumn raspberries. Cold-hardy salad greens are harvested throughout much of the year.

Kingsbury Slaw

SERVES 8 TO 10

The wonderful thing about this salad is that you can make it year-round using mostly local ingredients (even in Vermont). At Kingsbury Market Garden, they harvest cilantro and scallions from early spring through late fall. In late spring, the harvesting of napa cabbage begins; by early summer, savoy and red cabbage appear; and during the winter, the market garden relies on green storage cabbage (substituting red onions for scallions and pickled cherry bombs from the summer garden for fresh chiles). This slaw is great on its own or delicious in a sandwich or wrap. This recipe is great for a big crowd at a barbecue or picnic.

1 head napa or savoy cabbage, finely shredded (6 to 7 cups)

1/2 head red cabbage, finely shredded (2 to 3 cups)

6 scallions, thinly sliced

1 serrano or jalapeño pepper, stemmed, seeded, and finely chopped

1/4 cup chopped fresh cilantro

1/3 cup fresh lime juice (2 to 3 limes)

1/4 cup extra-virgin olive oil, plus extra if needed

Kosher salt and freshly ground black pepper

In a large bowl, combine the napa cabbage, red cabbage, scallions, serranos, cilantro, and lime juice. Drizzle with olive oil and toss to coat. Season with salt and pepper to taste. Cover and refrigerate for 1 hour before serving.

Kingsbury Market Garden

EARTH SKY TIME COMMUNITY FARM

Earth Sky Time Community Farm, located in Manchester, is a small community-based, year-round certified organic farm. The farm not only grows vegetables, orchard fruit, herbs and flowers on about 10 acres of land, but also runs a commercial kitchen and wood-fired bakery. All of their products are vegetarian, globally inspired, homemade prepared foods such as Vermont Goldburgers, hummus, and salsa. They bake a wide range of artisanal breads (mostly sourdough) in a Llopis oven, which is a wood-fired brick oven made in Spain. The owners, Oliver and Bonnie Levis, sell their produce and value-added products at their on-site farm stand, as well as at farmers' markets.

Red Cabbage and Carrot Slaw with Cilantro Vinaigrette

SERVES 6

This vibrant slaw uses cilantro-infused vinegar, which must steep for four days, so prepare accordingly.

Vinaigrette

1/2 cup fresh orange juice
1/2 cup Cilantro-Infused Vinegar (recipe follows)
2 tablespoons Vermont honey
1 tablespoon grated ginger
1 tablespoon fresh lime juice
3 tablespoons toasted sesame oil,
    plus extra to taste
Kosher salt and freshly ground black pepper

Cabbage and Carrot Slaw

4 cups finely shredded red cabbage
    (about 1/2 head)
2 cups shredded carrots (3 to 4 carrots)
2–3 tablespoons toasted sesame seeds

1. To make the vinaigrette: Whisk together the orange juice, vinegar, honey, ginger, and lime juice in a small bowl. Slowly whisk in the oil until well combined. Season with salt and pepper to taste.

2. To make the cabbage and carrot slaw: Combine the cabbage and carrots in a large bowl. Drizzle with the vinaigrette and toss to coat. Season with salt and pepper to taste. Cover refrigerate for 2 to 3 hours before serving. Garnish with toasted sesame seeds, if desired.

Cilantro-Infused Vinegar

1 1/2 cups fresh cilantro leaves, lightly crushed
1 cup Vermont apple cider vinegar

Place the cilantro in a 16-ounce glass jar with a tight lid. Add the vinegar and seal. Let sit at room temperature for 4 to 5 days. Strain the vinegar through a fine-mesh strainer into a clean jar. Cover and refrigerate for up to 2 weeks.

Earth Sky Time Community Farm

THE ESSEX RESORT & SPA

Nestled on 18 acres between vistas of the beautiful Green Mountains and the splendor of Lake Champlain is The Essex, Vermont's culinary resort and spa. In addition to a full-service spa, salon, fitness center, and their unique and sophisticated restaurant, Amuse, the Essex offers fun instruction in the four kitchen classrooms of Cook Academy.

Turkey Waldorf Salad

SERVES 4

This Waldorf salad is a great twist on an old classic that was originally served at the Waldorf Astoria Hotel in 1893. Turkey breast is a moist and flavorful stand-in for chicken, and grilling provides a nice change from the usual oven-roasted method. This salad is also a perfect way to use Thanksgiving turkey leftovers.

2 pounds skinless, boneless turkey breast, trimmed, cut into 4 pieces, and pounded thin

1/2 cup Caesar salad dressing, preferably homemade (recipe follows)

3 tablespoons light mayonnaise

Zest and juice of 1 lemon

1 1/2 tablespoons chopped fresh sage

1/8 teaspoon celery salt or celery seeds

Kosher salt and freshly ground black pepper

2 large apples, such as Red Delicious, cored and diced

2 cups halved red or green grapes

2 celery ribs, diced

1/3 cup walnut halves

1/4 cup minced red onion

1 head romaine lettuce, trimmed, washed, dried, and leaves separated

1. Place the turkey cutlets in a large zipper-lock plastic bag and add the dressing. Seal the bag and place in the refrigerator for 1 hour, turning the bag over at least once to distribute the marinade evenly.

2. In a small bowl, whisk together the mayonnaise, lemon zest, sage, and celery salt. Season with salt and pepper to taste.

3. In a large bowl, combine the apples, grapes, celery, walnuts, and onion. Sprinkle with lemon juice and toss to coat.

4. Preheat a gas or electric grill to medium heat. Remove the turkey cutlets from the dressing, place on the grill, and and cook, turning once, until just cooked through, about 6 minutes. Let cool, then slice on the bias into thin slices.

5. Add the mayonnaise mixture to the apple mixture and toss to coat evenly. Arrange the lettuce leaves on four plates and scoop the salad into the center of lettuce. Place the turkey slices on top and serve at once.

Variation: If you do not own a grill, heat 1 1/2 tablespoons olive oil in a large nonstick skillet over medium heat. Add the turkey cutlets, in batches if necessary, and cook, turning once, about 6 minutes.

Shawn Calley of The Essex Resort & Spa

Caesar Salad Dressing

4 garlic cloves, peeled
1 teaspoon anchovy paste
1/2 cup fresh lemon juice (3 lemons)
1 1/2 teaspoons Dijon mustard
1 1/4 cups canola oil
2/3 cup grated Parmesan cheese
1 teaspoon Worcestershire sauce, or to taste
1 teaspoon freshly ground black pepper
1/2 teaspoon kosher salt

Pulse the garlic and anchovy paste in a food processor until the garlic is minced. Add the lemon juice and mustard and pulse until well combined. While the machine is running, gradually add the oil, Parmesan, Worcestershire sauce, pepper, and salt. Serve immediately, or transfer to a container with a lid and refrigerate for up to 3 days. Makes 2 cups.

Pamela Cohan

WOODSTOCK FARMERS' MARKET

The Woodstock Farmers' Market is a busy year-round specialty food and fresh food market. Not only do they provide their Upper Valley community with wholesome fresh foods, they also serve their "far-away" customers via their website. The market offers great food that ranges from take-out prepared dinners and lunches to farm-fresh ingredients, such as Vermont cheeses, local eggs, organic local produce, all-natural meats, and everything in between.

For the past 20 years, customers have relied on the Woodstock Farmers' Market to be their champion for quality foods. Staff travel to local and regional farms and visit with food producers and wholesalers from the world over to select the best available items. Their belief is that anyone can create great food, but it all starts with using the best and freshest ingredients you can find. Luckily, some of the best sources are found right here in Vermont.

Today, more than ever, knowing where your food comes from is paramount. The dedicated staff takes the job of "bringing the food to the people" seriously. There is great concern for the food chain; where the product comes from, how it's delivered to the marketplace, and who the producers are. The customers love that connection and feel it's one of the most important things they can do for themselves and for their community.

Bow Thai Pasta Salad

SERVES 6 TO 8

In 1992, Amelia Rappaport, a New England Culinary Institute graduate, was hired to start the prepared foods department for the Woodstock Farmers' Market. She made Bow Thai Pasta Salad occasionally, in rotation with other pasta salads. Seventeen years later, Amelia is a part owner in the business and by popular demand Bow Thai Pasta Salad is made daily for their prepared salad case. This recipe makes more dressing than you will need for the pasta; extra dressing will keep, refrigerated, for up to three weeks. It can be used as salad dressing, a marinade for chicken, or other with other pasta or rice noodles.

Salt
1 pound farfalle
2/3 cup canola oil
1/2 cup soy sauce
1/2 cup rice vinegar
1/3 cup chili oil
2 tablespoons sesame oil
2 large garlic cloves, finely minced
1/4 teaspoon cayenne pepper
1 1/2 cups creamy peanut butter
1/2 cup chopped red bell pepper
1/2 cup thinly sliced scallions
1/4 cup sesame seeds, toasted

1. Bring a large pot of salted water to a boil. Add the pasta and cook until al dente, about 8 minutes. Drain the pasta, transfer to a large bowl, and let cool completely.

2. In a medium bowl, whisk together the canola oil, soy sauce, vinegar, chili oil, sesame oil, garlic and cayenne pepper. Whisk in the peanut butter until smooth.

3. Add 1 cup of the dressing to the pasta and stir to coat; add more dressing as needed. Season with salt to taste, sprinkle with peppers, scallions, and sesame seeds, and serve.

Amelia Rappaport and the Woodstock Farmers' Market

Wheat Berry Salad with Fresh Herbs

SERVES 4 TO 6

Cedar Circle Farm served this salad at their ninth annual Strawberry Festival in June 2011 to show how delicious whole grains can be. More than a dozen people asked for the recipe that day—including a few kids! Wheat berries are the entire wheat kernel, minus the hull. The staff at Cedar Circle likes the heirloom wheat berries grown on the farm, but any organic variety will work. Chewy cooked wheat berries give this salad a lovely depth and a nutty flavor, and you can vary the vegetables and herbs according to the season and what's in your garden. Radishes and fresh mint are nice additions. If you don't have walnuts, pine nuts would be a good substitute. If you are unable to find a kohlrabi bulb, you can substitute 1/3 cup lightly steamed chopped broccoli stems and 1/4 cup lightly steamed chopped golden turnip.

Vinaigrette

5 tablespoons brown rice vinegar, preferably organic
1 tablespoon fresh lime juice
1 tablespoon stone-ground mustard
1 teaspoon kosher salt
1/2 teaspoon freshly ground black pepper
6 tablespoons extra-virgin olive oil

Salad

1 cup hard wheat berries, preferably organic
2 celery ribs, diced
1 small kohlrabi bulb, peeled and diced
2 scallions, thinly sliced
3/4 cup walnuts, toasted and chopped
1/2 cup dried cranberries (optional)
2/3 cup chopped fresh parsley
1/3 cup coarsely chopped basil (optional)
Kosher salt and freshly ground black pepper

1. To make the vinaigrette: Whisk together the vinegar, lime juice, mustard, salt, and pepper in a small bowl. Whisking vigorously, add the oil in a slow, steady stream.

2. To make the salad: Bring 2 1/2 quarts salted water to a boil in a large saucepan. Add the wheat berries and cook uncovered, until tender, but still chewy, 1 to 1 1/4 hours.

3. Drain the wheat berries through a colander, then transfer to a large bowl. Add the vinaigrette and stir to coat. Stir in the celery, kohlrabi, scallions, walnuts, cranberries, if desired, and parsley and basil, if desired. Season with salt and pepper to taste. Serve warm or at room temperature.

Alison Baker and Cedar Circle Farm

Original General Store Blue Cheese Dressing

MAKES 4 CUPS

The Original General Store, located along historic country Route 100 in Pittsfield, just minutes from the Killington ski area, offers an extensive "down home" menu and experience. Chef Kim Kennedy and her husband, Doug, utilize local products and purveyors. They are committed to creating home-grown recipes and daily specials that appeal to any appetite. This creamy dressing has great layers of flavors and could easily be used as a dipping sauce for fresh veggies as well.

2 cups sour cream
1 cup mayonnaise
6 ounces blue cheese, crumbled (1 1/2 cups)
1/2 cup buttermilk
1 teaspoon white pepper
1 teaspoon dry mustard
1/8 teaspoon garlic powder
Hot sauce
Kosher salt and freshly ground black pepper

In a large bowl, whisk together the sour cream, mayonnaise, blue cheese, buttermilk, white pepper, mustard, and garlic powder. Season with hot sauce, salt, and pepper to taste.

Original General Store

Tyler Place Maple Balsamic Vinaigrette

MAKES ABOUT 3 CUPS

This is a very versatile dressing that is just as good as a marinade for chicken or pork tenderloin as it is drizzled over a bed of local mesclun greens. Make sure to use a high-quality balsamic vinegar in this dressing.

2 tablespoons coarsely chopped garlic
2 tablespoons coarsely chopped shallots
1/4 cup balsamic vinegar
1/4 cup pure Vermont maple syrup
1 1/2 tablespoons Dijon mustard
1 teaspoon dried oregano
1/4 teaspoon freshly ground black pepper
1 cup canola oil
1 cup extra-virgin olive oil
Hot water, as needed

Pulse the garlic and shallots in a food processor until they are minced. Add the vinegar, maple syrup, mustard, oregano, and pepper and pulse until well combined. While the machine is running, gradually add the oils until a creamy dressing forms. Season with salt and pepper to taste. If the dressing is too thick, add hot water, a little at a time, until the desired consistency is achieved.

The Tyler Place Family Resort

VEGETABLES

GREEN MOUNTAIN GARLIC

In 1979, when Bob and Cindy Maynard first moved to Waterbury, they had no idea how much organic garlic would influence their lives. Over the years, Green Mountain Garlic has evolved from a home garden into what is now their current farm. After lengthy conversations with organic garlic farmers who sold seed garlic, the two realized that there was a need for organic garlic and decided to grow their own.

When the youngest of their three children left for college, the Maynards converted the old hay field on their 100-acre Waterbury property into an organic garlic farm. Today, the farm offers 12 different types of hardneck and softneck garlic, all certified organic by Vermont Organic Farmers (VOF).

Winter Squash with Roasted Garlic

SERVES 6

3 1/4 pounds butternut squash
4 tablespoons (2 ounces) unsalted butter, softened
1 1/2 large garlic heads, roasted (recipe follows)
3 1/2 tablespoons pure Vermont maple syrup
1/2 teaspoon freshly ground white pepper, plus extra
1/4 teaspoon grated nutmeg
Salt
1 1/2 teaspoons minced fresh thyme leaves

1. Preheat the oven to 425 degrees.

2. Halve the squash lengthwise and remove the seeds and strings. Rub the inside of each half with 1 tablespoon butter. Place, skin side down, in a large roasting pan and add enough water to generously cover the bottom of pan. Roast until the flesh is fork-tender, about 45 minutes. Let stand until cool.

3. Meanwhile, squeeze the garlic flesh from the skins into a food processor.

4. When the squash is cool enough to handle, scoop out the flesh and place it in the food processor with the garlic. Add the remaining 2 tablespoons butter, maple syrup, 1/2 teaspoon pepper, and nutmeg and purée until smooth. Season with salt and pepper to taste and pulse to incorporate. Transfer to a serving bowl, sprinkle with thyme, and serve.

Green Mountain Garlic

Roasted Garlic

MAKES 2 HEADS

This is one of the easiest and tastiest of garlic treats. Roasting caramelizes garlic slightly and makes it mild and sweet. Roasted garlic has a creamy texture, is wonderful as a spread, and can be used in a variety of dressings and sauces. You can substitute it in any dish that calls for garlic. What you don't use can be kept in the refrigerator for up to 10 days.

2 large garlic heads
Olive oil
Water

Preheat the oven to 350 degrees. Slice off the top portion of the heads and peel off just the outer papery layers of skin. Place the heads face up in a baking dish or garlic baker and sprinkle with oil and a bit of water. Bake until the cloves feel soft when pressed, about 1 hour

Green Mountain Garlic

FIVE CORNERS FARMERS' MARKET

The Five Corners Farmers' Market, located in the heart of downtown Essex Junction, is a successful outdoor shopping area that provides fresh local food, entertainment, and summertime bliss to the community. There are plenty of places to park and it is within biking or walking distance for many residents.

Every Friday afternoon, from June to October, approximately 30 local vendors sell their wares. Shoppers may choose from local fruits, vegetables, herbs, flowers, gluten-free foods, fresh baked goods, cheeses, grass-fed beef, natural pork and chicken, wine, and mouth-watering prepared foods.

Braised Red Cabbage

SERVES 6 TO 8

The smell of this flavorful recipe takes chef Courtney Contos back to her childhood, all the way to her grandmother's kitchen in Germany. Today, Contos enjoys the braised red cabbage with beef rouladen, roast chicken, or pork. It is a great vegetable to make ahead.

2 tablespoons (1 ounce) unsalted butter
1 medium sweet onion, such as Vidalia or
    Walla Walla, thinly sliced
2 pounds red cabbage (1 medium head), shredded
Kosher salt and freshly ground black pepper
1 1/2 cups fresh or frozen whole cranberries
1 cup Vermont apple cider
1 bay leaf
5 juniper berries
1 cinnamon stick
1 large tart apple, cored and diced
3 tablespoons dark brown sugar
3 tablespoons Vermont apple cider vinegar

1. Melt the butter in a large stockpot over medium heat. Add the onion and cook until tender and slightly translucent. Add the cabbage, 1 teaspoon salt, and 1/2 teaspoon pepper and sauté, stirring occasionally, for 5 minutes.

2. Add the cranberries, cider, bay leaf, juniper berries, and cinnamon stick. Cover and cook, stirring occasionally, until the cabbage is tender, about 1 hour.

3. Add the apple, sugar, and vinegar, stirring until well combined. Cover and continue cooking until the apple is very tender, about 10 minutes. Remove the bay leaf and cinnamon stick, season with salt and pepper to taste, and serve.

Courtney Contos for the Five Corners Farmers' Market

Cumin-Roasted Tri-colored Carrots with Chevre

SERVES 6

If you ask most people what color a carrot is, the immediate response is usually "orange." However, the very first carrots, which were grown over 1,000 years ago, were actually purple, red, and yellow. Today these many-colored carrots have made a comeback. They vary slightly in sweetness and crispness from standard orange carrots, but they can be prepared the same way. If you are unable to find rainbow carrots, your typical carrot will also work well for this dish.

12 rainbow carrots, assorted colors, scrubbed, thick ends halved lengthwise, and cut into 2-inch pieces
2 tablespoons olive oil
1/2 teaspoon ground cumin
Kosher salt and freshly ground black pepper
1 tablespoon Vermont apple cider
1 1/2 ounces goat cheese, crumbled (1/3 cup)
1 tablespoon minced fresh cilantro

1. Preheat the oven to 400 degrees. Lightly oil a baking sheet and set aside.

2. Place the carrots in a large bowl, add the olive oil, cumin, 1 teaspoon salt, and 1/2 teaspoon pepper until evenly coated.

3. Place the carrots in a single layer on the prepared baking sheet. Roast, tossing occasionally, until tender and golden brown, about 30 minutes.

4. Sprinkle the carrots with the cider and salt to taste, and toss to coat. Transfer the carrots to a platter and sprinkle the goat cheese and cilantro over the top. Serve.

Tracey Medeiros

Squash Blossom Fritters with Taleggio, Truffle Oil, and Honey

SERVES 4

This is a great recipe that marries local ingredients, the squash blossoms and honey, with some of the best Italy has to offer, the truffle oil and Taleggio cheese (a cow's milk cheese similar to Brie, but earthier). Because the blossoms are one of the restaurant's signature dishes, Chef Cleary features the edible flowers whenever he can get them (which, fortunately is about 10 months of the year). If you don't have zucchini or summer squash in your own garden, look for squash blossoms at your local farmers' market.

8 cups canola oil
2 1/2 cups all-purpose flour
1 1/2 cups soda water
4 ice cubes
12 squash blossoms
4 ounces Taleggio or Brie cheese cut into
    12 equal pieces
1/4 cup white truffle oil, or to taste
1/2 cup Vermont honey, or to taste

1. Place the oil in a heavy-bottomed stockpot and heat to 350 degrees.

2. In a medium bowl stir together 2 cups of the flour and the soda water until the mixture resembles a thin pancake batter. Add the ice cubes and set aside.

3. Place the remaining 1/2 cup flour in a shallow bowl. Carefully open the squash blossoms and remove the stamen (the male reproductive part) from the inside of each blossom. Stuff each blossom with a piece of Taleggio and gently twist the end of blossom to enclose the cheese. Dredge the blossoms in the flour then quickly dip in the batter to thinly coat. (Make sure to hold the blossoms by the leaves along the stem so the cheese does not fall out.)

4. Immediately place three or four blossoms in the hot oil and fry until golden brown, about 2 minutes per side. Using a slotted spoon, remove the blossoms and drain on paper towels. Season with salt to taste. Repeat with the remaining blossoms. Place three squash blossom fritters on each serving plate, drizzle with the truffle oil and honey, and serve immediately.

L'Amante Ristorante

FOOTE BROOK FARM

Although Tony Lehouillier started Foote Brook Farm in 1997, his farming roots go back at least three generations. From 1955 to 1985, the site of the present Foote Brook farm was the Lehouillier Dairy Farm. Tony's mother, Polly Lehouillier, planted gardens, built greenhouses, and ran a farm stand out of the old dairy barn. Tony, along with some friends and partners, started out by growing a few varieties of vegetables and selling them to local restaurants, small co-ops, farmers markets and his mom's farm stand. Since then, Foote Brook Farm has grown to 45 acres producing 145 varieties of fruit and vegetables, sold at two farmers' markets, a retail stand, and through lots of small local accounts.

Tony and his wife, Joie, pride themselves on meeting the high standards of organic certification. Their employees (who call themselves Footebrookers) are the heart and soul of the farm. Every Friday the Lehouilliers look forward to sitting down with their staff and sharing the day's events and future plans, over some deliciously prepared farm-fresh food.

Stuffed Collard Greens

SERVES 6

These stuffed collard greens were first prepared for one of the Friday afternoon Footebrookers' meals. The collard greens' versatility makes it possible to stuff the leaves with a variety of local products.

1 tablespoon olive oil
2 medium onions or 1 bunch white early bunching onions with greens, chopped
2 (4-ounce) links sweet or spicy sausage
1 bunch collard greens, stems removed
2 cups whole-milk ricotta cheese
1 head garlic, minced
5 plum tomatoes, chopped

1. Preheat the oven to 350 degrees. Lightly oil a 9 x 13-inch baking pan and set aside. Fill a large bowl with ice water and set aside.

2. Heat the oil in a medium skillet over medium-high heat. Add the onions and sausage, breaking up the sausage with a fork, and cook until the onions are soft and translucent and the sausage is browned, about 7 minutes.

3. Meanwhile, fill a 6-quart stockpot halfway with water and bring to a boil over medium-high heat. Add the collards and blanch for 2 to 3 minutes. Using a slotted spoon, transfer the collards to the prepared ice bath and let cool completely. Drain the collards thoroughly and pat dry with paper towels.

4. Working in batches, lay the collard greens out on a work surface. Stir the ricotta and garlic together to blend and then spread a thin layer of the ricotta mixture on one side of each collard leaf. Spread about 2 tablespoons of the sausage mixture over the cheese.

5. Loosely roll up the collard greens lengthwise, being careful to keep the mixture inside of each bundle; carefully tie each roll with butcher's twine, securing the ends and center portion to form an oblong roll, or secure with toothpicks. Transfer to the prepared pan. Top with the tomatoes and bake for 25 minutes. Serve.

Foote Brook Farm

VALLEY DREAM FARM

Located in Pleasant Valley, in the lap of Mount Mansfield, Valley Dream Farm is a certified organic diversified farm that grows fruits, vegetables, flowers and herbs. The owners, Joe and Anne Tisbert and their family, believe in being good stewards of the land and protecting the environment by using sustainable farming methods. Preserved agriculturally through the American Farmland Trust, Valley Dream Farm is dedicated to building a better community, encouraging and inspiring other community members to do the same. They have donated over 50,000 pounds of produce to local food shelves and Salvation Farms.

Roasted Roots

SERVES 8

Feel free to alter the amounts in the seasoning mix to suit your taste, and to experiment with other root vegetables such as rutabagas, sweet potatoes, and garlic. There is no need to peel the potatoes, turnips, parsnips, or carrots. To ensure even cooking, cut the vegetables so they are uniform in size. Leftovers taste great reheated or added to soup.

8 ounces red beets, cut into 1-inch pieces

8 ounces red potatoes, cut into 1-inch pieces

8 ounces golden turnips, cut into 1-inch pieces

8 ounces parsnips, cut diagonally into
   1-inch pieces

8 ounces carrots, cut diagonally into
   1-inch pieces

1 small onion, cut into 1/3-inch wedges

3 garlic cloves, sliced

1 tablespoon chopped fresh parsley,
   plus extra for sprinkling

1 teaspoon chopped fresh thyme,
   plus extra for sprinkling

1 teaspoon chopped fresh rosemary,
   plus extra for sprinkling

1/2 teaspoon garlic salt

Salt and freshly ground black pepper

1/4 cup olive oil

1. Preheat the oven to 400 degrees. Lightly oil a 9 x 13-inch baking dish and set aside.

2. Place the beets, potatoes, turnips, parsnips, carrots, onion, garlic, parsley, thyme, rosemary, garlic salt, and 1/4 teaspoon pepper in a large bowl. Drizzle the oil over the vegetables and toss to combine, making sure to coat all the vegetables well.

3. Spread the vegetable mixture into the prepared baking dish. Roast, stirring every 15 minutes, until the vegetables are fork-tender and golden brown, 45 to 50 minutes.

4. Season with salt and pepper to taste. Sprinkle with additional parsley, thyme, and rosemary and serve.

Valley Dream Farm

Grilled Coconut Delicata Squash

SERVES 4

This recipe, a family favorite, was inspired by the potential health benefits of coconut oil and the Lehouilliers' love of coconut, as well as their need for dishes that are simple enough to make while chasing after two small children.

2 pounds delicata squash (about 3 medium)
   halved lengthwise, seeded, and cut crosswise
   into 1/2-inch-wide slices

1/4 cup organic extra-virgin coconut oil

Kosher salt

1/3 cup shredded coconut, toasted

1. Toss the squash with the coconut oil in a medium bowl and season with salt to taste.

2. Heat a grill to medium-high and grill the squash until tender, about 3 minutes per side. Top with the shredded coconut and serve.

Foote Brook Farm

THE PITCHER INN

The Pitcher Inn has been welcoming guests since the early 1850s. It was originally a simple country inn where weary travelers who ventured over treacherous mountain paths from Granville, Lincoln, or Roxbury would stop to rest. The inn has evolved over the decades, providing hearty meals and welcoming guests who vacation in the quaint, quiet village of Warren. It is affilitated with Relais & Chateaux, the international association of luxury hotels and restaurants.

Today's Pitcher Inn epitomizes hospitality, grace, and Vermont charm. Each room represents select aspects of the state; its history, character, sports, and social structure are all intertwined with the comforts discerning travelers expect of a small luxury hotel.

The inn's restaurants, Tracks and 275 Main, have also grown with the times. Vermont and the Mad River Valley boast an amazing variety of farmers, artisanal cheesemakers, orchards, apiaries, and brewerie. This diversity of incredible products provides inspiration for executive chef Susan Schickler and her culinary team. Both the inn's restaurants rely on fresh, seasonal ingredients and are supported by a wine cellar boasting more than 500 selections.

Turnip-Potato Gratin

SERVES 8 TO 10

This dish is served in the upstairs dining room during the late summer and early fall. The inn uses local turnips, Vermont Creamery crème fraîche and Cabot Clothbound Cheddar, aged at least 10 months in the cellars at Jasper Hill Farm. The cheddar has a delicate balance of sharpness and nuttiness that lends a caramelized sweetness to the dish. Aleppo chili pepper has the salty roundness and perfume of a sundried tomato, with an added kick.

2 tablespoons (1 ounce) unsalted butter, softened

8 ounces (about 8 slices) smoked bacon, sliced crosswise into 1/4-inch strips

4 medium Yukon Gold potatoes (about 2 pounds), peeled and sliced 1/8 inch thick

Kosher salt

Aleppo chili pepper

8 ounces Vermont cheddar cheese, shredded (2 cups)

4 small purple-top turnips, peeled and sliced 1/8 inch thick

1 large white onion, peeled and sliced 1/8 inch thick

2 cups heavy cream

1 cup crème fraiche

Grated nutmeg

Chopped fresh chives

1. Preheat the oven to 350 degrees. Coat a 10 x 15-inch baking dish with 2 tablespoons butter; set aside.

2. Sauté the bacon in a medium skillet over medium heat until crisp, about 6 minutes. Using a slotted spoon, transter to paper towels to drain.

3. Arrange the potatoes evenly on the bottom of the prepared dish, overlapping the slices. Season with salt and Aleppo pepper to taste, then sprinkle with one-third of the bacon and one-third of the cheese. Repeat with the turnips and then the onions, seasoning each with salt and Aleppo pepper to taste, and sprinkling with bacon and cheese. Gently pour the cream over top, being careful not to disturb the layers.

4. Bake the gratin until the vegetabless are very tender, about 1 1/4 hours.

5. Remove the gratin from the oven and spread the crème fraiche over the top. Return to the oven and bake until lightly browned and bubbly, about 10 minutes. Let rest for 10 minutes, then sprinkle with nutmeg and chives to taste, and serve.

The Pitcher Inn

LAZY LADY FARM

Lazy Lady Farm, owned by Laini Fondiller, is in the town of Westfield, near the Canadian border.. When Fondiller graduated from college she wanted to try something new , so she went to work on dairy farms. In 1981, she traveled to Corsica, France, where she stumbled into the cheesemaking business, and her love of cheese began. Fondiller remained in France for over two years, working at various goat cheese operations where she honed her craft.

When she returned home, Fondiller began adapting the recipes she had learned to make her own cheeses. She has been making cheese for more than 24 years now, milking more than 40 registered Alpine goats and producing more than 10,000 pounds of cheese a year. Fondiller's interest in politics has moved her to give many of her cheeses politically inspired names.

Lazy Lady Farm Three-Cheese au Gratin Potatoes

This au gratin recipe has a flavorful blend of three cheeses layered throughout the dish. It is creamy and rich, with a good bite. It's a perfect dish for autumn, when all three of these distinctive cheeses are available.

8 ounces russet potato, sliced 1/8 inch thick
8 ounces Yukon Gold potato, sliced 1/8 inch thick
Salt and freshly ground black pepper
2 tablespoons (1 ounce) unsalted butter
2 tablespoons all-purpose flour
2 garlic cloves, minced
1 1/2 cups heavy cream
8 ounces Lazy Lady Farm's Lady in Blue cheese
4 ounces Lazy Lady Farm's Mixed Emotion cheese
4 ounces Lazy Lady Farm's Tomme Delay cheese
1 tablespoon chopped fresh thyme, plus sprigs for garnish

1. Preheat the oven to 375 degrees. Lightly grease a 9 x 13-inch baking dish or similar sized casserole dish with butter or spray with nonstick cooking spray. Arrange the sliced potatoes in the prepared baking dish, season with salt and pepper to taste, and set aside.

2. Melt the butter in a medium saucepan over medium-low heat. Stir in the flour, whisking constantly, until thickened and pale golden in color. Stir in the garlic. Add the cream gradually, whisking until smooth. Remove from the heat and stir in the Lady in Blue, Mixed Emotion, 1/4 cup of the Tomme Delay, and the thyme. Season with salt and pepper to taste.

3. Carefully pour the cheese mixture over the potatoes. Lightly coat the dull side of a sheet of foil with nonstick cooking spray and cover the baking dish. Bake until hot and bubbly, about 1 hour. Remove the gratin from oven and sprinkle the remaining 1/4 cup of Tomme Delay over the top. Return to the oven and bake, uncovered, until the cheese is golden brown, about 10 minutes. Let rest for 10 minutes. Garnish with thyme sprigs and serve.

Juniper's at the Wildflower Inn for Lazy Lady Farm

Note: Lazy Lady Farm's Lady in Blue is a soft, creamy blue cheese made with raw cow's milk. It is available from September to May. Blythedale Farm has a similar Jersey Blue, as does Blue Ledge Farm; any soft and creamy blue cheese will work.

Note: Lazy Lady Farm's Mixed Emotion cheese is a delicious raw, soft, creamy cheese made from goat- and cow's milk. The cheese is available from June to December. Twig Farm Fuzzy Wheel raw goat/cow's milk cheese is a nice alternative.

Note: Lazy Lady Farm's Tomme Delay cheese is a raw goat's milk cheese that is firm and moist. It is available from May to November. A nice alternative is Consider Bardwell Farm's Manchester, a raw goat's milk cheese.

SQUARE DEAL FARM

In 1997, when Sarah Lyons and Ray Lewis bought their 146-acre farm in Walden, their dream was to develop the property for maple sugaring. The husband and wife team started off on a very small scale with approximately 250 taps. Today, the farm has around 6,000 taps. In addition to their maple sugar operation they raise Pinzgauer cattle, and pastured pigs.

Lyons and Lewis believe in the importance of sustainable agriculture and their dedication to the organic community is seen in every aspect of their farming practices. The farm's maple syrup and sugar are VOF-certified organic. This means that every step along the way has been checked to ensure that the farm manages their sugarbush sustainably—without the use of chemicals or pesticides. Everything that comes in contact with their sap, syrup, and sugar must conform to rigorous standards.

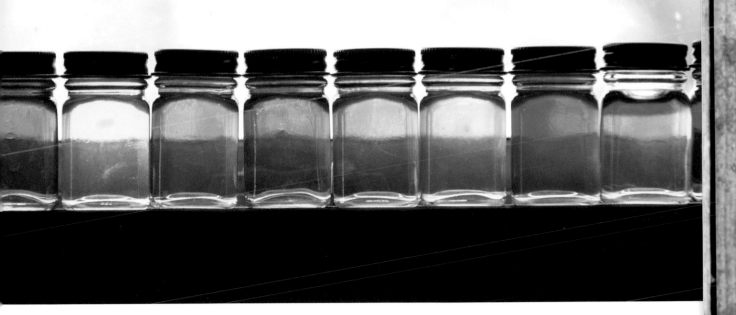

Maple-Glazed Sweet Potatoes

SERVES 6

To give the potatoes a richer caramelized look, after baking, place them under the broiler for 3 to 5 minutes.

3 medium sweet potatoes (about 2 pounds), scrubbed well
3 tablespoons (1 1/2 ounces) unsalted butter
1/4 cup pure Vermont maple syrup
1 teaspoon ground cumin
1/3 cup chopped walnuts
Sea salt and freshly ground black pepper
2–3 tablespoons thinly sliced scallions
Grated nutmeg

1. Preheat the oven to 350 degrees. Lightly grease a 9-inch square or 7 x 11-inch baking pan and set aside.

2. Place the sweet potatoes in a large pot of cold salted water. Bring to a boil over medium-high heat, then reduce the temperature and simmer until the potatoes are fork-tender, 20 to 30 minutes. Drain thoroughly in a colander and set aside.

3. When the potatoes are cool enough to handle, peel and cut them into 2-inch chunks. Place the potato chunks in a single layer in the prepared pan.

4. In a small saucepan, combine the butter, syrup, and cumin over medium-low heat, and simmer, stirring occasionally, for 3 minutes. Pour the maple mixture over the sweet potatoes and toss to coat evenly. Top the mixture with the walnuts and season with salt and pepper to taste. Bake until tender and lightly golden, 10 to 15 minutes. Sprinkle with the scallions and nutmeg to taste, and serve.

Square Deal Farm

BURLINGTON FARMERS' MARKET

The Burlington Farmers' Market is offered year-round. It consists of two markets; an outdoor market held in the warmer months, and an indoor market, which is opened during Vermont's chilly winters. Since 1980 the Burlington Summer Farmers' Market has been held every Saturday, from late spring through autumn, in downtown Burlington's City Hall Park. More than 90 stands overflow with seasonal produce, flowers, artisan wares, prepared foods, and much more.

The Burlington Winter Farmers' Market, which opened in 2008, has greatly benefited from the growing interest in buying local, as well as the fortune of many farms and studios nearby. Sheltered from the snowy Vermont weather, the indoor marketplace bustles with locals and visitors every other Saturday from November to April. Every one of the products available at the winter and summer farmers' markets is produced, grown, or crafted in the state of Vermont.

Zucchini Spread

MAKES 3 CUPS

Since zucchini has a very high water content, it is important to squeeze out as much moisture as possible before processing it. Serve this spread with crackers, bread rounds, or fresh raw vegetables.

3 cups finely shredded zucchini (about 2 medium zucchini)
8 ounces reduced-fat cream cheese, softened
1/4 cup chopped fresh cilantro
2 tablespoons extra-virgin olive oil
2 tablespoons lemon juice plus 1/2 teaspoon grated lemon zest
1 tablespoon grated Parmesan cheese
2 garlic cloves, minced
Salt and freshly ground white pepper

1. Wrap the zucchini in a clean dish towel and squeeze out the excess moisture. Process the zucchini, cream cheese, cilantro, oil, lemon juice, Parmesan, and garlic in a food processor until smooth, scraping down the sides of the bowl as needed. Spoon the mixture into a serving bowl, cover, and refrigerate for at least 1 hour or overnight.

2. Season the spread with salt and pepper to taste, sprinkle with lemon zest, and serve.

Sue Wells for the Burlington Farmers' Market

POMYKALA FARM

Pomykala Farm is a small family-run operation located on the Lake Champlain Islands in northern Vermont. The owners, Bob and Jane Pomykala, purchased their first piece of farmland in 1981, and their second in 1989. They felt that the islands were an ideal place to grow crops because Lake Champlain offers tempering effects from the extremes of weather. The lake holds the heat, which helps to make their fall last longer. The Pomykalas grow fruits, vegetables, herbs, and flowers on 70 acres. They also cultivate row crops and use cover crops to blanket out weeds, improve soil production, and build fertility.

Asparagus and Brown Rice

SERVES 4 AS A MAIN COURSE OR 6 AS A SIDE DISH

Jane Pomykala, co-owner of Pomykala Farm, likes to make this hearty meal in spring, when asparagus first appears on the scene. This simple dish is bright with citrus notes from the lemon zest and juice, as well as a subtle nuttiness from the brown rice and Parmesan cheese.

1 1/2 cups short- or medium-grain brown rice
3 1/2 cups low-sodium chicken broth
1 tablespoon unsalted butter
1 1/2 pounds asparagus, trimmed and sliced
    diagonally into 1-inch pieces
1 small bunch scallions, white and green parts,
    chopped
1 ounce Parmesan cheese, grated (1/2 cup)
1 teaspoon grated lemon zest plus
    1 tablespoon juice
Kosher salt and freshly ground black pepper
1 1/2 teaspoons chopped fresh thyme

1. Place the rice in a fine-mesh strainer and rinse thoroughly. Place the rice and broth in a medium saucepan and bring to a simmer over medium heat. Cover tightly, reduce the heat to low and cook until tender and most of the liquid has been absorbed, 40 to 45 minutes.

2. Melt the butter in a medium skillet over medium heat. Add the asparagus and green onions and sauté, stirring occasionally until tender, 6 to 8 minutes. Transfer to a medium bowl and add the rice. Stir in the Parmesan and lemon zest and juice. Season with salt and pepper to taste, sprinkle with thyme, and serve.

Pomykala Farm

FIDDLEHEAD BREWING COMPANY

Matt Cohen, the owner of Fiddlehead Brewing Company, was an anthropology major at Ithaca College who began making beer in his dorm using a home-brewing kit. The idea that most cultures make their own fermented beverages always fascinated him. This led Cohen to try and replicate some of these beverages, causing him to become involved in the science of fermentation.

After graduating from college, Cohen was looking for a career that spoke to both his interests in science and creativity. For Cohen, craft brewing was the perfect marriage of both creativity and craftsmanship, combined with hard science. He quickly realized that crafting beer was his life's calling.

Cohen honed his brewing skills while working for the Magic Hat Brewing Company as their head brew master. After 13 years with the company, Cohen decided to follow his dream and branch out on his own to start the Fiddlehead Brewing Company in Shelburne. The company's mission is to use as many local ingredients as possible to produce high-quality beer with the true beer connoisseur in mind.

Beer-Battered Fiddleheads

SERVES 4 TO 6

Serve these fiddleheads with Orange-Basil Dipping Sauce (page 181).

8 cups canola oil
8 ounces fiddleheads, trimmed
3/4 cup all-purpose flour
2 teaspoons baking powder
1 teaspoon garlic powder
3/4 teaspoon freshly ground black pepper
1/2 teaspoon salt
1/8 teaspoon dry mustard
3/4 cup IPA beer, such as Fiddlehead
1 large egg, lightly beaten
2 tablespoons club soda

1. Heat the oil in a large, heavy-bottomed saucepan over medium-high heat to 350 degrees. (The oil should measure about 3 inches deep.)

2. Wash the fiddleheads under cold running water and dry thoroughly with paper towels. In a medium bowl, stir together the flour, baking powder, garlic powder, pepper, salt, and dry mustard. Add the beer, egg, and club soda and stir until just combined.

3. Quickly dip each fiddlehead into the batter, soaking about 5 seconds. Drop small batches into the hot oil and fry until golden brown, turning occasionally to brown on all sides, 1 to 2 minutes. Using a slotted spoon, remove the fiddleheads and drain on paper towels. Serve immediately.

Fiddlehead Brewery

Fresh "Springy" Spring Rolls

MAKES 12 LARGE ROLLS, SERVING 6

This recipe is one of Jill Kopel's go-to appetizers. Spring rolls are really fun to make with kids. It is a great way to get them to eat more green veggies, without realizing it! Serve these spring rolls with your favorite Asian-style dipping sauce, such as duck sauce or a soy-ginger sauce, and sliced avocado on the side, if desired.

2 ounces cellophane noodles

1 tablespoon safflower oil

1 large sweet onion, minced

3 heads baby pak choy, chopped

3–4 tablespoons tamari

3 garlic cloves, minced

3 carrots, peeled and shredded

1 cup shredded salad turnips

5 scallions, thinly sliced

1 tablespoon grated ginger

1 teaspoon rice vinegar

12 rice-paper wrappers

3 cups micro greens

1/4 cup chopped fresh cilantro

1/4 cup chopped fresh mint

1/4 cup chopped dry-roasted peanuts

1 tablespoon sesame oil

1. Place the noodles in a large bowl and pour in enough hot water to cover. Let the noodles soak until they are soft and flexible, about 30 minutes. Drain, cut into 1 1/2-inch lengths and set aside.

2. Heat the oil in a medium skillet over medium heat. Add the onions and sauté, stirring often until soft, about 5 minutes. Add the pak choy, tamari, and garlic and sauté, stirring often, until soft, about 5 minutes. Remove from the heat and let cool completely.

3. In a medium bowl, combine the carrots, turnips, scallions, ginger, and rice vinegar.

4. Heat 2 cups water in a medium saucepan until hot but not boiling. Add 1 rice-paper wrapper, turning occasionally until softened, about 30 seconds. Using a slotted spoon, remove the wrapper and lay flat on clean, dry kitchen towels. Repeat with the remaining wrappers.

5. Place 1/4 cup micro greens on each wrapper. Place about 1 tablespoon of the onion mixture and 1 tablespoon of the carrot mixture on the greens. Divide the cilantro, mint, peanuts, and sesame oil among the wrappers and top each wrapper with some noodles.

6. Working one at a time, fold the bottom of each wrapper up over the filling and roll into a tight cylinder, folding in the sides as you go. Place the rolls, seam side down, on a plate. Cover with a damp towel until ready to serve.

New Leaf Organics

FOOD WORKS

Food Works is an nonprofit educational organization located in Montpelier. It was founded to address the root causes of hunger by returning children, families, and communities back to the land through gardening and food and nutrition education. In 2001 Food Works purchased the property now known as the Two Rivers Center, and began the process of turning an historic, but neglected farm into a home for its programs and a vision for the future.

Food Works' programs and initiatives reflect the belief that the best way to help people out of the cycle of hunger, and dependence on the hunger relief system, is to make healthy local foods and food education more available to those in need. Not only do Food Works' programs increase access to fresh local foods among vulnerable populations, they teach skills to increase self-sufficiency and empower people to make more informed decisions about dietary and lifestyle choices.

Winter Root Pancakes

MAKES 20 (3-INCH) PANCAKES

This recipe grew out of a Food Works' project to integrate food and nutrition education into the curriculum at Barre City Elementary and Middle School. One December, the first-grade teachers were reading to students about holiday celebrations and recipes from around the world. They talked about potato latkes and decided to use this recipe, but substitute local root crops stored at the Two Rivers Center's root cellar, making different kinds so the students could compare and contrast. So began the adventure into preparing many kinds of root cakes, which the students created, taste-tested and rated, followed up by some math problems using the resulting data. Serve these pancakes with fresh sprouts (sunflower, broccoli, alfalfa, radish, or pea); applesauce and sour cream; tomato chutney; or summer pesto and steamed tender greens.

1 large celeriac root (about 1 1/2 pounds), peeled, grated, and squeezed dry

1 russet or Idaho potato (about 12 ounces), peeled and grated

1 large parsnip (about 8 ounces), peeled and grated

1 large sweet onion (about 12 ounces), peeled and grated

1/4 cup whole-wheat flour, plus extra as needed

2 large eggs, lightly beaten

2 tablespoons chopped fresh thyme, basil, rosemary, basil, or parsley, or a combination

Kosher salt and freshly ground black pepper

2 ounces Vermont cheddar cheese, shredded (1 cup) (optional)

2 tablespoons grated Parmesan cheese (optional)
1/4 cup sunflower oil
2 tablespoons (1 ounce) unsalted butter

1. Preheat the oven to 275 degrees.

2. In a large bowl, mix together the celeriac root, potato, parsnip, onion, flour, eggs, herbs, and salt and pepper to taste. Fold in the cheddar and Parmesan, if using. If the batter seems too thin, add additional flour as needed.

3. Heat 1 tablespoon of the oil and 1/2 tablespoon of the butter in a large skillet over medium-high heat. Using a 2-inch ice cream scoop or 1/4-cup measure, drop the mixture onto the prepared griddle. Using a fork, flatten into pancakes and cook on one side until nicely browned, about 4 minutes. Flip the pancakes and cook until golden brown, about 3 minutes.

4. Transfer the pancakes to an ovenproof dish and keep warm in the oven. Repeat with the remaining oil and butter, and remaining pancake mixture, in three more batches. Serve.

Food Works at Two Rivers Center

YOUR FARM

In 2006, Kevin and Laura Channell purchased an empty hay field consisting of 28 acres of fertile sandy loam soil, on the Connecticut River in the town of Fairlee. Today, Your Farm is a VOF-certified organic farm, where over 100 different varieties of vegetables are grown on about 10 acres of the property. The Channells strive to farm in a sustainable manner by rotating crops, practicing erosion control, building soil health, and reducing off-farm inputs. All the produce is grown without the use of any chemical pesticides, herbicides, or synthetic fertilizers. Produce from Your Farm is sold through CSA memberships, the Norwich Farmers' Market, local restaurants and small grocers. Kevin and Laura consider it a privilege to steward this piece of prime farmland and share the bounties of the soil with local communities.

Summer Stuffed Heirloom Tomatoes

SERVES 4

One of Your Farm's favorite tomatoes is the Brandywine. The farm grows this special heirloom variety because of its amazing flavor, large size, and beefy texture. These tomatoes are delicious stuffed with an array of other vegetables from the peak summer harvest.

4 large Brandywine tomatoes
1/3 cup plus 2 tablespoons extra-virgin olive oil
2 garlic cloves, minced
1 teaspoon chili powder
Kosher salt and freshly ground black pepper
1 large sweet onion, chopped
3/4 cup chopped yellow summer squash
3/4 cup chopped zucchini
3/4 cup chopped, peeled eggplant
3/4 cup chopped red or green bell pepper
2 tablespoons grated Parmesan cheese
4 ounces fresh mozzarella cheese, cut into
    4 slices
2 tablespoons chopped fresh basil

1. Preheat the oven to 375 degrees.

2. Cut out and discard a cone-shaped section from the stem end of each tomato, being careful not to go all the way through. Place the tomatoes cut side up in a 9 x 13-inch baking dish.

3. In a small bowl, mix together 1/3 cup of the olive oil, 1 teaspoon of the garlic, the chili powder, 1/2 teaspoon salt, and 1/2 teaspoon pepper. Brush the tomatoes with garlic oil mixture, completely coating each one.

4. Heat the remaining 2 tablespoons oil in a large skillet over medium heat. Add the onion, summer squash, zucchini, eggplant, pepper, and the remaining garlic. Season with salt and pepper to taste and sauté until the vegetables are soft and translucent, 10 to 12 minutes. Stir in the Parmesan and spoon the vegetable mixture into each tomato until heaping full. Scatter any extra filling around the tomatoes. Drizzle the remaining garlic-oil mixture over the stuffed tomatoes and top each tomato with 1 slice mozzarella.

5. Bake the tomatoes until they are slightly softened and heated through, 15 to 20 minutes. Garnish with the chopped basil and serve.

Your Farm

Variation: Add 8 ounces ground beef or lamb, cooked, to the stuffing mixture and serve the tomatoes on a bed of pasta.

SANDWICHES, PIZZA, AND SAVORY PIES

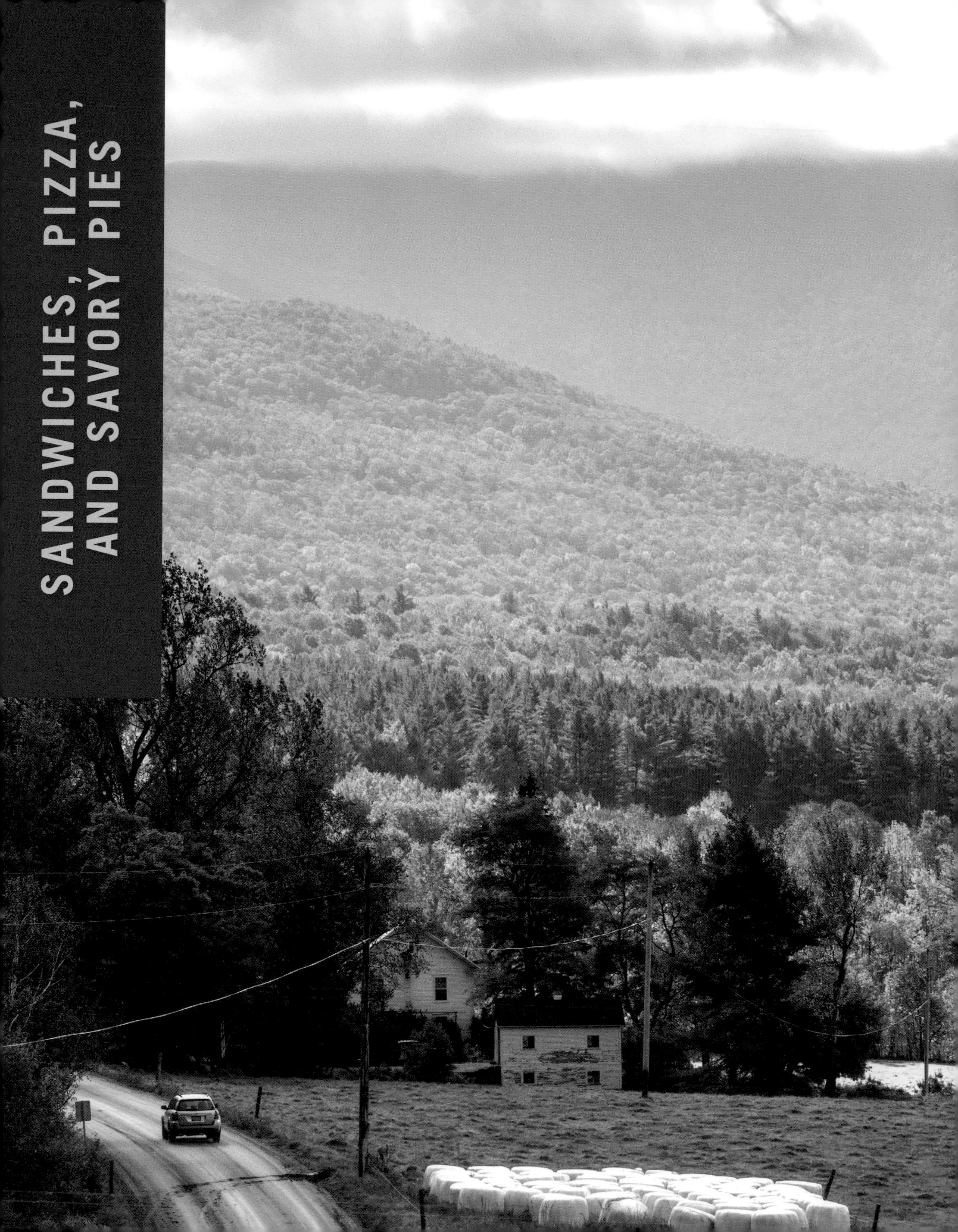

FULL MOON FARM

Rachel Nevitt and David Zuckerman farm with a passion, growing great food in a responsible way. Their farm, Full Moon Farm, is a stunning 155-acre diversified farm located in Hinesburg. Nevitt and Zuckerman grow 40 to 45 fruits and vegetables, ranging from beautiful heirloom tomatoes to fragrant muskmelons, sweet corn to daikon radishes, all VOF-certified. The husband-and-wife team also raises certified organic pastured pork and certified organic pastured chickens, which they sell to their CSA members, as well as at the Burlington Farmers' Market, and, occasionally, wholesale. Occasionally, they offer their meat for wholesale, giving the lucky consumer a rare opportunity to enjoy their products. Nevitt and Zuckerman strongly feel that it is important for people to meet the farmers who use the best organic practices to grow their food. As they say, "We are absolutely committed to connecting consumers to their local food sources and producers."

Rachel's Caprese Sandwich with Heirloom Tomatoes, Extra-Sharp Cheddar Cheese, and Basil

SERVES 4

At Full Moon Farm this sandwich is made with bread from Good Companion Bakery (in nearby Vergennes), extra-sharp cheddar cheese from Cabot Creamery, and heirloom tomatoes and basil from the farm. This sandwich is also called "Rachel's Summer Joy." It makes a delicious luncheon dish and is ideal for a hearty snack.

4 slices 1/2-inch-thick rustic farm bread
4 ounces extra-sharp cheddar cheese,
    thinly sliced
2–3 large heirloom tomatoes, cut into
    1/3-inch-thick slices
8–16 large basil leaves, torn into pieces
Olive oil
Salt and freshly ground black pepper

1. Adjust an oven rack to the top position and heat the broiler. Lightly toast the bread slices. Layer the tomato slices, basil leaves, and cheddar cheese on each slice. Drizzle with olive oil and season with salt and pepper to taste.

2. Place the sandwiches on a baking sheet and broil them until the cheese melts. Serve.

David Zuckerman and Rachel Nevitt of Full Moon Farm Inc.

CONSIDER BARDWELL FARM

Consider Bardwell Farm, located in West Pawlet, is a 300-acre goat and cow dairy farm, as well as an artisan cheesemaking operation. Consider Stebbins Bardwell founded the farm in 1864; it was the first cheesemaking co-op in Vermont. During the 1860s, local farmers would bring all their morning milk to the farm where it was made into cheese, which was later shipped to Albany, New York, and the Boston area.

In 2000, Angela Miller and her husband, Russell Glover, purchased the farm. They had a plan to revitalize the tradition of helping small, local farmers process their milk into cheese. The couple bought goats in 2002, and with the help of cheesemaker Peter Dixon, started experimenting with goat's milk cheese. The farm was officially licensed to sell cheese in 2004.

Today, the farm makes three kinds of goat's milk cheese from their own herd of 90 Oberhaslis goats—a Swiss Alpine breed. They also make three kinds of cow's milk cheese from the 20 Jersey cows that they co-own with their next-door neighbor. In addition, the farm uses the milk from two cow dairy farms located nearby.

All of their cheeses are made from raw milk, except for their fresh goat cheese. This cheese is sold within one week of being made; therefore, it needs to be pasteurized. The farm has five aging caves where cheeses are aged for three months. There are also some cheeses that may take as long as two years to age.

The Animal Welfare Approved Program certifies the farm. This certification ensures that all the farm animals live as closely as possible to their natural habitat, eating grass on pasture, rotationally grazing and foraging, and breeding only in their appropriate season. All of the farm's cheeses are made by hand, in small batches, from milk that is antibiotic- and hormone-free. The cheeses have all been named after places located around Consider Bardwell Farm. Currently, the farm has five cheesemakers and produces 80,000 pounds of cheese a year.

Pawletti

MAKES 1 SANDWICH, SERVING 1 TO 2

At the Consider Bardwell Farm Café, the star attraction is a grilled cheese sandwich; one weekend, the café served 350 of them! The key to the success of this dish is high-quality ingredients. This mouthwatering sandwich is prepared with local Rupert Rising Pain au Levain, by Jed Mayer, and the farm's very own prize-winning raw Jersey cow's milk cheese, called Pawlet. It's their version of a panini. They offer it with organic bread-and-butter pickles and sliced apple, or with thin slices of onion, tomato, and prosciutto. Mustard is served on the side, of course.

1 1/2 teaspoons unsalted butter, softened
2 slices rustic peasant bread
3 thin slices sweet onion
3 thin slices tomato
1–2 thin slices prosciutto
Freshly ground black pepper
1 (3-ounce) slice Pawlet cheese or any other
      mild raw cow's milk cheese
Coarse-grain or Dijon mustard

1. Preheat a grill pan over medium-high heat or preheat a panini press. Spread one side of each slice of bread with butter and place buttered side down on a cutting board. Layer one side of the bread with the onion, tomato, and prosciutto. Season with pepper to taste. Top with the cheese and the second slice of bread.

2. Place the sandwich on the grill pan or panini press. If using a pan, weigh down with a heavy skillet and cook until golden brown and the cheese has melted, 3 to 4 minutes per side. If using a panini press, grill according to the manufacturer's directions. Cut the sandwich in half and serve immediately, with mustard on the side.

Angela Miller of Consider Bardwell Farm

AMERICAN FLATBREAD COMPANY

In 1985, George Schenk constructed an outdoor stone oven and tried making flatbread. The experiment was a success and a new business was born. Five years later, he built American Flatbread's first bakery at Lareau Farm, a late 18th-century farm in Waitsfield, in the Mad River Valley. Since then, the franchise has expanded to include restaurants in Middlebury, Burlington, and New York City, as well as a frozen flatbread business. In 2006, the company purchased the Inn at Lareau Farm, which is once again a working farm.

Through its years of growth, American Flatbread has kept the same goals: to create simple, wholesome flatbreads baked in a primitive, wood-fired earthen oven, and to feature organic ingredients raised and harvested by local farmers. By focusing on a simple menu, the restaurants can explore the boundaries of artisinal pizza making while maintaining the quality and integrity of what they serve. And by partnering with neighboring farmers, the company has been able to establish a sustainable, community-based farm-to-plate network.

Harvest Flatbread

SERVES 4 TO 6

This pizza is inspired by ingredients that are common in Vermont, such as new potatoes, tender spinach, smoked bacon, sweet maple syrup, and sharp cheddar cheese. If you don't own a pizza stone, you can use a flat (or upside down rimmed) baking sheet. A baking sheet or cutting board can also stand in for a pizza peel.

2 tablespoons unsalted butter
1 large sweet onion, thinly sliced
Kosher salt and freshly ground black pepper
1 1/4 pounds new potatoes (red or gold), thinly sliced
2 tablespoons olive oil
5 slices uncured bacon
Coarse cornmeal, as needed
1 pound prepared pizza dough, preferably organic
Garlic-Infused Olive Oil (recipe follows)
2 cups packed fresh baby spinach
2 cups shredded roasted or grilled chicken breast (about 3 chicken breasts)
8 ounces sharp or extra-sharp Vermont cheddar cheese, shredded (2 cups)
1 ounce Parmesan cheese, grated (1/2 cup)
Pure Vermont maple syrup

1. Position the oven racks in the upper third and lower third of the oven and place a baking stone on the rack. Preheat the oven to 450 degrees. (The stone should preheat for 45 minutes.)

2. Melt the butter in a large skillet over medium heat. Add the onion and stir to coat. Spread into an even layer and cook, stirring occasionally, for 10 minutes. Sprinkle with salt to taste, reduce the heat to medium-low, and cook until the onion is nicely browned, about 30 minutes.

3. Meanwhile, place the potatoes in a medium bowl and drizzle with oil; toss to coat well. Season with salt and pepper. Spread the potatoes onto a baking sheet and roast on the lower oven rack, stirring halfway through, until the potatoes are fork-tender, 20 to 25 minutes.

4. Cook the bacon in a medium skillet over medium-high heat until lightly cooked, about 3 minutes. Transfer to paper towels to drain. Coarsely chop the bacon.

5. Sprinkle cornmeal onto a pizza peel and place the dough on the peel. Using your hands, stretch the dough into a 14 x 16-inch rectangle, and brush with garlic-infused oil to taste. Season lightly with salt. Arrange the potatoes evenly over the dough, leaving a 1-inch border, then layer the spinach and onions over the potatoes. Sprinkle evenly with the chicken and bacon, then sprinkle the cheddar and Parmesan over the top. Drizzle the entire pizza with maple syrup.

6. Slide the pizza onto the baking stone and bake until the edge of the crust is lightly crisp and the cheese is lightly browned, 20 to 25 minutes.

American Flatbread Company

Garlic-Infused Olive Oil

MAKES 1/2 CUP

1/2 cup extra-virgin olive oil
4 garlic cloves, thinly sliced

Heat the oil in a small saucepan over medium heat. Add the garlic and cook until fragrant, but not browned, 2 to 3 minutes. Let the oil cool, then cover and let steep for 1 hour. Strain the oil into a sterilized jar or bottle; discard the garlic. Use within 24 hours.

American Flatbread Company

KNOLL FARM

Knoll Farm is an organic family-run farm owned by Helen Whybrow and her husband, Peter Forbes. They grow highbush organic blueberries and raise purebred Icelandic sheep for breedstock, wool, and grass-fed meat. The couple also runs a nonprofit organization called the Center for Whole Communities, which they founded in 2003. The Center for Whole Communities offers leadership development retreats that focus on the environmental and social justice movements. Through these programs, Whybrow and Forbes help leaders from diverse fields, such as community development and urban conservation, find ways to work together to foster a strong relationship between people and the environment.

Blueberry Goat Cheese Pizza with Caramelized Onions and Rosemary

SERVES 4 TO 6

One of Knoll Farm's signature dishes is a wood-fired blueberry, goat cheese, rosemary pizza, which is made in their outdoor mud oven. The pizza has a nice combination of sweet and savory. It has a creamy tang from the goat cheese (Knoll Farm uses Vermont Butter and Cheese Creamery brand) and a sweet earthiness from caramelized onions coupled with blueberries. All of these ingredients, combined with the woody pine flavor from the fresh rosemary, make this pizza a real treat. If you don't own a pizza stone, you can use a flat (or upside-down rimmed) baking sheet. A baking sheet or cutting board can also stand in for a pizza peel.

3 tablespoons (1 1/2 ounces) unsalted butter
2 large sweet onions, sliced thin
Kosher salt
Coarse cornmeal, as needed
1 pound pizza dough, preferably whole-wheat
2 tablespoons olive oil, or as needed
8 ounces fresh goat cheese, crumbled, at room temperature (2 cups)
1 1/2 pints blueberries
3 tablespoons chopped fresh rosemary
Vermont honey

1. Place a baking stone in the oven and preheat the oven to 450 degrees. (The stone should preheat for 45 minutes.)

2. Melt the butter in a large skillet over medium heat. Add the onions and stir to coat. Spread the onions into an even layer and cook, stirring occasionally, for 10 minutes. Sprinkle with salt to taste, reduce the heat to medium-low, and cook until the onions are nicely browned, about 30 minutes.

3. Sprinkle coarse cornmeal onto a pizza peel and place the dough on the peel. Using your hands, stretch the dough into a 14 x 16-inch rectangle, and brush with the oil. Season lightly with salt. Sprinkle the goat cheese, then the blueberries and onions, on the crust. Top with the rosemary, leaving a 1-inch border, and drizzle with honey.

4. Slide the pizza onto the baking stone and bake until the edge of the crust is slightly crisp and lightly browned, 20 to 25 minutes.

Knoll Farm

CONANT'S RIVERSIDE FARM/ RIVERSIDE PRODUCE

In 1854, Samuel Conant purchased Conant's Riverside Farm. At that time the farm consisted of about 500 acres of cropland, forest, and pasture bordering the Winooski River. Today, the primary focus of the farm continues to be dairy. The sixth generation of Conant farmers now works on about 1,000 acres, which includes a combination of croplands and woodlands. They milk about 400 Holstein cows, and grow and selling sweet corn and other produce at their farmstand. They also market their own USDA-inspected ground beef during the produce season. The Conants are committed to continuing a tradition of sustainable environmental practices. Conant's Riverside Farm is a proud member of the Agri-Mark Dairy Co-operative, which supplies milk for such food producers such as Cabot Creamery.

Fresh Corn Quiche

SERVES 6 TO 8

This light and creamy quiche is a nice departure from the traditional quiche with cheese.

3 large eggs, lightly beaten
1/2 small onion, coarsely chopped
1 tablespoon all-purpose flour
1 teaspoon kosher salt
1/2 teaspoon freshly ground black pepper
1 1/3 cups half-and-half
3 tablespoons (1 1/2 ounces) unsalted butter, melted
2 cups fresh corn kernels (cut from 2 to 3 ears corn) or frozen, thawed
1 tablespoon chopped fresh thyme or basil
1 (9-inch) prepared whole-wheat piecrust

1. Preheat the oven to 375 degrees.

2. Process the eggs, onion, flour, salt and pepper in a food processor until the onion is finely chopped. Add the half-and-half and butter and process until just blended. Pour into a large bowl and stir in the corn and thyme. Pour the filling into the prepared crust.

3. Bake until the filling is slightly puffed and the top is golden brown, about 50 minutes. Remove from the oven and let cool slightly before serving.

Conant's Riverside Farm/Riverside Produce

JASPER HILL FARM

Brothers Andy and Mateo Kehler grew up summering on the edge of secluded Caspian Lake in the sleepy village of Greensboro. Their great grandfather had been a visitor to that area in the early 1900's. The brothers' long, emotional connection to the Northeast Kingdom made them decide to try to make a life there. When the opportunity arose in 1998, the two impulsively decided to buy a farm in Greensboro. They used the next three years to work on a business plan, gain the necessary experience to succeed as cheesemakers, and decide how best to use their farm's land.

Mateo spent two years in Europe working with farmstead cheesemakers in England, France, and Italy. After leaving Europe, he returned home. During the years, 2002 to 2003, the brothers built a small cheese plant and began making cheese. Since then, they have begun raising a herd of 45 Ayrshire cows, which they milk. Andy and Mateo have also started ripening cheeses for other cheesemakers. This is actually another one of their businesses, known as the Cellars at Jasper Hill.

The Cellars at Jasper Hill is the first business of its kind in the United States. To achieve their goal, the brothers needed to blast out a hillside and pour monolithic concrete to create a structure that consists of seven vaulted tunnels, which are 22,000 square feet in size. These tunnels are nestled beneath the pastures where cows graze. In that space, the Kehler's mature cheese for other cheesemakers.

Andy and Mateo are trying to assist dairy farmers who would like to transition from making commodity milk to the production of cheesemaking. By not having to make the investment in cheesemaking for their aging facilities, the dairy farmers increase the values of their farms. The Cellars at Jasper Hill offers the dairy farmer the labor to actually ripen the cheese. The brothers have a sales and marketing team to help the farm move their product. This frees the farmer from having to deal with the logistics necessary for getting the cheese to market and receiving payment. The Cellars at Jasper Hill basically take these tasks off the farmer's plate. This allows the producers o focus on the most important aspects of their trade—the quality milk production and cheesemaking techniques.

Part of the idea and inspiration for the Cellars at Jasper Hill evolved from Mateo's exposure to the cheese industry in England and France. What they are doing is an adaptation of what already exists in Europe although, their business is pretty different in some respects from anything that might exist in England or France.

What the brothers are really looking at doing is creating a revival on their landscape in Greensboro. They are the latest crop of optimists. The two of them believe that there is a market out there for high quality products and they are essentially in the business of putting their high value products into that pipeline. Andy and Mateo can see that this is an agricultural and economic development project—cheese is just a vehicle to achieve these goals.

Caramelized Onion and Bayley Hazen Blue Galette

SERVES 4 TO 6

This free-form tart is meant to have a rustic look, so don't worry if it is not perfect. The dough can be made up to one day ahead; just wrap and refrigerate. Bring the dough to room temperature before proceeding.

1 1/4 cups all-purpose flour

8 tablespoons (4 ounces) salted butter, cut into pieces and chilled

1/4 cup crème fraiche

1/4 cup ice water, plus extra as needed

2 tablespoons olive oil or bacon fat

4 medium yellow onions, peeled and thinly sliced

Pinch granulated sugar

2 garlic cloves, minced

1/2 teaspoon finely chopped fresh rosemary or thyme

5 ounces blue cheese, preferably Bayley Hazen Blue Cheese, crumbled (1 1/4 cups)

1 large egg yolk, lightly beaten

1. Place the flour in a large bowl. Cut in the butter with a pastry cutter, two butter knives, or with your fingers, until the mixture begins to form pea-sized pieces. Combine the crème fraiche and ice water and add in a steady stream while mixing the dough with your fingertips. If necessary, add a bit more water until the dough holds together, but do not overmix. Turn the dough out onto a clean, floured work surface and form into a ball. Wrap in plastic wrap or waxed paper and refrigerate for at least 20 minutes.

2. Meanwhile, preheat the oven to 400 degrees. Heat the oil in a large skillet over medium heat. Add the onions and sugar and cook for 2 minutes. Reduce the heat to medium-low and continue to cook, stirring frequently, until the onions are soft and golden, 35 to 40 minutes. Add the garlic and rosemary and cook for 1 minute.

3. On a floured work surface, roll the dough out into a 13-inch round. Transfer the dough to an ungreased baking sheet. Evenly spread the onion mixture over the dough, leaving a 1 1/2-inch border. Evenly sprinkle the cheese over the top. Fold the border over the filling, pleating the edges as you go around. The center will be open. Brush the crust with the beaten egg yolk.

4. Bake the galette until the crust is golden brown and the cheese is sizzling, about 30 minutes. Remove from the oven and let cool for 5 minutes before cutting and serving.

Jasper Hill Farm

FLOWERPOWER VT

Anne Flack-Matthews' passion for farming began as a child. Her grandmother, an immigrant from Prussia, taught her how to garden and became her inspiration. Flack-Matthews grew up helping out in her family's vegetable garden and raising a lot of her own food. For her, the satisfaction of being outside and seeing things grow was magical.

The love of gardening was in her blood and continues to be a strong presence in her life. Throughout her younger years Flack-Matthews somehow always managed to have a garden, beginning with 4H Club and continuing with a college community plot.

When she moved to a rural area in Pennsylvania, she bought 20 Araucana chickens at an Amish auction. This breed, native to Chile, lays eggs with light blue shells. Her three young children very much enjoyed taking care of the pear-shaped chickens with tufted "ears."

Ten years ago Flack-Matthews and her family moved to Vermont, where they bought a defunct llama farm, on a south-facing slope in Ferrisburgh. Flack-Matthews named the farm FlowerPower VT because it symbolized what the 1960s meant to her: peace, love, and understanding. Soon she bought a tiller and began planting flowering perennials, herbs and vegetables. The farm's main focus was growing organic flowers, which were sold at various farmers' markets. Creating flower arrangements for weddings and local events also kept Flack-Matthews very busy. Still, she felt that something was missing: her beloved Araucana chickens.

Following her dream, she purchased 100 Araucana chicks. Using chicken wire, she sectioned off part of the farm to create a large area for the chicks to eat grass, bugs and worms. Eventually, certified organic blue eggs were added to her onsite, year-round milk house farm stand and farmers market offerings. Loyal customers couldn't get enough of the delicious dark golden yolks. FlowerPower VT has also added Americana chickens to their happy group. This American breed is mixed in to add intelligence, health, and laying power to the flock.

The farm's organic certification reflects that the hens are fed organic grains, which are free of genetically modified grains, toxic insecticides and lake-polluting fertilizers. Presently, the farm has 450 laying hens, which range in the fields during the summer.

Flack-Matthews says, "Never give up, follow your dreams and believe in yourself—that's me! My community is becoming what I envisioned. The interaction has been the most rewarding part, by far. I have muscles, sunburn, sore shoulders, and a smile."

Farm Quiche

SERVES 8

This quiche recipe showcases the farm's fresh, delicious Araucana eggs. The rich, creamy filling is studded with baby spinach, cherry tomatoes, and Gruyère cheese.

1 1/2 tablespoons butter
2/3 cup chopped shallots (about 3 medium)
1 1/2 cups packed chopped fresh baby spinach
Coarse salt and freshly ground white pepper
6 large eggs, beaten
1 cup whole milk
1/2 cup heavy cream
1 1/2 teaspoons finely chopped fresh thyme
1/8 teaspoon grated nutmeg
1 (9-inch) whole-wheat pie crust, chilled
6 ounces Gruyère cheese, shredded (1 1/2 cups)
8 cherry tomatoes, halved

1. Preheat the oven to 375 degrees.

2. Melt the butter in a large skillet over medium-low heat. Add the shallots and sauté until tender, 3 to 4 minutes. Add the spinach and cook until just wilted, 2 to 3 minutes. Season with salt and pepper to taste. When cool enough to handle, transfer the spinach mixture to a paper towel and squeeze out any excess water. Set aside.

3. Whisk together the eggs, milk, cream, thyme, nutmeg, and salt and pepper to taste.

4. Spread the spinach mixture evenly over the bottom of the pie crust. Sprinkle 1 cup of the Gruyère on top of the spinach and carefully pour the egg mixture over the cheese. Sprinkle with the remaining cheese and arrange the tomatoes over filling. Bake until the egg mixture is still slightly wiggly in center, about 40 minutes. Let cool for 15 minutes, then cut into wedges and serve.

FlowerPower VT Farm

THISTLE HILL FARM

Thistle Hill Farm's philosophy evolved as a result of its owners' sense of responsibility for the working landscape of Vermont. Owner John Putnam grew up in Vermont but was on the periphery of farming. His grandfather pastured Jersey heifers and had an amazing wood lot, where Putnam worked during the summer when he was younger. He also threw a ton of hay bales for a neighbor and took care of horses for him at the Green Mountain Horse Association.

When John and his wife, Janine, got their own place, it was a run-down farm. They cleaned up the property, building the barns themselves. The farm is now fully functional and has been producing organic milk for 17 years and making organic cheese for 11 of those years.

Janine was one of the first certified organic milk producers in the state of Vermont. The Putnam family has never used chemicals, hormones, or antibiotics on the farm. The husband and wife team have no employees, except for incidental help. They want to include their family, neighbors, and local consumers in their endeavors. The two believe that living in Vermont means they are obligated to help protect the state's unique environment, which includes preserving its working landscape and quality of life, as well the integrity of the cheese and milk that they work so hard to create. John and Janine hope that they are doing their small part.

Tarentaise Bread Pudding

SERVES 12

Tarentaise cheese is smooth and dense, with a slightly nutty flavor and a natural rind.

4 tablespoons (2 ounces) unsalted butter
1/2 cup minced onion
2 garlic cloves, minced
1 tablespoon chopped fresh thyme
4 cups fresh whole-wheat bread crumbs
4 cups chicken stock
3 ounces Tarentaise cheese, shredded (3/4 cup)
1 large egg plus 2 large egg yolks, lightly beaten
Kosher salt and freshly ground black pepper

1. Preheat the oven to 350 degrees. Coat twelve 6-ounce ramekins with nonstick cooking spray; set aside.

2. Melt the butter in a small skillet over medium heat. Add the onion and cook, stirring occasionally, until soft and translucent, about 5 minutes. Add the garlic and cook, stirring often for 1 minute. Stir in the thyme and set aside.

3. In a large bowl, stir together the onion mixture, bread crumbs, stock, cheese, egg and yolks, and salt and pepper to taste until fully combined.

4. Divide the mixture into the prepared ramekins. Place in a roasting pan, add enough hot water to come halfway up the sides of the ramekins and cover the pan with foil. Poke small holes in the foil to allow steam to release.

5. Bake 15 minutes, then carefully rotate the pan and bake an additional 15 minutes. Carefully remove the foil and bake until the puddings are golden brown, 10 minutes. Serve immediately.

Carpenter and Main Restaurant for Thistle Hill Farm

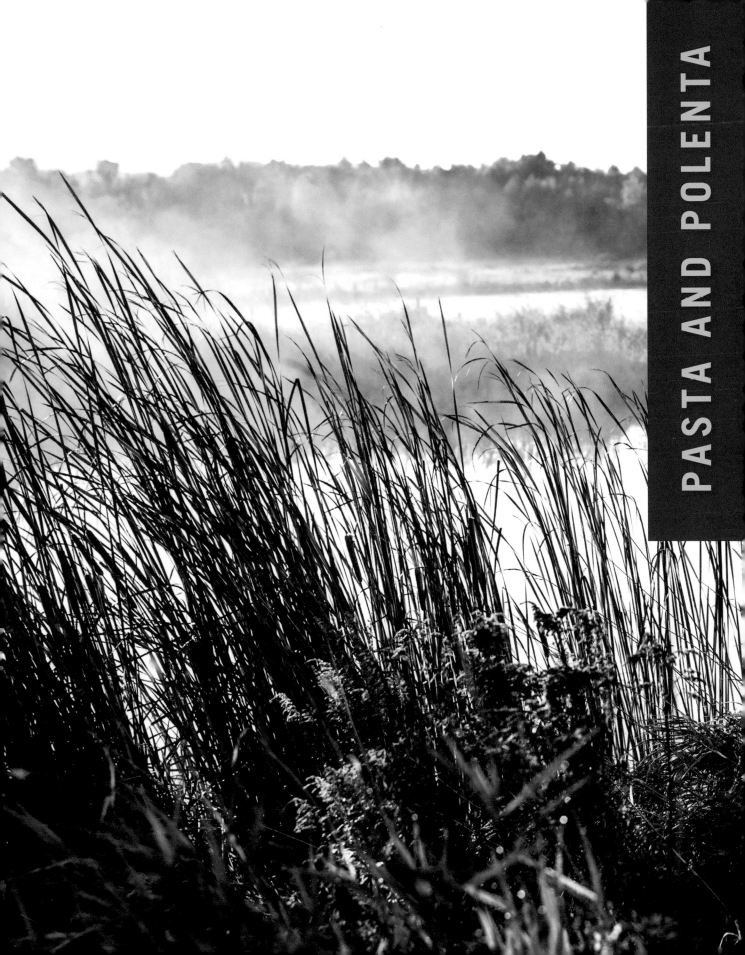

L'AMANTE RISTORANTE

In 1995, after attending the New England Culinary Institute in Vermont, Kevin Cleary cooked at some of the most highly acclaimed Italian restaurants in the Boston area, including Pignoli and the Tuscan Grill. He then spent four months in Italy working in the kitchens of the Michelin two-star Ristorante San Domenico in Imola and the chef-owned Osteria di Rendola in the green hills of Chianti. Upon returning to the states, Kevin landed the sous chef position at Il Capriccio and then, in 1999, he and wife, Kathi, opened L'Amante Ristorante in Gloucester, Massachusetts. In 2003, Kevin and Kathi moved L'Amante to Burlington, Vermont. The food is regional Italian and the wine list, consisting of 130 selections, focuses mainly on the north of Italy.

Orecchiette with Caramelized Turnips, Tuscan Kale, and Cracked Pepper

SERVES 4

Chef Cleary often uses produce from Half Pint Farm, located in the Intervale in Burlington. This very simple dish uses only a very few ingredients, so it is essential that everything be as fresh as possible. Tuscan kale, also called cavolo nero, lacinato, or dinosaur kale, is slightly sweeter than curly kale. Fusilli, tubettini, orzo, or coralli pasta can be used in place of the orrecchiette. Although this is a vegetarian dish, you can spice it up with hot Italian sausage, if desired.

Salt

1 pound orecchiette

1/4 cup canola oil

2 medium turnips, peeled and cut into 1/4-inch dice

1 pound Tuscan kale, stems and center ribs removed, roughly chopped

2 garlic cloves, minced

1/2 teaspoon red pepper flakes

Freshly cracked black pepper

8 tablespoons (4 ounces) unsalted butter

2/3 cup grated Parmigiano-Reggiano cheese, plus extra for garnish

1. Bring 6 quarts salted water to a boil in a large pot over medium-high heat. Add the pasta and cook until al dente, about 8 minutes. Drain the pasta, reserving 3/4 cup of the pasta water. Set aside.

2. Meanwhile, heat the oil in a large saucepan over medium-high heat until hot but not smoking. Add the turnips and reduce the heat to medium. Cook, stirring often, until the turnips are tender and golden, about 6 minutes.

3. Add the kale and cook, stirring often, until the kale is very tender, about 8 minutes. Add the garlic and red pepper flakes, and cook, stirring often, 1 minute. Add the reserved pasta water as needed and season with cracked pepper to taste. Add the butter and stir gently until melted.

4. Add the pasta to the kale mixture and toss with tongs until the pasta is well coated. Stir in the Parmigiano-Reggiano. Season with salt and additional cracked pepper to taste.

5. Divide the pasta into warm bowls, sprinkle with additional cheese, if desired, and serve.

L'Amante Ristorante

Mediterranean Couscous Pilaf

SERVES 4 TO 6

Serve with Moroccan-Style Chicken with Apricots and Almonds (page 130).

4 cups low-sodium chicken broth
2 tablespoons olive oil or duck fat
1/2 cup chopped yellow onion
1/2 cup chopped red bell pepper
1 garlic clove, minced
1 1/2 cups Mediterranean or Israeli couscous
1/2 teaspoon dried oregano
1 1/2 teaspoons grated lemon zest
Salt and freshly ground black pepper
Chopped fresh parsley

1. Bring the chicken broth to a boil in a medium saucepan over medium-high heat. Remove from heat, cover the pot, and set aside.

2. Meanwhile, heat the oil in a large saucepan over medium heat. Add the onion and pepper and cook, stirring often, until the onion is soft and translucent. Add the garlic and cook for 1 minute more. Stir in the couscous and cook until lightly browned, 3 to 4 minutes, stirring frequently.

3. Stir in the chicken broth and oregano, cover, and reduce the heat to low. Simmer until the broth is absorbed and the couscous is tender, 10 to 12 minutes. Add the lemon zest. Transfer to a bowl, fluffing the couscous with a fork or spoon. Season with salt and pepper to taste, sprinkle with parsley, and serve.

Ariel's Restaurant

Penne with Creamy Smugglers' Notch Vodka Sauce

SERVES 4 TO 6

Penne pasta with vodka sauce (penne alla vodka) is a classic that is fun to bring out now and again. This dish is smooth and lightly creamy, with a hint of sweetness from the Smugglers' Notch vodka, and a slight nuttiness from the freshly grated Parmigiano-Reggiano cheese. The key to this dish is using very fresh ingredients, from the spinach to the shrimp and scallops, making sure not to overcook the seafood. To prevent a flare-up, be sure to remove the skillet from the heat before adding the vodka.

Kosher salt and freshly ground black pepper
1 pound whole-wheat penne
3 tablespoons olive oil
1 pound jumbo shrimp (16/20 count), peeled and deveined
12 ounces sea scallops (20/30 count), tendons removed
8 slices prosciutto, coarsely chopped
2 tablespoons minced shallot
2 garlic cloves, minced
3 plum tomatoes, seeded and cut into thin strips
3 cups baby spinach
1/3 cup Smuggler's Notch vodka
1 1/4 cups natural marinara sauce
1 cup heavy cream
2 ounces Parmigiano-Reggiano or Pecorino Romano cheese, grated (1 cup), plus extra for serving
2 tablespoons chopped fresh basil

1. Bring a large pot of salted water to a boil, add the pasta, and cook until al dente, 6 to 7 minutes. Drain in a colander and set aside.

2. Meanwhile, heat the oil in a large skillet over medium-high heat. Add the shrimp and scallops and cook, 1 to 2 minutes on each side. Season with salt and pepper to taste. Add the prosciutto and continue to cook until the scallops are caramelized, about 2 minutes.

3. Reduce the heat to medium, add the shallot, garlic, tomatoes, and spinach, and cook for 1 minute. Remove the skillet from the heat and carefully add the vodka. Return to medium heat and cook until the alcohol burns off, about 2 minutes. Add the marinara sauce and heavy cream and simmer for 2 minutes. Stir in 1/2 cup of the cheese until melted and smooth. Add the pasta to the sauce and cook until heated through. Season with salt and pepper to taste.

4. Transfer the pasta to a large bowl and sprinkle with the remaining 1/2 cup cheese, tossing to incorporate. Sprinkle with the basil and serve with additional cheese.

Chef Peter McLyman of the Country Club of Vermont for Smugglers' Notch Distillery

Ricotta Gnocchi

SERVES 4

This is a very easy ricotta gnocchi recipe that Lee Duberman has taught to her cooking classes. Everyone loves it because it looks so much more difficult to make than it really is. Duberman either makes her own ricotta (recipe follows) or buys Turkey Hill Farm's flavorful ricotta, which is produced just a few miles from Ariel's restaurant. Duberman often serves the gnocchi in the spring with asparagus, leeks, and morel mushrooms, but it's also great in summer with chanterelles and corn, or in the fall and winter months with roasted root vegetables. The gnocchi can be made ahead of time; after boiling and cooling them, transfer to zipper-lock plastic bags and freeze.

Gnocchi

4 teaspoons salt

2 cups (1 pound) whole-milk ricotta cheese, preferably homemade

2 large eggs, lightly beaten

2 ounces Parmigiano-Reggiano cheese, grated (1 cup), plus extra for serving

1 tablespoon chopped fresh thyme or tarragon, plus extra for garnish

1/2 teaspoon grated nutmeg (optional)

1 1/4 cups all-purpose flour

Sauce

1/4 cup extra-virgin olive oil

1 cup heavy cream

4 tablespoons (2 ounces) unsalted butter

4 fresh sage leaves, finely chopped

Salt and freshly ground black pepper

1. Lightly oil a baking sheet and set aside. Bring 6 quarts water and 1 tablespoon of the salt to a boil in a large stockpot.

2. In a medium bowl, stir together the ricotta, eggs, Parmigiano-Reggiano, thyme, nutmeg (if using) and the remaining 1 teaspoon salt. Add the flour and stir until a wet and sticky dough begins to form. Turn out onto a floured surface and knead until the dough just comes together. Cut the dough into 8 equal pieces and set aside on a lightly floured baking sheet.

3. Lightly flour a clean work surface and roll each piece of dough into a 1/2-inch-thick rope. Cut each rope into 1-inch pieces. Add the gnocchi in batches, two ropes at a time, to the boiling water. Cook until the pasta has floated to the surface, about 2 minutes per batch. Using a small sieve or slotted spoon, transfer the gnocchi to the prepared baking sheet. Repeat with the remaining gnocchi. Spread the gnocchi out on the baking sheet and let cool until ready to use.

4. To make the sauce: Heat 2 tablespoons of the oil in a large nonstick skillet over medium-high heat until hot. Add half of the gnocchi and sauté, lightly tossing, until golden brown. Transfer to a large bowl and cover to keep warm. Repeat with the remaining 2 tablespoons oil and remaining gnocchi. Reduce the heat to medium and add the cream, butter, and sage to the skillet. Cook until the sauce reduces slightly, about 5 minutes, then pour over the gnocchi and toss to coat. Season with salt and pepper to taste. Sprinkle the gnocchi with chopped thyme and serve with additional Parmigiano-Reggiano cheese.

Ariel's Restaurant

Variation: After transferring both batches of sautéed gnocchi to the bowl in step 4, add one or two of the following ingredients: 1/2 cup blanched diagonally sliced asparagus, 1/2 cup blanched English peas, 1 small bunch sautéed or grilled wild leeks (ramps), 1 cup blanched fiddlehead ferns, 1 bunch blanched chopped spinach, 1/2 cup sautéed wild or cultivated mushrooms, or 1/4 cup pine nuts, toasted and chopped. Make the sauce and combine as directed.

Simple Ricotta Cheese

MAKES 4 CUPS

This recipe is super simple to make and well worth the minimal effort.

1 gallon whole milk
1 quart buttermilk

1. Line a fine-mesh strainer with a double layer of cheesecloth and set over a large bowl.

2. Combine the milk and buttermilk in a heavy stockpot and heat over medium heat, stirring occasionally, until the mixture begins to steam. Reduce the heat to low and continue to cook until the curds separate from the whey, and a 1- to 2-inch layer of curds floats to the top. Ladle the curds into the prepared strainer and Let drain at room temperature for 1 to 3 hours. Use immediately or cover and refrigerate.

Ariel's Restaurant

HERMIT'S GOLD WILD EDIBLES

At a very young age, Colin McCaffrey began foraging for wild edibles in the Connecticut River Valley of Vermont. His mother showed him how to cook milkweed shoots and roast dandelion roots, aa well as harvest wild berries, nettles, and fiddleheads. His first taste of wild mushrooms was freshly picked inky caps sautéed in butter. McCaffrey spent hours in the woods hunting, fishing, and learning the names of wildflowers and the properties of herbs. After settling in central Vermont, he has spent the past two decades learning the woods around his home and beyond, seeking out the best edible plants and fungi, which he sells to local co-ops and restaurants such as Hen of the Wood in Waterbury and Frida's Taqueria in Stowe. His "day job" is record producer, songwriter, and musician.

Spaghetti and Porcini Mushroom Meatballs

SERVES 4

This recipe is one of McCaffrey's favorite ways of using the porcini and *Boletus edulis* mushrooms that he harvests and dries all summer. The intense, earthy flavor of the dried porcini mushroom is a wonderful compliment to grass-fed beef. Colin has made these meatballs with a brown gravy served on mashed potatoes as well as in a tomato sauce with pasta. Each approach brings out different subtleties of spice and mushroom flavor.

1/2 ounce dried porcini mushrooms, not rehydrated

1 teaspoon paprika

1 teaspoon ground cumin

1/2 teaspoon salt

1/2 teaspoon freshly ground black pepper

1/4 teaspoon grated nutmeg

1/8 teaspoon curry powder

1 pound ground beef, preferably grass-fed

1/2 cup finely ground bread crumbs or panko

1/4 cup finely grated Parmigiano-Reggiano cheese, plus extra for serving

1 large egg, lightly beaten

1 large garlic clove, minced

2 tablespoons olive oil

3 cups good-quality tomato-basil pasta sauce

12 ounces whole-wheat spaghetti

1. Pulse the mushrooms, paprika, cumin, salt, pepper, nutmeg, and curry powder in a food processor until well combined.

2. In a large bowl mix the mushroom-spice mixture, beef, bread crumbs, Parmigiano-Reggiano, egg, and garlic until just combined. Using your hands, form into 16 meatballs.

3. Heat 1 tablespoon of the oil in a large skillet over medium-high heat. Add half of the meatballs and cook, turning until browned on all sides, about 7 minutes. With a slotted spoon, transfer the meatballs to a plate. Repeat with the remaining oil and remaining meatballs. Return all the meatballs to the skillet. Add the pasta sauce and simmer until the meatballs have reached an internal temperature of 140 degrees, about 15 minutes.

4. Meanwhile, bring a large pot of salted water water to a boil, add the pasta, and cook until al dente, 6 to 7 minutes. Drain in a colander. Place the pasta in a large bowl and top with the meatballs and sauce. Serve with additional grated Parmigiano-Reggiano cheese, if desired.

Hermit's Gold Wild Edibles

Alpen Macaroni

SERVES 8 TO 10

Thistle Hill Tarentaise cheese is smooth-textured, subtly nut-flavored and naturally rinded. Serve this rich dish with a green salad and a nice crusty baguette.

1 pound macaroni
2 medium potatoes, unpeeled, cut into 1/4-inch cubes
8 ounces (about 8 slices) bacon
1 large onion, chopped
3 garlic cloves, minced
2 tablespoons (1 ounce) unsalted butter
2 tablespoons all-purpose flour
6 ounces Tarentaise cheese, shredded (1 1/2 cups)
1–1 1/2 cups light cream
2 teaspoons dry mustard
Kosher salt and freshly ground black pepper
Cayenne pepper
Chopped fresh thyme or parsley, for garnish

1. Preheat the oven to 350 degrees. Lightly grease a 10 x 15-inch baking dish with butter or coat with nonstick cooking spray; set aside. Bring a large pot of salted water to a boil, add the macaroni, and cook until al dente. Drain in a colander and set aside.

2. Place the potatoes in a medium saucepan and cover with cold, salted water. Bring to a boil over medium-high heat and cook until the potatoes are just tender. Drain in a colander and set aside.

3. Cook the bacon in a medium skillet over medium-high heat until crisp, 5 to 6 minutes. Let the bacon drain on paper towels, then coarsely chop it. Pour off all but 2 tablespoons of the bacon fat from the skillet, then add the onion and cook over medium-high heat, stirring occasionally, until soft and translucent, about 5 minutes. Add the garlic and cook, stirring occasionally, for 1 minute.

4. Melt the butter in a medium saucepan over medium-low heat. Whisk in the flour and cook until the mixture has thickened and the flour is a pale golden color. Remove from the heat and stir in the bacon, 1 cup of the Tarentaise, the cream, and dry mustard. Season with salt and pepper to taste.

5. In a large bowl, stir together the macaroni, potatoes, and cheese mixture and transfer to the prepared dish. Lightly coat the dull side of a sheet of foil with nonstick cooking spray and cover the baking dish.

6. Bake the macaroni and cheese until hot and bubbly, about 20 minutes. Remove the dish from oven and sprinkle the remaining 1/2 cup cheese and cayenne pepper to taste over the top. Return to the oven and bake, uncovered, until the cheese is golden brown, about 10 minutes. Let rest for 10 minutes, sprinkle with thyme, and serve.

Thistle Hill Farm

Pasta with Veal and Pancetta Bolognese

SERVES 6 TO 8

This hearty, rustic dish has a rich robust veal flavor with pork undertones. The pancetta adds a nice contrast of spice and salt without the smoky flavor of bacon.

1/4 cup extra-virgin olive oil
1 medium Spanish onion, diced
5 garlic cloves, minced
4 ounces pancetta, finely chopped
2 pounds ground veal
8 ounces ground pork
1 cup dry white wine
2 cups puréed tomatoes
1/2 cup heavy cream
1/8 teaspoon grated nutmeg
1 bay leaf
2 tablespoons (1 ounce) unsalted butter
1 tablespoon chopped fresh rosemary
1/4 cup chopped fresh parsley
Kosher salt and freshly ground black pepper
1 pound tagliatelle, fettuccine, or rigatoni
Grated Parmigiano-Reggiano cheese

1. Heat the oil in a large pot over medium heat. Add the onion and cook, stirring occasionally, until soft and translucent, about 10 minutes. Add the garlic and cook for 1 minute. Add the pancetta, veal, and pork, increase the heat to medium-high, and cook, breaking up with a fork, until the meat is browned. Add the wine and bring to a boil, scraping up the brown bits from the bottom of the pot. Continue cooking until most of the wine has evaporated, 4 to 5 minutes. Add the tomatoes, cream, nutmeg, and bay leaf and reduce the heat to low.

Simmer, uncovered, stirring occasionally, for 45 minutes to 1 hour. Remove and discard the bay leaf. Stir in the butter, rosemary, and parsley and season with salt and pepper to taste.

2. Meanwhile, bring a large pot of salted water to a boil, add the pasta, and cook until al dente. Drain, reserving 1/4 cup pasta water and return the pasta to the pot. Add the sauce and cook, stirring frequently, until heated through. If the sauce seems dry, stir in the reserved pasta water as needed. Serve with Parmigiano-Reggiano cheese.

The Belted Cow Bistro

Pasta with Goat Cheese and Roasted Tomatoes

SERVES 4 TO 6

Blue Ledge Farm was established in the year 2000. It is a small family-owned and operated goat, dairy, and cheesemaking operation. Their mission is to create a high-quality product built on the cornerstones of respect for the consumer, land, and animals, as well as the local community. This soft-textured pasta dish is creamy, fresh and aromatic, with a nice lingering tanginess from the goat cheese. The plump, juicy kalamata olives give it a meatlike taste. Substitute whole-wheat penne pasta for added protein and fiber if you prefer. Just be sure make sure to cook the pasta al dente because it will cook more when the starchy pasta water is incorporated.

2 1/2 pounds cherry tomatoes, halved,
    or whole grape tomatoes
2 tablespoons olive oil
Salt and freshly ground black pepper
1 pound penne

6 ounces fresh goat cheese, crumbled
    (1 1/2 cups)
1/2 cup pitted Kalamata olives, halved
3/4 cup chopped fresh basil, plus extra
    for garnish
2 teaspoons fresh lemon juice
1/3 cup grated Parmesan cheese

1. Preheat the oven to 425 degrees.

2. Place the tomatoes on a baking sheet, drizzle
   with olive oil, and season with salt and pepper
   to taste. Roast for 15 minutes and set aside.

3. Bring 6 quarts of salted water to a boil in a
   large pot over medium-high heat. Add the
   pasta and cook just until al dente. Drain the
   pasta, reserving 2/3 cup of the pasta water.

4. While the pasta is cooking, combine the
   tomatoes, goat cheese, olives, basil, and lemon
   juice in a large bowl. Add the hot pasta and
   toss, mixing well. Slowly add the reserved
   pasta water as needed, stirring until the
   sauce is creamy. Season with salt and pepper
   to taste.

5. To serve, spoon pasta into warm bowls and
   top with Parmesan. Garnish with basil and
   serve at once.

Blue Ledge Farm

BELLA FARM

Rachel Schattman did not grow up on a farm. She got her first taste of farming at the Putney School, a boarding high school on a dairy and small vegetable farm in Putney, Vermont. Students were required to do farm work, and Schattman found great joy in being outdoors, working in the rich soil.

She began working at a farm near her home during school breaks, and her passion for growing things continued to bloom, along with her love for Vermont's tight-knit farming community.

After earning a master's degree from the University of Vermont, Schattman and a friend, Kelli Brooks, started a certified organic farm at the Intervale in Burlington. The Intervale's farm program offers farmers the opportunity to keep their initial costs low by providing an area to farm, shared space in their greenhouses and coolers, and the use of tractors and farm implements. Schattman and Brooks christened their new venture "Bella Farm." Soon seven varieties of garlic, eight types of basil, and an intriguing assortment of culinary herbs were springing up through the Intervale's rich organic soil. They decided to use some of their garlic and basil crop to create a dairy- and nut-free pesto. Because pesto freezes well, it could be made during the summer, frozen, and sold throughout the winter.

The Intervale enabled Schattman to gain technical and business skills, as well as the experience needed to start a farm of her own. Bella Farm is now located on about 20 acres of south-facing slope in Monkton. Schattman and her partner, Patrick Rowe, have a beautiful view of the hills from their newly constructed home and fields. The farm is certified organic, and four of their acres are used for vegetables, herbs, and cover crops. Schattman believes in using cover crops such as buckwheat to manage weeds and pests, and increase soil fertility. She continues to make her signature pesto at home in her certified kitchen. On a typical day, the basil is picked in the morning and processed by afternoon. Bella Farm produces between 2,500 and 3,000 six-ounce units of pesto per season. It is sold frozen at the Burlington Farmers' Market or thawed in the "hippie cooler" at City Market, Onion River Co-op in Burlington.

For Schattman, the quality of the food she produces is of the utmost importance, as is making that food accessible to all members of the community. With the help and support of family, friends, and Rowe, she welcomes each day with unswerving dedication and optimism that she is truly making a difference.

Schattman explains, "Farming is a fascinating and continuously challenging process that is extremely rewarding for me. My body may get tired, but I am never, ever bored!"

Sage and Cherry Tomato Polenta

SERVES 4

Like many recipes from Bella Farm, this polenta was inspired by seasonal abundance; in this case, a bumper crop of cherry tomatoes. This dish is quick, easy, and satisfying.

4 cups water
1/2 teaspoon kosher salt
1 tablespoon unsalted butter
1 cup coarse- or medium-ground polenta
1/2 teaspoon olive oil
1 cup cherry or grape tomatoes, halved
1 tablespoon minced fresh sage
1/2 cup shaved Parmigiano-Reggiano cheese,
    plus extra for serving
Kosher salt and freshly ground black pepper
Chopped fresh parsley

1. Bring the water, salt and butter to a boil in a large saucepan over medium-high heat. Whisking constantly, add the polenta in a slow, steady stream. Continue stirring until the water returns to a boil. Reduce the heat to low and simmer, stirring occasionally with a wooden spoon, until thickened, 35 to 40 minutes. The polenta should pull away from the sides of the pan.

2. Meanwhile, heat the oil in a small skillet over medium-high heat. Add the tomatoes and sage and cook for 3 minutes. Stir the tomatoes, sage, and Parmigiano-Reggiano into the warm polenta. Season with salt and pepper to taste, sprinkle with parsley and additional cheese, and serve.

Rachel Schattman of Bella Farm

TWIN FARMS

Twin Farms, nestled among 300 acres of rolling hills in Barnard, is the former estate of Nobel Prize–winning author Sinclair Lewis and his journalist wife, Dorothy Thompson. Thompson kept Twin Farms until she was no longer physically able to live there. The property has changed hands several times since then; today's ownership now includes several partners. It is Vermont's only luxury five-star, all-inclusive resort and spa.

As the executive chef, Ted Ask oversees all aspects of the Twin Farms' culinary experience. His philosophy revolves around the changing seasons, locally grown herbs and vegetables (some from Twin Farms' own gardens), and honoring each guest's dietary preferences. There is no set menu so each day is a different culinary story. A questionnaire is sent to guests when they make their reservation. This way the restaurant is made aware of each guest's dietary restrictions, food allergies, and preferences. When guests sit down to eat, they do not have to order. Their meal arrives all to their liking.

Twin Farms Red Polenta with Wildcrafted Oyster Mushroom Broth

SERVES 4

Chef Ask says, "For this recipe we grow the 'Painted Mountain' variety of red corn in the Twin Farms garden—it has done very well in this climate. After picking, we dry the ears, then remove the kernels for storage. This allows us to grind polenta to order for our dishes and have the garden featured on our menus throughout the winter months. The caring hands of Les Hook and Nova Kim, from Wild Gourmet Food, provide the mushrooms, which are always picked with the thought of maintaining the land and preserving the wild mushroom patches for years to come."

Polenta

4 cups low-sodium chicken stock

1 cup coarse-ground or medium-ground polenta

Oyster Mushroom Broth

1 1/2 tablespoons olive oil

8 ounces wild oyster mushrooms, trimmed and coarsely chopped

3 cups vegetable stock

1 teaspoon chopped fresh thyme, plus 4 thyme sprigs for garnish

1 bay leaf

1–2 tablespoons dry sherry

Kosher salt and freshly ground black pepper

Garlic Chips

1 teaspoon olive oil

2 elephant garlic cloves, thinly sliced

1 cup ricotta cheese

Parsley leaves (optional)

1. To make the polenta: Bring the chicken stock to a boil in a large saucepan over medium-high heat. Whisking constantly, add the polenta in a slow, steady stream. Continue stirring until the stock returns to a boil. Reduce the heat to low and simmer, stirring occasionally with a wooden spoon, until thickened, 30 to 35 minutes. The polenta should pull away from the sides of the pan.

2. To make the oyster mushroom broth: Meanwhile, heat the oil in a large skillet over medium-low heat. Add the mushrooms and cook until soft and golden, about 6 minutes. Add the stock, thyme, and bay leaf and simmer until the liquid has reduced by half, about 12 minutes. Discard bay leaf. Stir in sherry and season with salt and pepper to taste.

3. To make the garlic chips: While the mushroom broth is simmering, heat the oil in a small skillet over medium heat. Add the garlic, and fry until golden brown on both sides, about 1 minute per side. Using a slotted spoon, remove the garlic and set aside on paper towels.

4. Spoon the polenta into bowls; top each serving with mushrooms, ricotta cheese, and garlic chips. Drizzle the mushroom broth over the polenta, garnish with thyme sprigs or parsley leaves, if desired, and serve.

Twin Farms

MAPLEBROOK FINE CHEESE

In 2003, Michael Scheps, a third-generation cheesemaker, began producing hand-stretched mozzarella in the kitchen of Al Ducci's Italian Pantry, an Italian-style delicatessen and food market, in Manchester Center. Scheps was stretching out mozzarella cheese and putting the balls out on the counter for Al Ducci's customers when Johann Englert walked into the store. Immediately, she was drawn to the display of mozzarella balls. Englert hadn't seen mozzarella displayed in that fashion since a trip to Italy years before, so she decided to buy some. She immediately fell in love with the cheese and felt that it was the best mozzarella that she had tasted in the United States.

A natural entrepreneur, Englert approached Scheps with the idea of selling his cheese to Boston chefs. Initially, Englert took 20 mozzarella balls to Boston; five of the gourmet shops that sampled them ordered more, and before long, Scheps was scrambling to keep up with the orders Englert generated. The following year, the pair saw enough potential in their budding business to purchase a cheese plant in Bennington, Vermont, and launched what is now Maplebrook Fine Cheese.

Through the use of Old-World cheesemaking traditions, the company now handcrafts seven cheeses—handmade mozzarella, smoked mozzarella, hand-dipped ricotta, whole milk feta, burrata, cheddar bites, and mozzarella in water.

Polenta Bites Stuffed with Smoked Mozzarella

MAKES ABOUT 40 PIECES

When you bite into this polenta-based hors d'oeuvre, there is the surprise of warm, gooey Maplewood Farm smoked mozzarella inside. These little snacks are hard to resist when topped with a dollop of concentrated tomatoes, garlic, and basil. They are elegant enough to serve at a wedding reception or at a casual get-together with friends at home.

Tomato Sauce

1 tablespoon olive oil
2 garlic cloves, minced
1 (14.5-ounce) can crushed tomatoes
Pinch crushed red pepper flakes, or to taste
1 tablespoon chopped fresh basil, plus extra for garnish
Granulated sugar
Kosher salt

Polenta

1 cup milk
1 cup yellow polenta or stone-ground cornmeal
1 teaspoon salt
Pinch grated nutmeg
Freshly ground black pepper
2 cups simmering water
2 tablespoons (1 ounce) unsalted butter
2 tablespoons grated Parmesan cheese, plus extra for garnish
4 ounces smoked mozzarella cheese, cut into 1/2-inch cubes

1. Place a rack in the center of the oven and preheat the oven to 425 degrees. Lightly coat a baking sheet with nonstick cooking spray and set aside.

2. To make the tomato sauce: Heat the olive oil in a medium saucepan over low heat. Add the garlic and cook until just fragrant, about 30 seconds. Add the tomatoes, red pepper flakes, basil, and 1 teaspoon sugar. Increase the heat to medium-low heat and cook until the sauce is thick enough to push to one side of the saucepan, about 15 minutes. Season with sugar and salt to taste, and set aside.

3. To make the polenta: Whisk together the milk, polenta, salt, nutmeg, and pepper to taste in a medium saucepan over medium heat. Whisking constantly, add the water and bring to a boil. Reduce the heat to medium-low and cook, stirring occasionally with a wooden spoon, until the polenta is thick, creamy and pulls away from the pan, about 15 minutes. Add the butter and Parmesan, stirring until melted. Let rest off the heat for 5 minutes.

4. Spoon the warm polenta into a pastry bag without a tip. Pipe the polenta into 1-inch-diameter mounds on the prepared baking sheet.

5. Pick up a mound of polenta and place one mozzarella cheese cube halfway into the center, shaping the polenta around the cheese. The cheese should be visible on the top with a layer of polenta underneath and all around. Repeat with the remaining polenta and mozzarella. The finished bites should be roughly 3/4 inch high by 1 1/4 inches wide.

6. Bake until the cheese is melted and the polenta is warmed through, about 15 minutes. Transfer to a serving platter, spoon a small amount of sauce on top of each piece of polenta, then sprinkle with additional Parmesan and basil. Serve immediately. (To reheat, cover with plastic wrap and heat in microwave until warmed through.)

Robert Titterton and Maplebrook Farm

POULTRY

Apple-Stuffed Chicken Breasts

SERVES 4

In this recipe, pan-seared airline chicken breast is stuffed with a good raw cow's milk cheese, caramelized apples, and topped with Calvados sauce. An airline chicken breast is a boneless skin-on breast that has an attached wing joint. The name was popularized in the 1960s, when commercial airlines would serve chicken breast halves in this style. Although the recipe specifies this particular cut, the dish works just as well with boneless, skin-on breasts and requires less preparation time. Use any firm but moist raw cow's milk cheese here; Orb Weaver Farm makes a delicious raw cow's milk cheese, as does Consider Bardwell Farm.

4 airline chicken breast halves, trimmed
Kosher salt and freshly ground black pepper
3 tablespoons canola oil
2 tablespoons (1 ounce) unsalted butter
2 Granny Smith apples, peeled, cored,
    and cut into thin slices
1 tablespoon granulated sugar
4 ounces raw cow's milk cheese, shredded (1 cup)
1/4 cup chopped onion
1/4 cup chopped celery
1/4 cup chopped carrots
1 tablespoon chopped fresh thyme,
    plus sprigs for garnish
3 garlic cloves, minced
2/3 cup Calvados, Apple Jack,
    or other apple brandy
1/2 cup Vermont apple cider

1. Preheat the oven to 375 degrees. Lightly grease a baking sheet and set aside. Using a sharp boning knife, carefully remove the bones and cartilage from the underside of each chicken breast. The only bone remaining in the breast should be the wing joint bone. Cut horizontally through the center of each chicken breast to within 1 inch of the opposite side, creating a pocket. Season the chicken with salt and pepper to taste.

2. Heat the oil in a large skillet over medium-high heat. Add the breasts and brown on all sides, about 4 minutes per side. Remove the breasts from the skillet and place on the prepared baking sheet.

3. Melt 1 tablespoon of the butter in a medium skillet over medium-low heat. Add the apples and sugar and sauté until golden brown and slightly softened, about 10 minutes. Add the cheese and set the pan aside.

4. Spoon an equal amount of apple-cheese mixture into the pocket of each chicken breast. Bake the chicken for 20 minutes.

5. Meanwhile, melt the remaining 1 tablespoon butter over medium heat in the same skillet used for the chicken. Add the onion, celery, carrots, and thyme and sauté until the onion is soft and translucent, about 10 minutes. Add the garlic and sauté for 2 minutes. Whisk in the Calvados, scraping the bottom of the skillet. Whisk in the apple cider and simmer until the liquid is reduced by half. Strain the sauce through a fine-mesh strainer, discarding the vegetables, and season with salt and pepper to taste.

6. Place the chicken on a large platter, pour the sauce over the chicken, garnish with thyme sprigs, and serve.

Juniper's at the Wildflower Inn

MISTY KNOLL FARMS

Misty Knoll Farms is a family-owned and operated farm, producing the finest naturally raised free-range turkeys and naturally raised chickens available in Vermont.

As stewards of Vermont's working landscape owners John Palmer and Rob Litch treat their farm as a precious, irreplaceable resource, following sustainable farming practices to ensure that their cropland will be productive for future generations. The two raise their birds with the utmost care, feeding them whole grains, free of antibiotics and animal by-products. Their chickens range free in spacious, specially designed enclosures. Their turkeys, when old enough to withstand Vermont's cool nights, are sheltered in open barns with free range access to lush pasture, sunlight, and fresh water. The result— healthy, nutritious, and flavorful birds, nature's way.

By processing the turkeys and chickens on-site, in their own USDA-inspected facility, they subject the birds to minimal stress. Palmer and Litch carefully grade them by hand to assure that only the finest birds are available for sale.

Coq au Vin

SERVES 4

David Merrill, executive chef at the Burlington Country Club, created this recipe for cooks who love to entertain. The wine tenderizes the chicken and the bacon gives a deep flavor. Add a variety of seasonal vegetables for a great one-pot meal. Spoon over wide noodles or roasted garlic mashed potatoes.

1 cup all-purpose flour
Kosher salt and freshly ground black pepper
1 (3-pound) whole chicken, cut into 8 pieces and trimmed
1/4 cup olive oil
8 ounces bacon, diced
8 ounces white mushrooms, trimmed and halved
1 pound pearl onions, peeled
4 carrots, peeled and coarsely chopped
3 garlic cloves, coarsely chopped
2 cups Burgundy wine
4 cups chicken stock
6 sprigs fresh thyme
2 bay leaves

1. In a medium bowl, stir together the flour, 1 1/2 teaspoons salt, and 1 teaspoon pepper. Dredge the chicken pieces in the flour and shake off any excess.

2. Heat 2 tablespoons of the oil in a Dutch oven over medium-high heat. Add the chicken skin side down and brown, 3 to 4 minutes per side. Transfer the chicken to a platter.

3. In the same pot, cook the bacon over medium-high heat until crisp, about 5 minutes. Transfer the bacon with a slotted spoon to paper towels. Pour off all but 2 tablespoons of the bacon drippings and add the remaining 2 tablespoons olive oil, the mushrooms,

onions, and carrots. Cook, stirring occasionally, until light golden brown, about 5 minutes. Add the garlic and cook, stirring frequently, for 1 minute.

4. Pour in the wine and stock and bring to a boil over medium-high heat. Return the chicken to the pot and stir in the reserved bacon, thyme and bay leaves. Cover the pot and simmer over medium heat until the chicken is tender and the breasts register 160 degrees and thighs register 175 degrees, about 45 minutes. Remove the thyme sprigs and bay leaves, season with salt and pepper to taste, and serve.

David Merrill of the Burlington Country Club for Misty Knoll Farms

Chicken Paprika

SERVES 4

Eric Seitz, co-owner of Pitchfork Farm, got this hearty, earthy recipe from his Hungarian grandmother. Serve with Hungarian Nokedli (page 32).

8 bone-in, skin-on chicken thighs, legs, or split breasts, trimmed
Kosher salt and freshly ground black pepper
Garlic powder
2 tablespoons olive oil
1 large sweet onion, thinly sliced
1 green bell pepper, stemmed, seeded and thinly sliced
1 red bell pepper, stemmed, seeded and thinly sliced
2 1/2 cups low-sodium chicken broth
2 tablespoons sweet Hungarian paprika
1 large tomato, seeded and chopped
1/2 cup sour cream

1 tablespoon all-purpose flour
Chopped fresh parsley

1. Season the chicken with salt, pepper, and garlic powder to taste. Heat the oil in a large skillet over medium-high heat. Add half of the chicken pieces and brown, about 3 minutes per side, then transfer to a platter. Repeat with the remaining chicken.

2. Add the onion and bell peppers to the empty skillet, reduce the heat to medium and cook, stirring often, until the onion is soft and translucent, about 10 minutes. Return the chicken to the skillet, add the broth and paprika, and bring to a simmer. Cover and cook until the chicken has cooked through, about 30 minutes.

3. Remove the chicken from the skillet and stir in the tomatoes. Whisk together the sour cream and flour and stir into the sauce; cook until heated through. Season with salt to taste, sprinkle with parsley, and serve.

Pitchfork Farm

CLOUDLAND FARM

Cloudland Farm was originally a 2,000-acre dairy farm, when Bill Emmons's grandfather and great grandfather purchased the property in the early 1900s. Today, the diversified family-run farm consists of just over 1,000 acres, 4 miles from the town of Woodstock. The current owners, Bill and his wife, Cathy, raise Black Angus beef cattle, pastured chickens and turkeys, pigs, horses, and vegetables, as well as running a certified tree farm and the Cloudland Farm Country Market.

Raising happy, healthy animals and producing wholesome food is very important to the Emmons family. The owners of Cloudland Farm pride themselves on being good stewards of the land, while producing the most nutritious feed for their animals. The farm uses no growth hormones or antibiotics, except in rare cases of life-threatening illness. All of their animals are pastured. During the winter months, the animals feed on hay that is produced on the farm, without the use of chemical fertilizers.

Cloudland Farm also offers an on-farm restaurant, which is open for dinner on Thursday and Saturday nights. The restaurant utilizes local food, most of which is organic. All of the meat served comes from the farm, as does a portion of the produce. The menu is limited to one prix fixe meal, selected and prepared by the chef, Nick Mahood. With advance notice, Mahood happily accommodates dietary restrictions or vegetarian preferences.

Chicken Breasts Stuffed with Chevre and Sautéed Ramps Served with Pickled Ramps and a Rhubarb Gastrique

SERVES 4

When ramps are no longer available, you can substitute a combination of 18 wild scallions and 6 garlic bulbs (small fresh heads of garlic with stalks). Reserve two garlic bulbs, including the lower end of the stalks, and 8 scallions for pickling. Chef Mahood uses Vermont Butter and Cheese Creamery goat cheese in this dish. Serve with wild rice or pilaf, if desired.

Rhubarb Gastrique

1 cup granulated sugar
1/2 cup red wine vinegar
1/2 cup water
3 cups finely chopped rhubarb
1 teaspoon chopped fresh sage
Kosher salt and freshly ground black pepper

Sautéed Ramps

12–14 ramps, cleaned, green leaves discarded
4 tablespoons unsalted butter
Kosher salt and freshly ground black pepper

Chicken

4 (6-ounce) boneless, skin-on split chicken breasts, trimmed
8 ounces goat cheese
Kosher salt and freshly ground black pepper, to taste
3 tablespoons canola oil
Pickled Ramps (recipe follows)

1. Preheat the oven to 400 degrees. Lightly grease a baking sheet and set aside.

2. To make the rhubarb gastrique: Bring the sugar, vinegar, and water to a boil in a medium nonreactive saucepan. Add the rhubarb, and sage and boil until the rhubarb is soft and the mixture has thickened, 5 to 10 minutes. Let cool for 10 to 15 minutes, then transfer to a blender or food processor and process until smooth. Season with salt and pepper to taste, spoon into a bowl, and set aside.

3. To make the sautéed ramps: Slice the bulbs and stalks into small rounds and slice the leaves into narrow strips. Melt the butter in a medium skillet over medium heat, add the bulbs and stalks and sauté until soft and tender. Add the leaves and cook until just wilted. Season with salt and pepper to taste. Let cool completely.

3. To make the chicken: Using a small sharp knife, cut horizontally through the center of each chicken breast, to within 1 inch of opposite side, creating a pocket. Spoon one-quarter of the sautéed ramps and one-quarter of the goat cheese into the pocket of each chicken breast. Season each chicken breast liberally with salt and pepper to taste.

4. Heat the oil in a large skillet over medium-high heat. Add the breasts and brown on both sides, about 4 minutes per side. Transfer the breasts to the prepared baking sheet, skin side up and bake for 20 to 25 minutes.Let rest for 5 minutes. Top with the rhubarb gastrique and pickled ramps and serve.

Cloudland Farm

Pickled Ramps

8–10 ramps, cleaned, green leaves discarded
1/3 cup water
1/3 cup white wine
1/3 cup white wine vinegar
1/3 cup granulated sugar
2 teaspoons salt

Place the ramp bulbs in a 16-ounce glass jar with a tight lid. Combine the water, wine, vinegar, sugar, and salt in a saucepan and bring to a boil over medium-high heat. Cook, stirring frequently, until the sugar is dissolved. Pour over the ramps and seal jar. Let cool to room temperature, then refrigerate for at least 3 hours.

Chef Nick Mahood of Cloudland Farm

Green Chicken

SERVES 4

In this dish, you may use any type of fresh herb—or a combination of herbs—with delicious results, so try whatever you have and enjoy the green!

1 cup loosely packed fresh herbs, such as basil, Thai basil, cilantro, or mint

1/4 cup extra-virgin olive oil

1 teaspoon grated lemon zest plus 1/4 cup juice (2 lemons)

2 garlic cloves or 2 garlic scapes, coarsely chopped

Kosher salt and freshly ground black pepper

4 (6-ounce) boneless, skinless chicken breasts, trimmed and cut into 1-inch strips

1. Combine the herbs, oil, lemon zest and juice, garlic, and salt and pepper to taste in a food processor or blender and purée until a smooth paste forms.

2. Place the chicken strips in a large zipper-lock plastic bag, add the herb paste, and stir to coat. Seal the bag and refrigerate for at least 30 minutes or up to 12 hours. Remove the chicken from the refrigerator 30 minutes before grilling.

3. Preheat a gas or electric grill to medium heat. Clean the grill grate and brush with oil. Place the chicken on the grill, cover, and cook, until cooked through, about 4 minutes per side.

Note: For an alternate method of preparation, put the raw marinated chicken and your favorite veggies on skewers to create flavorful kabobs. You may also spread the herb paste underneath the skin of a whole chicken before roasting it in the oven.

Sterling College

Moroccan-Style Chicken with Apricots and Almonds

SERVES 4

This is an old favorite of Lee Duberman's, which she has made for every restaurant that she has owned. It is rich, earthy, and inexpensive to make. The dish is best made with chicken thighs, preferably from high-quality local chickens. Pomegranate molasses is syrup made from reduced pomegranate juice; it can be found at Middle Eastern markets or in the international aisle at the supermarket. If you don't feel like firing up the grill, you can cook the chicken indoors using a grill pan. Serve this chicken on a bed of Mediterranean Couscous Pilaf (page 110).

Chicken and Marinade

2 tablespoons olive oil

3 garlic cloves, minced

1 tablespoon ground coriander

1 1/2 teaspoons ground cinnamon

1/4 cup Vermont honey

1/4 cup pomegranate molasses

8 boneless, skinless chicken thighs (about 2 3/4 pounds), trimmed

1 teaspoon kosher salt

Sauce

4 cups low-sodium chicken stock

2 carrots, peeled and sliced thin

1/2 cup chopped dried apricots

1 tablespoon cornstarch

1/4 cup cold water

Salt and freshly ground black pepper

1/4 cup chopped toasted almonds

1. To make the chicken and marinade: Heat the oil in a medium saucepan over medium heat. Add the garlic, coriander, and cinnamon, and cook, stirring the mixture often, for about 1 minute. Stir in the honey and molasses and heat until just bubbling. Pour half of the mixture into a small bowl and set aside to cool. Reserve the remaining marinade mixture in the saucepan.

2. Sprinkle the thighs with salt to taste, place them in a large zipper-lock plastic bag and add the cooled marinade from the bowl. Sprinkle with salt, seal the bag and refrigerate for at least 2 hours or up to 24 hours.

3. Heat a gas or electric grill to high heat. Lightly grease the grill grate with nonstick cooking spray. Place the chicken on the grill, cover, and cook until the meat registers 175 degrees, 4 to 5 minutes per side. Transfer the chicken to a platter and let rest.

4. To make the sauce: While the chicken is cooking, add the chicken stock to the remaining marinade mixture in the saucepan. Bring to a boil over medium-high heat, then reduce the heat and simmer for 10 minutes, stirring often. Add the carrots and apricots and continue to simmer until the carrots are tender, about 20 minutes.

5. Whisk the cornstarch and water together, then whisk the mixture into the sauce and cook until thickened, about 1 minute. Season with salt and pepper to taste. Pour the sauce over the chicken, sprinkle with the almonds, and serve.

Ariel's Restaurant

STONEWOOD FARM

Stonewood Farm is located in Orwell, on Vermont's western border. It is one of the largest turkey farms in New England, raising about 29,000 birds a year. The farm has been in the Stone family for generations, and they take great pride in raising all-natural turkeys that are free of hormones and antibiotics. Their birds are not caged but are housed in open-air barns, an arrangement that offers them lots of natural sunlight and fresh air, while protecting them from predators and disease. The farm's mission is to provide the people of Vermont and its surrounding states with quality turkeys that are humanely raised.

Cranberry and Turkey Sausage Stuffing

SERVES 12 TO 16

As with any stuffing recipe, the ingredients and flavor possibilities are endless—feel free to experiment. This recipe makes enough stuffing to fill an 18- to 20-pound turkey, with some extra stuffing left over. After stuffing the turkey (loosely, as the stuffing will expand when cooked), spoon the extra stuffing into an 8-inch square pan, dot with 1 tablespoon butter, and bake as directed.

1 (15-ounce) package all-purpose seasoned bread stuffing mix
6 tablespoons (3 ounces) unsalted butter
2 cups finely chopped yellow onions (about 2 small onions)
2 cups finely chopped celery (about 4 ribs)
1 Granny Smith apple, cored and chopped
2 garlic cloves, minced
2 teaspoons chopped fresh sage
2 teaspoons chopped fresh rosemary
1 teaspoon salt
1 tablespoon olive oil
1 pound mild turkey sausage, casings removed
1 cup mashed jellied cranberry sauce
1 cup Vermont apple cider, plus extra as needed
2 large eggs, lightly beaten

1. Preheat the oven to 350 degrees. Lightly butter a 9 x 13-inch baking dish and set aside. Place the bread stuffing mix in a very large bowl.

2. Melt 4 tablespoons of the butter in a large skillet over medium heat. Add the onions, celery, and apple and cook, stirring often, until the vegetables are soft and translucent, about 10 minutes. Stir in the garlic, sage, rosemary, and salt and cook for 1 minute. Add the vegetable mixture to the bread stuffing.

3. In the same skillet, heat the oil over medium heat. Add the sausage and cook, crumbling with a fork, until browned, about 7 minutes. Using a slotted spoon, transfer to the bowl with the bread stuffing.

4. Add the cranberry sauce, cider, and eggs to the bread stuffing. Gently mix all the ingredients together; do not overmix. Season with salt and pepper to taste. If the mixture seems too dry, add more cider until the desired consistency is reached.

5. Spoon the stuffing into the prepared baking dish. Cut the remaining 2 tablespoons butter into small pieces and distribute them evenly over the stuffing. Cover with foil and bake for 25 minutes. Uncover and bake until golden brown on top, about 10 minutes. Serve.

Stonewood Farm

Warm Chicken, Tomato, and Mozzarella Napoleon with Basil Oil and Balsamic Glaze

SERVES 4 TO 6

This recipe makes more basil oil than you will need for the chicken; the remaining oil can be used for salad dressing or a marinade.

1 cup chopped fresh basil
1 cup olive oil
1 cup all-purpose flour
3 large eggs, lightly beaten
2 cups panko bread crumbs
4 skinless, boneless chicken breasts (about 2 1/2 pounds), trimmed and halved lengthwise
3 tablespoons canola or vegetable oil
2 large tomatoes, sliced
1 (8-ounce) ball fresh mozzarella, sliced
Aged balsamic vinegar, for drizzling

1. Preheat the oven to 350 degrees. Spray a 9-inch square baking dish with nonstick cooking spray and set aside. Combine the basil and olive oil in a small bowl and set aside.

2. Place the flour in a shallow bowl, the eggs in a second bowl, and the panko in a third bowl. Dip each piece of chicken in the flour, then the eggs, and finally the panko. Heat the vegetable oil in a large skillet over medium-high heat until hot but not smoking. Add the chicken in batches and cook until browned, 4 to 5 minutes per side.

3. Arrange half of the chicken in the prepared dish. Layer the tomato slices and cheese slices over the chicken, and then top with the remaining chicken. Bake until the chicken has cooked through and the cheese has melted, about 20 minutes. Drizzle with the basil oil and balsamic vinegar and serve.

West Mountain Inn

Roasted Chicken with Chilled Heirloom Tomato Purée and Scallion Rice Cakes Topped with Crispy Kale

SERVES 4

Black Krim tomatoes are really the best for this dish, given their low acidity and high sugar. They ripen so nicely during the summer months and create an amazing chilled purée. Other good choices include Paul Roberson, Moskovich, or Mountain Princess. This recipe has a wide variation of textures and flavors, from the crispy, salty kale, and light but substantial rice cakes to the juicy, savory chicken and the sweet, acidic tomato purée.

1 cup sushi rice

2 teaspoons seasoned rice vinegar

1/4 cup chopped scallions

1 (3 1/2-pound) whole chicken, giblets discarded

9 tablespoons olive oil

Kosher salt and freshly ground black pepper

6 medium heirloom tomatoes

4 garlic cloves, minced

1 teaspoon red pepper flakes, plus extra to taste

1/4 cup chopped fresh cilantro

2 tablespoons red wine vinegar

1 bunch kale, stemmed and chopped

3 tablespoons vegetable oil

1. Preheat the oven to 375 degrees. Place the rice in a medium saucepan, add 1 cup water and bring to a simmer over medium heat. Cover tightly, reduce the heat to low and cook until tender, 30 to 35 minutes. Stir in the seasoned rice vinegar, let cool slightly, then stir in the scallions. Let cool completely.

2. Rinse the chicken and pat dry with paper towels. Rub with 3 tablespoons of the olive oil and season generously inside and out with salt and pepper. Place breast side up in a roasting pan. Roast the chicken, basting every 15 minutes, until the skin is golden brown, the juices run clear, and the chicken breast reaches an internal temperature of 160 degrees, about 1 1/4 hours. When the chicken is cool enough to handle, using two forks or your fingertips, shred or pull the meat from the bones and set aside.

3. Meanwhile, score the tomatoes and lay on a lined baking sheet. Sprinkle with 1 tablespoon olive oil and salt to taste and roast for 45 minutes or until the tomatoes are shriveled but tender. Let cool.

4. To make the garlic and chili oil: While the tomatoes and chicken are cooking, gently heat 4 tablespoons olive oil in a small saucepan over medium heat. Add the garlic and red pepper flakes and cook until the garlic is fragrant, but not colored, 2 to 3 minutes. Let the oil cool to room temperature.

5. When the tomatoes are cool enough to handle, place them in a blender, add the cilantro, garlic and chili oil, vinegar, and 1 teaspoon salt and purée until smooth. Season with salt and additional red pepper flakes, if desired. Transfer to a bowl, cover and refrigerate.

6. Place the kale in large skillet with 1/4 cup water and cook over medium-high heat until the water has evaporated. Add the remaining 1 tablespoon olive oil and a pinch salt. Toss and lay on a parchment-lined baking sheet. Sprinkle with salt and roast in the oven for 30 minutes, or until dark green and crispy.

7. While the kale is roasting, wet your hands with warm water and, using a 2-ounce ice cream scoop, take one scoop of rice and form into a

disk. Repeat with the remaining rice to make 4 disks. Heat the vegetable oil in a large skillet over medium-high heat. Add the rice cakes and cook until the edges start to brown, about 3 minutes per side.

8. Ladle 1/4 cup of the tomato purée in an even circle on each plate. Place a rice cake in the center of the purée, then place some of the shredded chicken on top of the rice cake. Top with crispy kale and serve.

Pebble Brook Farm and Black Krim Tavern

FOWL MOUNTAIN FARM AND RABBITRY

Fowl Mountain Farm and Rabbitry, in Dummerston, is owned and operated by Chip and Carlene Hellus. In the last six years, they have created a diversified farm, on which they raise all-natural meat chickens, pheasants, turkeys, pigs, and rabbits as well as selling chicken eggs. The farm has an "approved source" on-site processing facility, which is overseen and monitored by the Vermont Departments of Health and Agriculture. For Chip and Carlene it is important to honor the animals' lives by allowing them to live as comfortably and naturally as possible. The animals are processed on-site to minimize their stress and maximize the meat's freshnesss.

Roasted Pheasant with Thyme-Roasted Sweet Potatoes and Sherry Cream

SERVES 2 TO 4

Ismail Samad, executive chef at the Gleanery, in Putney, welcomes the challenge of creating dishes around what is available locally. Creativity plays a crucial role in the way Chef Ismail prepares each recipe and is what makes his job fun and rewarding. The recipe concept for this pheasant dish started with a conversation with the owners of Fowl Mountain Farm and Rabbitry. If you can't find pheasant, you can substitute quail or chicken.

Sweet Potatoes and Pheasant

2 large (about 1 1/2 pounds) sweet potatoes, peeled and cut into 1-inch pieces
1 large sweet onion, cut into 1-inch pieces
5 tablespoons olive oil
4 tablespoons (2 ounces) unsalted butter, melted
8 sprigs fresh thyme
Kosher salt and freshly ground black pepper
1 (2- to 3-pound) pheasant, cut into 4 pieces and trimmed

Sherry Cream

1/3 cup dry sherry
1 shallot, sliced thin
2 teaspoons chopped fresh thyme, plus extra for garnish
Pinch red pepper flakes
1 cup heavy cream
Kosher salt and freshly ground black pepper

1. To make the sweet potatoes and pheasant: Preheat the oven to 350 degrees. Combine the sweet potatoes, onion, 2 tablespoons of the oil, 2 tablespoons of the butter, 4 sprigs of the thyme, and salt and pepper to taste in a large bowl, tossing to coat. Transfer to a baking dish and bake until the sweet potatoes are tender, about 40 minutes.

2. Increase the oven temperature to 400 degrees. Season the pheasant with salt and pepper to taste. Heat the remaining 3 tablespoons oil in a large skillet over medium-high heat until hot, but not smoking. Add the pheasant, skin side down, and sear for 2 to 3 minutes. Add the remaining 2 tablespoons butter and remaining 4 sprigs thyme, transfer the skillet to the the oven and cook the pheasant for about 25 minutes, flipping the pieces over halfway through the cooking time.

3. To make the sherry cream: While the pheasant is cooking, combine the sherry, shallot, thyme, and pepper flakes in a medium saucepan over low heat and simmer until the sauce is reduced by half. Slowly whisk in the cream and cook until the mixture is reduced by one-third. Season with salt and pepper to taste. Pour the mixture through a fine-mesh strainer and cover to keep warm.

5. Transfer the sweet potatoes to a microwave-safe bowl and microwave until hot. Divide the sweet potatoes and pheasant among four plates, spoon the sherry cream over the pheasant, sprinkle with chopped thyme, and serve.

Chef Ismail Samad of the Gleanery for Fowl Mountain Farm and Rabbitry

FISH AND SEAFOOD

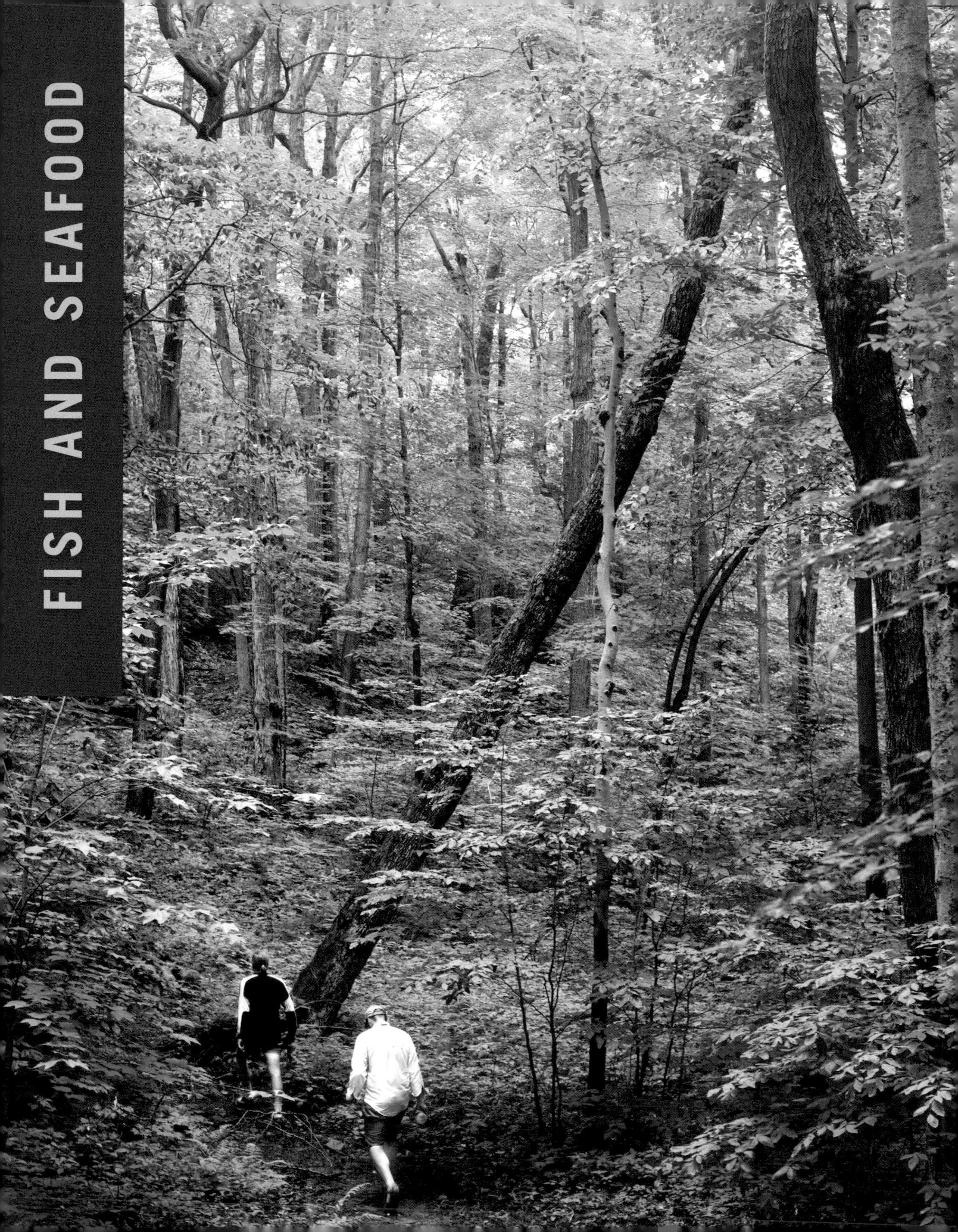

PISTOU

Pistou, located in Burlington, features contemporary American cuisine prepared with both classic and modern French technique. Chef and owner Max Mackinnon strives to serve the best possible food made with high-quality seasonal ingredients, in a welcoming environment. The menu at Pistou changes daily according to what local farmers have to offer, as well as what is available throughout the growing season. The wine list focuses on French and domestic offerings, and they love serving wines that are natural and/or biodynamic.

Butter-Poached Halibut with Forbidden Black Rice, Beet Dashi, and Fennel Salad

SERVES 6

This recipe uses black rice, also known as forbidden rice, as a base. Black rice has an appealing, very nutty flavor, which contributes to the complexity of the dish. The earthy beet dashi and sweet fennel salad complement each other, and the other ingredients, perfectly. Poaching the fish in butter gives it a luxurious texture and preserves its white color, which makes for a striking contrast with the purple-black rice. The beet dashi can be made a few hours ahead of time. Note that you may not need all the vinaigrette made in step 3; dress the salad according to your taste.

Forbidden Rice

4 cups water
2 cups black rice
2 sprigs fresh thyme
2 garlic cloves, peeled
2 star anise pods
1 teaspoon coriander seeds
1 tablespoon olive oil, or to taste
Kosher salt

Beet Dashi

2 quarts fish broth
1/3 cup bonito flakes
1 sheet of kombu
1 cup dried shiitake mushrooms
2 star anise pods
1 tablespoon coriander seeds
1/2 cup beet juice

Fennel Salad

2 fennel bulbs, stalks removed, bulbs trimmed
1/2 cup extra-virgin olive oil
1/4 cup fresh lemon juice (2 lemons)
1 tablespoon Vermont honey, plus extra to taste
1 tablespoon chopped fresh chives
1 tablespoon chopped fresh parsley
1/2 teaspoon celery seeds
Kosher salt and freshly ground black pepper

Poached Halibut

1/4 cup water
1 pound unsalted butter, cut into 1-tablespoon-sized pieces
3–3 1/2 pounds halibut, cut into 6 equal pieces

1. To make the rice: Bring water, rice, thyme, garlic, anise pods, and coriander seeds to a boil in a medium saucepan over medium-high heat. Reduce the heat to simmer; cover and cook until tender, about 30 minutes. Add olive oil and salt to taste, and fluff rice with a fork.

2. To make the beet dashi: Bring the fish broth, bonito flakes, kombu, shiitake mushrooms, star anise pods and coriander to a simmer in a medium saucepan over medium heat. Simmer for 40 minutes, then add the beet juice.

3. To make the fennel salad: Using a mandoline or sharp chef's knife, slice fennel bulbs very thin and place in a medium bowl. Whisk together oil, lemon juice, honey, chives, parsley, and celery seeds. Season with additional honey and salt and pepper to taste. Toss desired amount of vinaigrette with fennel and marinate in the refrigerator for about 30 minutes.

4. To make the poached halibut: Bring the water to a simmer in a large saucepan over medium-high heat. Slowly whisk in the butter. Add the halibut and cook, basting with butter, until just cooked through, about 20 minutes. Season with salt and pepper to taste.

To serve: Place rice in a shallow bowl, top with fish, add some of the dashi around the rice, and top with fennel salad.

Pistou

WhistlePig Whiskey and Molasses—Marinated Salmon Fillets

SERVES 4

This recipe is a great one to pull out when you are entertaining guests. It is very easy to prepare ahead of time. To prevent the fish from sticking, make sure the grill grate is very clean; scrape or brush it and oil it well just before cooking the salmon.

2 cups molasses
1/2 cup WhistlePig whiskey
1 tablespoon minced fresh ginger
1 garlic clove, minced
1 cup canola oil, plus extra for the grill
Kosher salt and freshly ground black pepper

4 (7-ounce) skinless salmon fillets

1. In a medium bowl, whisk together the molasses, whiskey, ginger, and garlic. Whisk in the canola oil until well combined. Season with salt and pepper to taste. Place the salmon in a large zipper-lock plastic bag, pour the marinade over the salmon, seal, and place in the refrigerator for 30 minutes, turning the bag over at least once to marinate evenly.

2. Heat a gas or electric grill to medium-high heat and generously brush the cooking grate with oil. Remove the salmon from the marinade and grill for 3 minutes. Using a large spatula, carefully flip the fillets over and grill for 3 more minutes. Serve.

Chef Peter McLyman of the Country Club of Vermont for WhistlePig Whiskey

Mussels with Brown Beans and Hard Cola

SERVES 2

Winter, spring, summer, or fall there is nothing more comforting than a bowl of steamed mussels paired with some crusty grilled bread to soak up the broth. A classic mussel dish usually involves white wine and garlic, but the combination can often overpower the taste of the mussels. The introduction of the hard cola began as a fun late-night experiment in the Bluebird Tavern kitchen that pleasantly surprised everyone when it worked so well. The spiked soda lends a more subtle, sweet balance to the dish and really allows the mussels to shine. Bluebird Tavern uses Prince Edward Island mussels, which are unsurpassed in quality, flavor, and consistency.

1 pound Canadian mussels

2 tablespoons canola oil

1/2 cup thinly sliced red onion

3 garlic cloves, minced

3 tablespoons canned black beans or pinto beans, drained and rinsed

Salt and freshly ground white pepper

2 tablespoons spicy ketchup

1/2 cup hard cola

1/3 cup dry white wine

3 tablespoons (1 1/2 ounces) unsalted butter

1 tablespoon chopped fresh parsley or cilantro

1 teaspoon salted corn nuts

Crusty bread

1. Rinse and scrub the mussels under cold running water, removing the beards with your fingertips or with sharp kitchen shears. Discard any mussels that may be broken or do not close when tapped.

2. Heat the oil in a large pot over medium heat. Add the onion, garlic, and brown beans, stirring often, and cook until onions are soft, 3 to 4 minutes. Season with salt and pepper to taste. Add the mussels and ketchup, gently stirring to coat. Cover the pot, increase the heat to high and cook until the mussels just start to open, about 2 minutes.

3. Add the cola, wine, and butter and cook until all the mussels have opened, 3 to 4 minutes, shaking the pot occasionally. Remove from the heat and discard any mussels that do not open. Stir in the parsley. Season with additional salt and pepper to taste. Garnish with corn nuts and serve immediately with crusty bread.

Bluebird Tavern

SMUGGLERS' NOTCH DISTILLERY

Smugglers' Notch Distillery, in Jeffersonville, is owned and operated by father-and-son team Ron and Jeremy Elliott. Ron is a retired business executive, while Jeremy is a pharmaceutical chemist.

Smugglers' Notch produces the highest-rated domestic vodka in America. It is made from a combination of sweet corn and winter wheat, which is sourced from Idaho and then blended with water from a local spring. Because vodka is 60 percent water, this local source gives the spirit a truly Vermont terroir. The filtration process used also sets this vodka apart from the others: All other vodkas produced in the United States are charcoal filtered, while the Elliots use a particulate filter, which allows the the vodka to retain some of its natural flavors. As a result, it has a hint of sweetness and smoothness.

The Elliotts have expanded their spirit line to include a premium single-barrel, double-aged amber rum. The rum is aged for three years in charred white oak barrels and then transferred to four-year-old whiskey barrels to finish off the process. The whiskey barrels infuse complex whiskey overtones, while giving each batch its own subtle characteristics and distinctive flavor profile. Gin is the distillery's newest offering.

Grilled Shrimp with Smugglers' Notch Vodka and Mango Cocktail Sauce

SERVES 6

This recipe came to Chef Peter McLyman on a warm summer's day when he wanted to make shrimp cocktail, but did not want to go the traditional route. Taking a cue from the season, he grilled the shrimp and paired it with a cool, refreshing mango sauce, which he spiked with Smuggler's Notch vodka. This sweet and smoky combination has become McLymann's go-to summer shrimp cocktail recipe.

Dried ancho chiles have a wonderful sweet, yet hot flavor, which adds delicious layers to the marinade. You can substitute a dried pasilla chile, if necessary. The versatile cocktail sauce also pairs perfectly with grilled pork tenderloin, grilled chicken breast, or a meaty white fish such as halibut or snapper.

Shrimp and Marinade

2 cups Italian or balsamic vinaigrette
1/2 cup chopped fresh cilantro leaves
1/3 cup canned diced green chiles, drained
2 tablespoons red pepper flakes
1/2 dried ancho chile, seeded, deveined, and coarsely chopped
1 1/2 tablespoons hot sauce, such as Sriracha or Tabasco
3 garlic cloves, chopped
2 teaspoons cayenne pepper
2 teaspoons ground cumin
2 teaspoons ground coriander
2 teaspoons chopped fresh ginger
1 1/2 pounds jumbo shrimp (16/20 count), peeled and deveined

Mango Cocktail Sauce

4 medium ripe mangos, peeled, pitted, and sliced

1/2 cup Smuggler's Notch vodka

2 tablespoons Grand Marnier

1 tablespoon red pepper flakes

1 teaspoon grated fresh ginger

1. To make the shrimp: Process the vinaigrette, cilantro, green chiles, red pepper flakes, ancho, hot sauce, garlic, cayenne, cumin, coriander, and ginger in a blender or food processor until smooth. Transfer the mixture to a large zipper-lock plastic bag, add the shrimp, seal, and refrigerate for 1 to 3 hours.

2. To make the mango cocktail sauce: While the shrimp is marinating, combine the mangos, vodka, Grand Marnier, red pepper flakes, and ginger in a clean blender or food processor and pulse until almost smooth. Transfer the sauce to a bowl, cover, and refrigerate for at least 1 hour.

3. Preheat a gas or electric grill or heat a grill pan over medium heat. Remove the shrimp from the marinade and grill for about 2 minutes per side.

4. Pour the cocktail sauce into a decorative bowl and place it on a platter. Arrange the shrimp around the bowl and serve.

Chef Peter McLyman of the Country Club of Vermont for Smugglers' Notch Distillery

Seared Day Boat Scallops, Braised Endive, Confit Potato, and Shaved Prosciutto with Orange Beurre Blanc

SERVES 4

Day boat scallops are harvested by hand and are untreated, or "dry." They are strongly preferred over "wet" scallops, or those treated with a chemical preservative. Pistou serves Maine Dayboat Scallops. The bright flavor of orange juice provides the perfect counterpoint to rich scallops and bitter endive in this elegant winter dish. Small balls of potato are cooked as a "confit" in duck fat until tender; their earthiness holds up well alongside the salty prosciutto and meaty shellfish. Be sure to zest the oranges before juicing them.

Confit Potatoes

1 1/2 pounds Yukon Gold potatoes (2 to 3 potatoes), peeled

2 tablespoons (1 ounce) duck fat or unsalted butter, melted, or 2 tablespoons extra-virgin olive oil

2 garlic cloves, chopped

2 sprigs fresh thyme

Kosher salt and freshly ground black pepper

Orange Beurre Blanc

1 1/2 cups fresh orange juice (3 oranges)

1 1/2 cups dry white wine

1 garlic clove, minced

1 teaspoon chopped fresh thyme

16 tablespoons (8 ounces) unsalted butter, cut into small cubes and chilled

Braised Endive

2 heads Belgian endive
2 1/2 tablespoons grapeseed oil
1/2 cup dry white wine
1/2 cup chicken stock
1 1/2 tablespoons grated orange zest
2 garlic cloves, minced
2 teaspoons chopped fresh thyme
Pinch saffron

Scallops

2 tablespoons extra-virgin olive oil
12 large sea scallops, tendons removed
8 prosciutto slices, thinly shaved (optional)
2–3 cups microgreens

1. To make the confit potatoes: Preheat the oven to 350 degrees. Using a melon baller, scoop the potato into balls. Place in a small ovenproof dish and toss with the duck fat, garlic, thyme, and salt and pepper to taste. Cook the potatoes until fork-tender, 35 to 40 minutes.

2. To make the orange beurre blanc: Meanwhile, combine the orange juice, white wine, garlic, and thyme in a small saucepan over medium-high heat and cook until the mixture is reduced to 1 cup, 12 to 15 minutes. Whisk in the butter and season with salt and pepper to taste. Cover and set aside.

3. To make the braised endive: Cut the endives in half lengthwise. Heat the oil in a medium skillet over medium-high heat. Add the endives cut side down and sear until nicely browned. Add the wine, chicken stock, orange zest, garlic, thyme, and saffron and bring to a boil. Reduce heat to a simmer and cook until endive is tender, 10 to 12 minutes.

4. To make the scallops: Rewarm the beurre blanc over low heat. Heat the oil in a large skillet over medium-high heat. Add the scallops and sear for 2 to 3 minutes on each side. Place three scallops on each plate, arrange an endive half between the scallops, and spoon some of the potatoes on the side. Drape two prosciutto slices over the scallops and drizzle with the orange beurre blanc. Sprinkle a handful of microgreens over the top and serve.

Pistou

RED CLOVER INN

Vermont is famous internationally as a food and dining destination, and the Red Clover Inn, along with its local farm partners, showcases premier Vermont farm-to-table dining. Chef Dennis Vieira has a close relationship with area farmers and purveyors, selecting fresh-from-the-farm meats, produce, and dairy products, as well as fresh game, for Red Clover's seasonally inspired menus. Vieira, who is first-generation Portuguese American with Azorean roots, has worked in some of the most innovative kitchens in America and abroad. His career is a study in the avant-garde approach to flavors. The appeal of leading an outdoor lifestyle combined with the abundance of fresh produce convinced Vieira to make Vermont his home.

Back Home–Style Portuguese Steamed Middleneck Clams

SERVES 4

This middleneck clam recipe is one of Chef Vieira's favorites, because it is so versatile. The dish is great on its own, over linguini pasta, or with grilled or pan-seared shrimp. Portuguese-style clams also pair very well with a simple fillet of roasted cod. Fiery piri piri peppers (also known as bird's eye peppers) are available at specialty food stores and some supermarkets; if you are unable to find them you can substitute jarred hot chili (cascabel) peppers or hot sauce.

20 middleneck clams
1 cup dry white wine
3 tablespoons olive oil
6 garlic cloves, crushed and chopped
1 tablespoon minced jarred piri piri peppers
1 tablespoon unsalted butter
3/4 cup chopped fresh parsley
Kosher salt and freshly ground black pepper
Crusty bread

1. Rinse and scrub the clams under cold running water. Discard any clams that may be broken or do not close when tapped.

2. Heat a large pot over medium-high heat. Add the clams, cover, and cook for 1 minute. Add the wine, olive oil, garlic, and peppers, gently stirring to coat. Cover the pot and simmer until the clams just start to open, 5 to 6 minutes.

3. With a slotted spoon, remove the clams and reduce the heat to medium. Stir in the butter and parsley. Season with salt and pepper to taste. Discard any clams that do not open. Season with salt and pepper to taste.

4. Place the clams in a serving bowl and serve with broth and crusty bread.

Red Clover Inn

WEST MOUNTAIN INN

Nestled on 150 mountainside acres overlooking the Battenkill Valley, the century-old West Mountain Inn has been welcoming travelers with warmth and hospitality for the last 30 years. Dining at the inn is a very important part of a guest's stay. Chef Jeff Scott prepares delicious New England fare with only the freshest ingredients. Everything served by the inn is made on-site using local organic produce, free-range meats and poultry, seasonal game, local cheeses and dairy products, and fresh fish, All the inn's breads, pastries, and desserts are homemade. Working directly with local organic farms and food producers, West Mountain Inn is helping maintain Vermont's rich agricultural heritage and provides a dining experience bursting with freshness and flavor.

Sautéed Sea Scallops in a Smoked Bacon and Maple Cream Sauce

SERVES 3 TO 4

Chef Scott uses Vermont Smoke and Cure bacon in this dish. These quick scallops make a perfect hot appetizer, or you can serve them with quinoa and a fresh green vegetable as a main course.

1 tablespoon olive oil
12 large sea scallops, tendons removed
3 ounces (about 3 slices) smoked bacon, minced
1/2 cup pure Vermont maple syrup
1/4 cup heavy cream
Kosher salt and freshly ground black pepper

1. Heat the oil in a large skillet over medium-high heat. Add the scallops and sear for 2 minutes on each side. Transfer to a plate and set aside.

2. Add the bacon to the empty pan and cook for about 1 minute. Add the maple syrup and heat for 1 minute. Slowly whisk in the cream and cook until heated through, about 1 minute. Return the scallops and any accumulated juices to the pan and warm through. Season with salt and pepper to taste and serve.

West Mountain Inn

Pan-Seared Salmon with Crabmeat and Sweet Potato Hash and Tomato Coulis

SERVES 4

The heart of this dish is the crabmeat and sweet potato hash. It was inspired by a cool September day, the colors of fall, and some fresh veggies. Since New England crab is considered some of the best around, Chef Scott wanted to find a way to combine it with local vegetables. The hash and coulis are equally as tasty when paired with any kind of fish.

2 sweet potatoes, peeled and diced
2 tablespoons (1 ounce) unsalted butter
1 medium onion, diced
2 tablespoons chopped garlic
4 medium tomatoes, cored and chopped
1 cup dry white wine
2 tablespoons arrowroot
2 tablespoons cold water
4 (7- to 8-ounce) skinless salmon fillets
1 cup diced red bell pepper
1 cup diced yellow bell pepper
8 ounces fresh crabmeat or frozen and thawed
1 tablespoon chopped fresh thyme
Kosher salt and freshly ground black pepper

1. Place the sweet potatoes in a medium saucepan and cover with cold, salted water. Bring to a boil over high heat and cook until the potatoes are tender, about 10 minutes. Drain and set aside.

2. Melt 1 tablespoon of the butter in a medium skillet over medium heat. Add the onion and stir to coat. Spread the onion in an even layer and cook, stirring occasionally, for 10 minutes. Sprinkle with salt, reduce the heat to medium-low, and continue cooking until the onion is nicely browned, about 10 minutes. Add 1 tablespoon of the garlic and cook for 1 more minute. Add the tomatoes and 1/2 cup of the wine and cook until the mixture is reduced by one-third, 20 to 25 minutes.

3. Heat the oven to 350 degrees. In a small bowl, whisk together the arrowroot and water. Whisk into the tomato mixture. Transfer to a food processor and purée until smooth. Season with salt and pepper to taste. Cover and keep warm.

4. Melt the remaining 1 tablespoon butter in a large skillet over medium-high heat. When the pan is hot, add the salmon and sear about 2 minutes on each side. Transfer the salmon to a baking sheet and bake for 15 minutes.

5. While the salmon is baking, add the peppers and remaining 1 tablespoon garlic to the empty skillet. Cook until the peppers are tender, about 3 minutes. Add the sweet potatoes, crabmeat, thyme, and remaining 1/2 cup wine and cook, stirring frequently, until the liquid is reduced by one-third, 10 to 15 minutes. Divide the hash among individual plates, place a salmon fillet on each portion of hash, and top with the tomato coulis. Serve.

West Mountain Inn

MEAT

WHISTLEPIG WHISKEY

WhistlePig Whiskey is a small craft distillery located on WhistlePig Farm, one of the oldest farms in Addison County. The company's flagship product, WhistlePig Straight Rye Whiskey, has won consistent acclaim—from Wall Street Journal's endorsement as one of the Top Five Whiskies of 2010 to Wine Enthusiast's highest rating ever for a rye whiskey at 96 points. WhistlePig Farm is however, more than just a craft distillery. The farm is being lovingly restored by WhistlePig's proprietor and founder, Raj Bhakta, whose objective is to redefine the model for sustainable agriculture in Vermont. WhistlePig Farm has introduced two pig breeds to Vermont (from Hungary and New Zealand) and is also the home of goats, horses, sheep, ducks, and a considerable 20-acre maple stand, which Bhakta intends to tap for syrup to be aged in whiskey barrels. Ultimately, Bhakta seeks to demonstrate that farming, when driven by entrepreneurial ambition, can be a lucrative and deeply satisfying undertaking. As WhistlePig Whiskey leads the revival of rye whiskey, WhistlePig Farm is not far behind with the shifting paradigms of modern day, sustainable agriculture.

New York Strip Steaks with WhistlePig Whiskey Demi-glace Sauce

SERVES 4

Chef Peter McLyman received some high-quality New York strip steaks that had some great marbling. He had just tasted WhistlePig Whiskey for the first time earlier that week and thought that it would complement the steaks beautifully. Peter brought some of that straight rye back to the kitchen and created his whiskey demi-glace. You can substitute white mushrooms, portobellos, or stemmed shiitake mushrooms for the cremini.

4 (10-ounce) New York strip steaks, about 1 inch thick, trimmed
Kosher salt and freshly ground black pepper
3 tablespoons olive oil
10 ounces cremini mushrooms, thinly sliced
1/4 cup finely chopped shallot
1 garlic clove, minced
1/3 cup WhistlePig whiskey
1 1/4 cups demi-glace or beef stock
1/4 cup heavy cream

1. Preheat the oven to 425 degrees. Season the steaks generously with salt and pepper.

2. Heat 2 tablespoons of the oil in a large ovenproof skillet over medium-high heat. When the oil is hot, add the steaks and sear 3 to 4 minutes on each side. Transfer the steaks to a baking sheet and bake until medium-rare, 6 minutes.

3. While the steaks are in the oven, add the remaining 1 tablespoon oil to the empty skillet and heat over medium heat. Add the mushrooms, shallot, and garlic and cook for 2 minutes. Remove the skillet from the heat and carefully whisk in the whiskey. Return the skillet to the heat and cook for about 2 minutes. Add the demi-glace and return to a simmer. Slowly whisk in the cream and cook until the sauce is slightly reduced. Season with salt and pepper to taste. Spoon the sauce over the steaks and serve.

Chef Peter McLyman of the Country Club of Vermont for WhistlePig Whiskey

Variation: Prepare a gas or electric grill and grill the steaks over medium-high heat, turning once, until medium-rare, 3 to 4 minutes. While the steaks are resting, prepare the whiskey demi-glace sauce in a skillet. Prepare demi-glace just as you would for skillet/oven preparation. Spoon the sauce over the steaks and serve.

Panko-Encrusted Minute Steaks

SERVES 4

The gravy in this recipe is very light, almost brothlike, which adds a nice textural contrast to the succulent meat and crispy panko bread crumbs. Add some garlic mashed potatoes and a fresh vegetable, and you've got the perfect country dinner. If possible, buy grass-fed beef for this recipe.

8 (4-ounces each) minute steaks, trimmed
Sea salt and freshly ground black pepper
1 tablespoon unsalted butter
1/4 cup plus 1 tablespoon olive oil
3 garlic cloves, minced
1 cup plus 1 1/2 tablespoons all-purpose flour
2 cups low-sodium beef broth
1/8 teaspoon Worcestershire sauce, or to taste
1 tablespoon chopped fresh thyme, or to taste
Pinch cayenne pepper
3 large eggs, lightly beaten
2 cups panko or homemade bread crumbs

1. Place each steak between sheets of parchment paper and, using a meat mallet, pound to 1/4-inch thickness. Season the meat with salt and pepper to taste.

2. Heat the butter and 1 tablespoon of the oil in a large skillet over medium heat until hot, but not smoking. Add the garlic and cook for 30 seconds. Add 1 1/2 tablespoons of the flour and cook for 30 seconds. Whisk in the stock, Worcestershire sauce and thyme, stirring constantly, until smooth and slightly thickened. Pour into a bowl and set aside. Carefully wipe out the pan with a paper towel.

3. In a medium bowl, stir together the remaining 1 cup flour and cayenne pepper. Place the eggs and bread crumbs in separate bowls. Dip each minute steak in the flour, then in the egg, and then in the bread crumbs. Set the steaks on a cooling rack.

4. Heat 2 tablespoons oil in the same skillet used for the sauce over medium-high heat until hot, but not smoking. Add two steaks and cook until the crust is nicely browned on both sides, 2 to 3 minutes per side. Transfer to a platter and repeat with the remaining 2 tablespoons oil and remaining steaks. Let the steaks rest for 5 minutes. While the steaks rest, warm the gravy, then serve the steaks and gravy together.

High Ridge Meadows Farm

SHAT ACRES FARM

The Shatney family has been raising Highland cattle on Shat Acres Farm in Greensboro Bend for over 40 years. They market their beef under the brand name Greenfield Highland Beef. The family has the oldest closed herd in the country, which means that they have not bought a cow in over 30 years, and their herd is the third-largest herd of Highlands in the United States. Today, the farm is considered to have some of the top Highland cattle genetics in the country.

The success of Shat Acres Farm stems from Carroll Shatney, who had an eye for cattle. He knew which bulls to use and which animals to cull. Carroll loved his Highlands and instilled that love in his son, Ray, who today owns the farm with Janet Steward. Ray's oldest daughter, Kelly, her husband, Matt, and their children are now working on the farm, the third and fourth generation to do so. Being a good steward of the land has always been part of the Shatneys' farm philosophy—"taking care of the land so your animals will have what they need." The owners feel an obligation to make sure that their animals are properly cared for and have a good life. The end result is that consumers have access to humanely raised, high-quality local meat.

Amber Ale–Braised Highland Beef Chuck Roast

SERVES 6

Because there is very little waste with Highland beef, if you are lucky enough to have access to Greenfield Highland Beef, you can use a 2- to 3-pound roast for this recipe; it will still serve six. Pair this roast with mashed potatoes for a delicious meal.

1 (3- to 4-pound) boneless beef chuck roast, trimmed
Kosher salt and freshly ground pepper
1/4 cup all-purpose flour
5 tablespoons canola oil
1 1/2 pounds yellow onions, thinly sliced
3 large garlic cloves, minced
1 tablespoon pure Vermont maple syrup
1 tablespoon tomato paste
1 1/2 cups low-sodium beef broth, or as needed
1 (12-ounce) bottle Vermont amber ale
1/4 cup apple cider vinegar
2 tablespoons chopped fresh parsley
4 sprigs fresh thyme
1 bay leaf
1 1/2 tablespoons whole-grain Dijon mustard
1 1/2 teaspoons cornstarch
2 tablespoons water

1. Preheat the oven to 325 degrees. Season the roast with salt and pepper to taste. Place the flour in a large, shallow bowl and dredge the roast in the flour.

2. Heat 3 tablespoons of the oil in a large Dutch oven over medium-high heat until hot but not smoking. Add the meat and brown on all sides, about 5 minutes per side. Transfer to a large plate and set aside.

3. Reduce the heat to medium and add the remaining 2 tablespoons oil. Add the onions and cook until soft and translucent, stirring often, about 8 minutes. Add the garlic, maple syrup, and tomato paste and cook for 1 minute. Add the broth, ale, vinegar, parsley, thyme, and bay leaf, scraping the bottom of the pot to loosen any brown bits.

4. Spread the mustard thinly over the entire roast and return it to the pot along with any accumulated juices. Bring to a boil over medium heat. Cover the pot and transfer it to the oven. Cook until the meat is fork-tender, about 3 hours, turning the roast over halfway through the cooking time.

5. Transfer the roast to a carving board and tent loosely with foil. Discard the bay leaf and thyme sprigs. Using a slotted spoon, transfer the onions to a plate and tent loosely with foil. With a spoon, skim any fat off the surface of the liquid and bring to a boil over medium-high heat. Continue to boil until the sauce is reduced slightly. Combine the cornstarch and water in a small bowl, then whisk the cornstarch slurry into the liquid. Simmer until the liquid thickens, stirring often, about 3 minutes. Season with salt and pepper to taste.

6. Cut the roast into thick slices, against the grain, or pull apart in pieces. Arrange the meat on a platter with the onions and pour a little of the sauce over the top. Serve, passing the remaining sauce at the table.

Tracey Medeiros and Greenfield Highland Beef

GRAZE

Graze is an online food delivery service, founded in 2010 by Christy Colasurdo and Julianna Doherty. It all began when Colasurdo visited Doherty in Vermont and returned home to Connecticut with a cooler full of local meats and cheeses. Doherty realized that there was a market in urban New England areas for wholesome, farm-fresh foods. She envisioned Graze as a business that would deliver the best Vermont artisanal food products to a customer's front door. Colasurdo, an intrepid foodie and writer who had been covering the farm-to-table movement, felt that the timing was right, and the two friends launched Graze, focusing their first efforts in Connecticut's Fairfield County. Today, the company makes deliveries in Connecticut, Massachusetts, New York, and Vermont.

The foods offered by Graze come from small family-run farms that produce their products in small batches, with care. The company works with farmers and producers who share their passion for protecting both the environment and their customers' health, and who believe in making it easier for families to source local, farm-fresh foods that don't contain artificial ingredients, pesticides, hormones, antibiotics, or excess preservatives.

Individual Holiday Beef Wellingtons

MAKES 2

This recipe is based on the classic, reinterpreted as individual portions for an elegant presentation. For additional portions, simply multiply the ingredients according to the number of guests you will be serving. If you are entertaining a small group, you only have to prepare the portions that are needed; this wastes less of an expensive cut of beef. The puff pastry and port reduction provide the drama. Graze uses all-natural, pasture-raised beef tenderloin from PT Farms in St. Johnsbury.

Duxelles

2 tablespoons (1 ounce) unsalted butter
6 tablespoons minced shallot or red onion
6 ounces white mushrooms, stemmed and minced
1 teaspoon chopped fresh thyme, plus thyme sprigs for garnish
Salt and freshly ground black pepper

Spinach

2 teaspoons olive oil
12 large spinach leaves

Beef Wellingtons

1 (17 1/4-ounce) package frozen puff pastry, thawed
2 teaspoons Dijon mustard
2 (6-ounce) pasture-raised filets mignon, trimmed
Kosher salt and freshly ground black pepper
1 large egg, beaten with 2 teaspoons water

Port Reduction Sauce

2 tablespoons chopped shallot
4 tablespoons (2 ounces) unsalted butter
2 cups port wine
Salt and freshly ground pepper

1. To make the duxelles: Melt the butter in a medium skillet over medium heat. Add the shallot and cook, stirring often, until soft and translucent, 2 to 3 minutes. Add the mushrooms and thyme and cook, stirring often, until golden brown, 5 to 6 minutes. Season with salt and pepper to taste and let cool.

2. To make the spinach: Heat the oil in a small skillet over medium-high heat. Add the spinach and cook until just wilted, about 2 minutes. Let cool slightly, then squeeze the spinach to remove any excess water. Set aside on paper towels to continue draining.

3. To make the Beef Wellingtons: Roll the pastry dough out and cut two 6-inch disks and two 8-inch disks. Spread 1 teaspoon mustard in the center of each 6-inch disks. Place the beef filets on the mustard and season the beef with salt and pepper to taste. Spread half of the mushroom duxelles over each filet and top with the spinach. Using a pastry brush or your fingertips, paint the inside edges of the puff

pastry with the egg. Cover with the 8-inch puff pastry disks. Being careful to press the air out, seal the edges together with your fingertips. Use the tines of a fork to crimp the edges. Trim any excess dough to create a neat round package. Brush the top and sides with the beaten egg.

4. Place the Beef Wellingtons on a parchment-lined baking sheet. Transfer to the freezer to allow the egg coating to dry and the pastry to set and chill, about 30 minutes. While the Wellingtons are in the freezer, preheat the oven to 400 degrees. Bake the Wellingtons until the pastry is golden brown, about 25 minutes for medium-rare. Let stand 10 minutes.

5. To make the port reduction sauce: While the Wellingtons are baking, melt 2 tablespoons of the butter in a medium skillet over medium heat. Add the shallot and cook, stirring often, until translucent, 2 to 3 minutes. Remove the skillet from the heat and add the wine. Return the pan to the heat and cook until the volume is reduced by half. Slowly whisk in the remaining 2 tablespoons butter. Season with salt and pepper to taste.

6. Cut each Beef Wellington in half, arrange on plates, and drizzle the sauce around and over the steak. Garnish with thyme sprigs.

Graze

THE FROZEN BUTCHER AT SNUG VALLEY FARM AND FIVE CORNERS FARMERS MARKET

The story of the Frozen Butcher at Snug Valley Farm springs from Helm and Nancy Nottermann's days as successful dairy farmers and Holstein breeders in the Northeast Kingdom. It was a natural transition for them to use their years of experience milking to raising Holstein steers for grass-fed beef. The duo had already been doing that for neighbors and family for years. In 2002, they made the plunge: The Frozen Butcher at Snug Valley Farm was born as the farmers' market arm of their grass-fed beef operation. The frozen meat products were transported from their farm in East Hardwick and displayed in solar-powered freezers, on a trailer with the distinctive logo of a mustached purple cow.

With no female bovines on the farm, the Nottermanns support local dairy farmers by purchasing 2-day-old Holstein bull calves at a premium price and raise them without hormones or stimulants. Dedicated to providing humane and natural care for their animals, they use herbal homeopathic remedies and natural milk replacer, supply calf cozies (jackets) to the sensitive newborns, and provide each with a roomy individual stall. As the friendly critters grow for a full two years, they graze on the farm's pastures in summer and eat its hay all winter, which makes for delicious grass-fed beef. The Nottermans also raise pork, buying piglets from a local farmer, raising

them on pasture and grain. Snug Valley Farm's third product, managed by their son, Ben, is the thousands of pumpkins sold from the front lawn. This arm of the farm started when Ben was six and paid most of his college tuition.

Being worthy stewards of the land and the environment is paramount to the Nottermans. Thus, they maximize the health of their pastures with intensive rotational grazing to provide the best grass possible for "the boys." They are committed to supporting area businesses, from the local family-run dairy farms where they purchase their calves to the farm supply stores, graphic designers and printers, nearby vegetable farms, and food co-op. The Nottermans strive to keep the Northeast Kingdom a vibrant and growing agricultural community.

Rolled Stuffed Beef (Rouladen)

SERVES 4

This recipe is from Swabia, the region in southern Germany where Helm Nottermann grew up. The area consisted of small farms, limited budgets, and great cuisine. Notterman's mother prepared delicious meals using mostly homegrown ingredients. Helm and his wife, Nancy, enjoy many of his mother's recipes using their own grass-fed beef. They like to use Vermont Smoke and Cure bacon in this recipe. To make slicing the beef easier, place it in the freezer for an hour. Good accompaniments include garlic mashed potatoes, roasted red potatoes, sweet potato fries, or homemade spaetzle.

2 pounds top round or flank steak, trimmed
Kosher salt and freshly ground black pepper
8 ounces bacon, finely chopped
1 large sweet onion, minced
1/2 cup chopped fresh parsley, plus extra for garnish
1/3 cup Dijon mustard
3 tablespoons canola oil
1 3/4 cups beef stock
2 tablespoons all-purpose flour
1 cup red wine
1 tablespoon Worcestershire sauce
1/4 cup sour cream

1. Cut the steak into two pieces, about 4 by 8 inches each. Then slice each piece in half horizontally, making a total of four thin pieces. Place each piece of meat between sheets of parchment paper and, using a meat mallet, pound to 1/8-inch thickness. Season with salt and pepper to taste.

2. Combine the bacon, onion, and parsley in a small bowl. Spread each piece of meat with the mustard, then divide the bacon mixture among the four pieces and spread out to cover the mustard. Loosely roll up the beef pieces lengthwise, being careful to keep the mixture inside of the bundles. Carefully tie each roll with butcher's twine, securing the ends and center portion to form an even oblong shape, or secure with toothpicks.

3. Heat the oil in a Dutch oven over medium-high heat. Add two of the beef rolls and brown on all sides, about 4 minutes per side. Transfer to a platter and repeat with the remaining two rolls. Reduce the heat to medium and add 1/4 cup stock to the pot. Scrape up any browned bits and and whisk in the flour, stirring until smooth. Whisk in the wine, Worcestershire sauce, and remaining stock until smooth. Add the beef rolls along with any accumulated juices, cover, and reduce the heat to low. Simmer for 1 1/2 to 1 3/4 hours.

4. Transfer the beef rolls to a warm platter. Whisk the sour cream into the broth mixture until smooth. Pour the sauce over the beef, sprinkle with parsley, and serve.

Helm Notterman of Snug Valley Farm

THE RELUCTANT PANTHER INN AND RESTAURANT

The Reluctant Panther Inn and Restaurant is southern Vermont's premier small luxury hotel. Located in the heart of historic Manchester Village, it has been in continual operation since the mid-1960s and offers 20 spacious, elegantly appointed rooms and suites and a top-rated gourmet dining experience. The Panther's restaurant specializes in contemporary American cuisine with an emphasis on locally sourced foods. CIA-trained chef Jonathan Cox creates a sophisticated dining experience that is unsurpassed in northern New England. A multiple-year, Wine Spectator Award–winning wine list complements the tasteful menu.

A partner with the Vermont Fresh Network, the restaurant relies upon local neighbors to provide a steady stream of fresh ingredients, including breads, cheeses, seasonal produce (locally foraged mushrooms, orchard fruits) and meats. In particular, the inn is fortunate to have its pork and Hereford beef supplied by Weston's Morgan Hill Farm, owned and operated by one of the hotel's managing partners. These ingredients, paired with artisanal wines, bolster the menus for an annual series of food and wine dinners.

The Reluctant Panther's name is a nod to the wild panthers that once roamed the nearby mountains despite the encroachment of humans. They symbolized the fierce, independent attitude of Vermonters, who fought against interference by the English King and from their neighbors to the east and west. At the Green Mountain Tavern, which stood on this site until 1897, Ethan Allen's Green Mountain Boys met and organized their resistance. The name *Reluctant Panther* was conceived in the 1960s; it pairs the reluctance of panthers to come down from the mountains with the historical symbolism of the property. The Reluctant Panther has been a Manchester institution ever since.

Pork Two Ways

SERVES 4 TO 6

Chef Cox is committed to producing a highly seasonal menu and autumn in Vermont is one of the most exciting times to do so. This dish is a perfect example of that approach, marrying the last of summer's produce and herbs with the warmer, deeper flavors of the coming winter. The restaurant uses pork belly from Morgan Hill Farm in Weston, Vermont. For a change of pace, you can substitute thinly sliced red cabbage for the Swiss chard.

For the Pork Loin

1 pound boneless pork loin, trimmed and tied
    with butcher's twine
Kosher salt and freshly ground black pepper
2 tablespoons canola oil
2 tablespoons (1 ounce) unsalted butter

Polenta

1/2 cup water
2 cups milk
1/2 teaspoon salt
2 tablespoons (1 ounce) unsalted butter
2/3 cup cornmeal
1/4 cup sour cream
1/8 teaspoon red pepper flakes, plus extra to taste
Kosher salt and freshly ground black pepper

Swiss Chard

1 bunch Swiss chard, stems and leaves
    separated, stems chopped and leaves
    sliced into 1-inch strips
2 tablespoons (1 ounce) unsalted butter
1 tablespoon brown sugar
1 tablespoon red wine vinegar

Kosher salt and freshly ground black pepper
Pork Belly Braise (recipe follows)
Apple-Sage Compote (recipe follows)

1. To make the pork loin: Preheat the oven to 325 degrees. Season the pork loin with salt and pepper to taste. In a large ovenproof skillet heat the oil over medium-high heat until hot but not smoking. Add the pork and brown on all sides, about 3 minutes per side. Add the butter, remove the skillet from the stovetop and let the loin rest in the skillet for 15 minutes. Transfer the skillet to the oven and cook until the internal temperature reaches 135 degrees, about 1 hour. Transfer to a cutting board and let rest for about 10 minutes.

2. To make the polenta: While the pork is cooking, combine the water, milk, and salt in a medium saucepan over medium-high heat and bring to a simmer. Whisking constantly, add the cornmeal in a slow, steady stream. Reduce the heat to low and simmer, stirring occasionally with a wooden spoon, until thickened, 35 to 40 minutes. The polenta should pull away from the sides of the pan. Stir the sour cream and red pepper flakes into the warm polenta and season with salt and pepper to taste.

3. To make the Swiss chard: Meanwhile, fill a medium saucepan with water and bring to a boil over medium-high heat. Fill a large bowl with ice water. Add the chard stems to the boiling water and blanch for 2 to 3 minutes. Using a slotted spoon, transfer the stems to the ice bath and let cool completely. Drain the stems and set aside. Melt the butter in a medium skillet. Add the chard leaves, stirring to coat. Cover and cook until wilted, stirring occasionally. Add the chard stems, brown sugar, vinegar, and salt and pepper to taste and cook until tender, about 5 minutes.

4. When the pork loin has rested 10 minutes, cut into thin slices. To serve, place 2 to 3 slices of pork loin on each plate and spoon some of the compote next to it. Spoon some of the polenta and Swiss chard onto each plate. Place 1 or 2 cubes of pork belly on the pork loin and drizzle the braising liquid over the pork, polenta, and Swiss chard.

The Reluctant Panther Inn and Restaurant

Pork Belly Braise

Start this braise the day before you intend to serve the roast.

1 tablespoon brown sugar

2 teaspoons salt

1 teaspoon freshly ground black pepper

1 teaspoon ground fennel seeds

1 pound pork belly

3 sprigs fresh thyme

1 fresh bay leaf

1 sprig fresh sage

2 tablespoons canola oil

1 large yellow or sweet onion, thinly sliced

1 large carrot, peeled and diced

1 celery rib, diced

2 (16-ounce) cans stout beer

1/2 cup molasses

1/2 cup Vermont apple cider

2 tablespoons Vermont apple cider vinegar

1. Combine the sugar, salt, pepper, and fennel seeds in a small bowl. Rub the spice mixture evenly over the pork belly, wrap it in plastic wrap, and refrigerate for 1 hour. Remove the pork belly from the refrigerator and gently rinse off excess rub with cold water.

2. Preheat the oven to 325 degrees. Tie the thyme, bay leaf, and sage together with butcher's twine or wrap in cheesecloth. Heat the oil in a Dutch oven over medium-high heat until hot but not smoking. Add the pork belly and brown on both sides, about 2 minutes per side. Add the onion, carrot, celery, beer, molasses, cider, cider vinegar, and herb bundle. Bring to a boil, cover the pot, and transfer to the oven. Cook until the pork belly is fork-tender, 2 to 3 hours. Let cool for about 30 minutes. Place in the refrigerator overnight.

3. The next day, remove and discard any fat from the top of the braise. Remove the pork belly and cut into small cubes. Strain the braising liquid into a saucepan and discard the vegetables. Cook the liquid over medium heat until it is reduced by half. Return the pork belly cubes to the liquid and heat through.

The Reluctant Panther Inn and Restaurant

Apple-Sage Compote

MAKES ABOUT 2 CUPS

This compote can be made up to a day ahead of time and reheated before serving.

1/2 cup water

1/2 cup Vermont apple cider

1/4 cup packed brown sugar

1 cinnamon stick

3 Granny Smith apples (about 1 pound), peeled, cored, and diced

4 fresh sage leaves, thinly sliced

Kosher salt and freshly ground black pepper

Combine the water, cider, sugar, and cinnamon stick in a medium saucepan and bring to a boil over medium-high heat. Reduce the heat and simmer, stirring occasionally, until the liquid has reduced by one-third. Add the apples and cook, stirring occasionally, until the mixture has thickened and the apples are very tender, about 15 minutes. Remove from the heat and add the sage and salt and pepper to taste. Remove the cinnamon stick before serving.

The Reluctant Panther Inn and Restaurant

VERMONT SALUMI

Peter Roscini Colman's experience in life, and passion for food, was the inspiration for his business, Vermont Salumi. Born in Assisi, in the Umbrian region of Italy, Peter moved to Vermont when he was 3 1/2 years old, where he was raised on an organic vegetable farm. Growing up, Peter split his time between working on his family's Cate Farm in Plainfield and taking annual trips to Italy to visit other family members. Peter always loved eating prosciutto while in Italy, but he felt it was an expensive product. It was during one of those visits to Italy, that Peter decided to learn how to cure his own meat. He expressed this desire to some of his family and friends, who recommended that Peter apply for apprenticeships with old-world butchers in Italy. Peter soon found himself in a butcher shop in Italy learning how to slaughter pigs and cure the meat.

Upon his return to Vermont, Peter felt that the state offered a business opportunity for dry-curing meats. Using the advanced curing techniques that he learned in Italy, Peter renovated the space in his family's barn to start Vermont Salumi. The company currently offers four types of sausages, which are made from local pork that is raised on pasture without hormones or antibiotics. The sausages are made by hand, in small batches, without the use of nitrates or preservatives.

Lentils with Vermont Salumi Daily Grind Sausages

SERVES 4

If you cannot find Vermont Salumi Daily Grind sausages, sweet Italian sausage is a fine substitute. Serve with a loaf of crusty bread.

1 pound Vermont Salumi Daily Grind sausages
6 cups water
1 tablespoon unsalted butter
1 small onion, minced
12 ounces French green lentils
1 bay leaf
Kosher salt and freshly ground black pepper
2 tablespoons olive oil, plus extra for drizzling
2 garlic cloves, minced
1 cup crushed tomatoes
1 tablespoon red wine vinegar
Chopped fresh parsley

1. Bring the sausages and 2 cups of the water to a simmer over medium heat. Cook, turning occasionally, until the sausages are plump and the water has reduced by half, about 12 minutes. Remove the sausages from the stovetop and tent with foil. Reserve 1 cup of the sausage liquid.

2. Melt the butter in a 2 1/2-quart saucepan over medium heat. Add the onion and sauté until soft and translucent, stirring often, about 10 minutes. Add the lentils, the remaining 4 cups water, the bay leaf, and just enough reserved sausage liquid to cover. Increase the heat to medium-high and bring to a boil. Reduce the heat to medium-low, partially cover, and simmer until tender, about 1 hour. Discard the bay leaf. Season with salt and pepper to taste. Cover and set aside.

3. Heat the oil in a medium skillet over medium heat. Add the sausages and cook until browned, about 6 minutes. Add the garlic and cook for 1 minute, stirring often. Transfer the garlic, tomatoes, and vinegar to the lentil pot and cook until heated through. Season with salt and pepper to taste.

4. Slice the sausages and arrange them over the warm lentils. Drizzle olive oil over the top and sprinkle with parsley. Serve.

Vermont Salumi

Newhall Farm Berkshire Pork Loin with Poached Apples

SERVES 6

During the fall at Newhall Farm, you will find apples and pork both ready for market; thus, this classic recipe combination. The key to this roast's juiciness is that it brines overnight, so be sure to start this recipe the day before you plan to serve it. Pork tenderloins can be used in place of the roast; just reduce the brining time to six hours. The poached apples can be made a day in advance. Refrigerate the apples and poaching liquid separately, then recombine and reheat them before serving.

Pork

1/2 cup apple brandy

1/2 cup whole-grain mustard

1/2 cup wildflower honey

1/4 cup salt

1 tablespoon chopped fresh sage

4 cups water

3 pounds boneless pork loin, trimmed

2 tablespoons olive oil

Poached Apples

8 cups Vermont apple cider

1/2 cup granulated sugar

1/2 cup dry white wine

1 small sprig fresh rosemary

1/2 vanilla bean, split

6 apples such as Cortland, Empire, or
    Granny Smith, peeled

Chopped fresh rosemary

Sauce (optional; recipe follows)

1. To make the pork: Whisk together the brandy, mustard, honey, salt, and sage in a large container until smooth. Whisk in the water. Submerge the loin, cover the container, and refrigerate overnight.

2. To make the poached apples: Combine the cider, sugar, wine, rosemary, and vanilla bean in a large stockpot. Add the apples, cover and bring to a boil over medium heat. Remove the rosemary and let cool for 1 hour. When the apples are cool, core and slice them and set aside. Reserve 1/2 cup plus 2 tablespoons of the poaching liquid if making the sauce.

3. Preheat the oven to 425 degrees. Set a rack in a roasting pan. Remove the pork from the brine and pat dry with a towel. Brush pork with oil and place on the roasting rack.

4. Roast the pork until it begins to brown, about 15 minutes. Lower the heat to 350 degrees and cook until the internal temperature reaches 135 degrees. Let rest for 15 minutes, then slice. Garnish the pork with the sliced apples, sprinkle with chopped rosemary, drizzle with sauce, if desired, and serve.

Sauce

2 1/2 cups veal stock or chicken stock

1/2 cup plus 2 tablespoons apple poaching liquid

1 sprig fresh thyme

2 teaspoons arrowroot

2 tablespoons (1 ounce) unsalted butter

Kosher salt

Combine veal stock, 1/2 cup of the poaching liquid, and thyme sprig in a medium saucepan and bring to a simmer over medium-low heat. In a small bowl, combine arrowroot and the last 2 tablespoons poaching liquid. Whisk arrowroot mixture into stock and cook until slightly thickened, about 15 minutes. Whisk in butter. Discard thyme sprig and season with salt to taste.

Newhall Farm

THE STOWE MOUNTAIN LODGE

The farm-to-table dining concept that prevails throughout the Stowe Mountain Lodge's food and beverage outlets takes advantage of the area's vast source of artisanal foods. The lodge's executive chef, Josh Berry, is dedicated to sourcing the freshest products in New England and has created relationships with local farmers, while also saturating the menu with dishes that are uniquely Vermont. Farm-to-table principles and local artisanal ingredients are second nature to Berry, as he grew up in New England and has always appreciated all the culinary assets that the region has to offer.

Pork Tenderloin Medallions Stuffed with Dried Fruit and Cheddar Cheese, Cranberry-Braised Red Cabbage, and Vanilla Whipped Sweet Potatoes

SERVES 8

For this colorful and savory meal, Chef Berry uses antibiotic- and hormone-free pork from Duclos & Thompson farm in Weybridge and Jasper Hill's Cabot Clothbound Cheddar. Note that you will need to start the cabbage the day before you plan to serve this dish. If you prefer a mild vanilla flavor in the sweet potatoes, use one vanilla bean instead of two.

Cranberry-Braised Red Cabbage

2 heads red cabbage, quartered, cored, and leaves separated
1 red onion, thinly sliced
2 cups fresh cranberries, roughly chopped
1 1/2 cups dry red wine
1/2 cup granulated sugar
Kosher salt
White pepper
Ground cinnamon

Vanilla Whipped Sweet Potatoes

8 sweet potatoes
2 tablespoons (1 ounce) unsalted butter
2 tablespoons brown sugar
2 vanilla beans
Kosher salt and white pepper

Pork Tenderloin Medallions

1 (2-pound) pork tenderloin

1 pound cheddar cheese, shredded (4 cups)

1 cup chopped fresh parsley

1 cup raisins

1/2 cup dried currants

1/2 cup dried cherries

Kosher salt and white pepper

1 cup all-purpose flour

5 large eggs, lightly beaten

2 1/2 cups panko bread crumbs

2 tablespoons (1 ounce) unsalted butter

1. To make the cranberry-braised cabbage: Chop the cabbage into bite-sized pieces. Place the cabbage, onion, and cranberries in a large container. Add the wine, sugar, and salt, pepper, and cinnamon to taste and toss to coat. Cover and let the cabbage marinate in the refrigerator overnight.

2. Preheat the oven to 350 degrees.

3. To make the vanilla whipped sweet potatoes: Place the sweet potatoes on a baking sheet lined with foil. Bake until fork-tender, about 1 hour. Let cool slightly, then slice in half and scoop the flesh into a medium bowl. Add the butter and sugar. Split the vanilla beans in half lengthwise using a paring knife. Scrape the seeds and pulp into the bowl with the potatoes. Mash with an old-fashioned masher or hand-held mixer until smooth, then season with salt and pepper to taste.

4. To make the pork tenderloin medallions: Slice the pork tenderloin into eight equal pieces. Place each piece of pork between sheets of parchment paper. Using a meat mallet, pound the meat to 1/2-inch thickness. Place the medallions in the refrigerator.

5. Combine the cheese, parsley, raisins, currants, and cherries in a medium bowl. Lightly oil a baking sheet.

6. Place one of the medallions on a clean work surface and spoon one-eighth of the filling in the center. Roll the pork around the filling and transfer to the prepared baking sheet. Repeat with the remaining pork and filling.

7. Place the flour, eggs, and bread crumbs in three separate shallow bowls. Season the medallions with salt and pepper. Dip each pork roll into the flour, shaking off excess, then the eggs, and then dredge in the bread crumbs.

8. Return the pork to baking sheet and roast until golden brown and cooked through, 20 to 25 minutes. Let rest for 5 minutes.

9. While the pork is roasting, melt the butter in a large skillet. Add the cabbage mixture, cover, and cook over medium-low heat until the cabbage is tender and most of the liquid is absorbed.

10. Slice the pork. Place a small mound of cabbage in the center of eight warm dinner plates, spoon a small amount of sweet potatoes next to the cabbage and top with a sliced roll of stuffed pork.

The Stowe Mountain Lodge

Note: The stuffing makes more than needed for this recipe. It also works well with chicken. Store tightly covered in the refrigerator for future use.

JERICHO SETTLERS' FARM

Christa Alexander and Mark Fasching started their year-round, diversified farm on leased land back in 2002. Since then, Jericho Settlers' Farm has grown to encompass 200 sprawling acres in the towns of Jericho and Richmond. Much of that acreage is grazing land for their cattle and sheep, which are 100 percent grass-fed. The couple also raises pigs, chickens, and vegetables.

Alexander and Fasching offer a year-round CSA and farm stand and participate in the Burlington Farmers' Market while also working with a small number of local chefs and restaurants. They embrace the daily, and seasonal, challenges that come with farming.

Cider-Braised Pork Chops with Apples and Onions

SERVES 6

It is very important to purchase bone-in blade-cut pork chops and not bone-in center-cut chops for this dish. The blade-cut pork chops will be tender and falling off the bone, rather than overcooked and tough. Serve with a fresh green vegetable such as kale or broccoli rabe and crusty bread on the side.

6 bone-in blade-cut pork chops, 1 inch thick, trimmed
Kosher salt and freshly ground black pepper
2 tablespoons olive oil
2 medium yellow onions, chopped
2 apples, such as Empire, Cortland, or McIntosh, cored and coarsely chopped
1 cup Vermont apple cider
1/2 cup chicken stock
2 tablespoons pure Vermont maple syrup
3 garlic cloves, minced
2 sprigs fresh thyme, plus extra sprigs for garnish

1. Preheat the oven to 300 degrees. Season the pork chops with salt and pepper to taste. Heat the oil in a large Dutch oven over medium-high heat. Add the chops and brown on both sides, in batches, about 2 minutes per side. Transfer the pork chops to a plate and set aside.

2. Reduce the heat to medium. Add the onions to the pot and cook, stirring often, until soft and golden, about 6 minutes. Add the apples, cider, stock, maple syrup, garlic, and thyme, stirring until well combined. Bring to a boil and continue to cook, whisking often, until the sauce is slightly reduced. Return the pork chops and accumulated juices to the pot. Cover cook until the meat is tender and falling off the bone, about 1 hour. Season with salt and pepper to taste.

3. Place the pork chops on individual plates and arrange the apples and onions around the meat. Top with the sauce and garnish with thyme sprigs. Serve.

Jericho Settlers' Farm

MISERY LOVES CO.

Misery Loves Co. is a team of restaurant veterans, Laura Wade, Nathaniel Wade, and Aaron Josinsky. They travel about the greater Winooski area in Big Red, a 1976 Winnebago camper converted into a mobile kitchen. The menu changes daily and the team is also available to cater a variety of parties, tailoring the menu to suit the event and planner's needs. Because they are a small independent company, Misery Loves Co. is able to work with all sorts of budgets, doing events for up to 200 guests. They not only have the flexibility to do food preparation in their mobile kitchen, but also are able to cook in an assortment of other culinary settings. They also opened a restaurant and bar in Winooski in the winter of 2012.

Korean Reuben

SERVES 8 TO 10

This recipe requires a smoker and some advance planning; the brisket must be started five days before it's served. You'll also need a couple of special ingredients. Insta Cure No. 1, a blend of salt and sodium nitrite, is available at sausagemaker.com or www.amazon.com. Gochujang is a chile-spice paste from Korea. It is sold at Asian markets, and some natural food stores. Chili garlic sauce, while not the same, can be substituted. The results are well worth the time and effort, however, for a quick version of this recipe, you can use a good-quality black pastrami.

Brine and Brisket

8 1/2 cups water

1 1/2 cups kosher salt

1 cup granulated sugar

3 tablespoons Insta Cure no. 1
    (for slow-cooking meats)

1 garlic head

1 tablespoon pickling spice

2 1/2 pounds fatty point brisket, trimmed

2 teaspoons freshly ground black pepper

2 teaspoons ground coriander

Pickled Mustard Seeds

3/4 cup water

3/4 cup rice wine vinegar

1/2 cup mustard seeds

1/4 cup granulated sugar

1 1/2 teaspoons kosher salt

Chili Mayo

1 cup mayonnaise, preferably Kewpie
    (Japanese mayonnaise)

2 tablespoons gochujang, or to taste
16–20 slices hearty rye bread
1 (15-ounce) jar kimchi

1. To brine the brisket: Combine the water, salt, sugar, Insta Cure, garlic, and pickling spice in a large stockpot and bring to a boil over medium-high heat. Let cool, then refrigerate until the brine is cold. Place the brisket in the brine, cover, and refrigerate for 3 days, turning the meat halfway through brining. Remove the meat from the brine and refrigerate, uncovered, overnight.

2. Set up the smoker according to the manufacturer's directions, using apple wood. Coat the meat with the pepper and coriander, place it in the smoker, and smoke slowly, maintaining a temperature of about 200 degrees, until the internal temperature of the meat reaches 150 degrees, about 8 hours.

3. When the meat is almost at 150 degrees, preheat the oven to 325 degrees. Transfer the meat to the oven and cook until the internal temperature of the meat reaches 190 degrees, about 45 minutes. Let the brisket cool, then wrap and refrigerate overnight.

4. To make the pickled mustard seeds: Combine the water, vinegar, mustard seeds, sugar, and salt in a medium saucepan and bring to a simmer over medium-low heat, stirring often, until the seeds are plump and tender and the liquid is absorbed, 25 to 30 minutes.

5. To make the chili mayo: Combine the mayonnaise, 1/4 cup of the pickled mustard seeds, and gochujang in a small bowl. Add additional mustard seeds to taste.

6. Slice the brisket against the grain. Spread each slice of bread with chili mayo. Layer the brisket and kimchi on half of the bread slices and top with the remaining bread slices. Serve.

Misery Loves Co.

BOYDEN VALLEY WINERY

Boyden Valley Winery, housed in a restored 1875 carriage barn on the Boyden family farm in Cambridge, is steeped in the culture and agricultural heritage of Vermont's Green Mountains. From the 10,000 grapevines that have been lovingly tended by the family for four generations the Boydens craft wines that feature only the finest fruit from the loamy soils of the Lamoille River Valley. The care with which they've nurtured the land lends itself to traditional winemaking, and the wines they produce are balanced and delicious.

The winery crafts a variety of high-quality international award-winning wines as well as ice wines and cream liqueurs. They welcome visitors year-round to taste their products and learn why they are making Vermont famous for wine.

Pork Tenderloin with Cassis and Soy Sauce Reduction

SERVES 4

The pork tenderloin with cassis and soy sauce reduction recipe was inspired by the winery's cassis wine. Made with Vermont-grown organic grown black currants, the cassis is aged in French oak barrels for two years, making it decadent and pleasing to the palate. Linda Boyden, who is originally from Montreal, created this dish as a reflection of her heritage, combining the rich and savory flavors found in traditional French fare. The sautéed fennel adds a great dimension with a nice sweetness and texture. The cassis (the French term for black currant wine) is aromatic and very flavorful—its fruitiness emerges nicely and lends an elegant soft finish to the sauce.

2 tablespoons olive oil
1 medium fennel bulb, top removed, cored and
    thinly sliced, plus 2 tablespoons chopped
    fronds for garnish
1/2 teaspoon red pepper flakes
1 pork tenderloin (about 1 1/4 pounds), trimmed
1/2 cup low-sodium soy sauce
1 cup pure Vermont maple syrup
1/2 cup black currant wine,
1 tablespoon unsalted butter
Kosher salt and freshly ground black pepper

1. Heat 1 tablespoon of the oil in a medium skillet over medium heat. Add the fennel and red pepper flakes and toss to coat with the oil. Cook the fennel, stirring occasionally, until soft, about 30 minutes. Season with salt and pepper to taste. Remove from the heat, cover, and set aside.

2. Heat the remaining 1 tablespoon oil in a separate medium skillet over high heat. Season the pork with salt and pepper to taste, place in the skillet, and brown on all sides, about 3 minutes per side. Reduce the heat to medium-low, cover, and cook until an instant-read thermometer registers 145 degrees, about 20 minutes. Transfer the pork to a plate and tent with aluminum foil.

3. Pour the soy sauce and maple syrup into the same skillet used for the pork. Cook, whisking frequently, over medium-low heat until the liquid is reduced by half, about 5 minutes. Increase the heat to medium-high and slowly whisk in the wine. When the sauce begins to boil, reduce the heat to medium and slowly whisk in the butter. Cook until the mixture is thick enough to coat the back of a spoon, 2 to 3 minutes. Add the fennel and cook just until heated through. Season with salt and pepper to taste.

4. Transfer the pork to a cutting board and cut into 1/2-inch-thick diagonal slices. Pour the sauce over pork, sprinkle with the reserved fennel fronds, and serve.

Boyden Valley Winery

EDEN ICE CIDER COMPANY

In April 2007, Eleanor and Albert Leger bought an abandoned dairy farm in West Charleston. A year earlier, while visiting Montreal, they had sampled ice cider and discussed making a similar product in Vermont. The two decided to knock down the decrepit farmhouse and replace it with a new building that would have a full- sized foundation and basement. In the basement of the rebuilt farmhouse, a small pressing operation and bonded winery were born. During the winter of 2007, they made their first batch of about 100 cases of ice cider, which sold out in a month and a half. The demand for their product gave the couple enough confidence to start Eden Orchards and the Eden Ice Cider Company.

All their products are made from traditional and heirloom varieties of apples that are grown in Vermont. The naturally cold weather conditions here concentrate the flavors and sugars of the fruit before fermentation. Envision going to an apple orchard in the fall and sampling a cup of fresh-pressed apple cider. The cider has a rich, sweet yet tart flavor, along with a wonderful apple aroma. This is the flavor and signature taste that the Legers want Eden Vermont Ice Cider to be known for. They focus on a product that has a great "apple nose," which gives the palate a wonderful first impression of freshness. The product must also have a balance of acidity for a nice tart finish.

These artisanal producers are dedicated to making a product with thought and care for the climate, community, and the planet on which we live. All their materials are recyclable and renewable, right down to using natural cork closures from cork trees in Portugal.

Pan-Roasted Berkshire Pork Chops with Vermont Ice Cider

SERVES 2

Vermonters are fortunate to have organic pasture-raised Berkshire pork in the area. These pork chops have a wonderful flavor and delicate texture. Apples and pork are natural culinary partners, as the acidity from the apples brightens the subtle meatiness of the pork. Eden Calville Blend Vermont Ice Cider is a perfect pairing for pork, offering a balance of sweetness and acidity.

2 (10-ounce) bone-in pork chops, 1 1/4 inches thick, trimmed
Sea salt and freshly ground black pepper
Freshly ground black pepper, to taste
1 1/2 tablespoons olive oil
2 tablespoons (1 ounce) unsalted butter
1/4 cup minced shallot
1 tablespoon chopped fresh thyme, rosemary or sage, plus 2 sprigs for garnish
2/3 cup Eden Calville Blend Vermont Ice Cider

1. Preheat the oven to 375 degrees. Season the pork chops with salt and pepper to taste.

2. Heat the oil in a medium ovenproof skillet over medium-high heat until hot but not smoking. Add the pork chops and brown, about 3 minutes per side. Cover the skillet with aluminum foil, transfer to the oven, and roast until an instant-read thermometer registers 150 degrees, about 10 minutes.

3. Transfer the pork chops to a plate and tent with foil.

4. Add 1 tablespoon of the butter to the pan juices in the skillet and melt over medium-high heat. Add the shallots and chopped thyme and cook, stirring often, until soft and golden, about 2 minutes. Remove the pan from the heat and carefully add the ice cider. Return the pan to the heat and bring the liquid to a gentle boil. Deglaze the pan, stirring frequently and scraping up bits from the bottom, until the liquid is reduced by half, about 4 minutes. Whisk in the remaining 1 tablespoon of butter until well incorporated. Season with salt and pepper to taste.

5. Place the pork chops on individual plates and spoon some of the sauce over each chop. Garnish with herb sprigs and serve.

Eden Vermont Ice Cider

Slow-Cooked Veal Shoulder with Savoy Cabbage and Wild Rice Blinis

SERVES 4

The late fall and winter harvests are the inspiration for this light braised dish. At Twin Farms, they use organic veal from Howvale Farm in Tunbridge and organic savoy cabbage from Fable Farm in Barnard. The Northern Spy Apples, from Champlain Orchards in Shoreham, along with cider vinegar from Gingerbrook Farm in South Washington, give the recipe a sweet, crisp acidity that is a nice contrast to the veal and blinis. This dish makes a great main course or appetizer.

Veal

1 pound veal shoulder, trimmed
Kosher salt and freshly ground black pepper
2 tablespoons olive oil
1/2 cup dry white wine
2 garlic cloves, roughly chopped
6 sprigs fresh thyme
1 bay leaf
2 1/2 cups beef stock, plus extra as needed

Vinaigrette

1/4 cup Vermont apple cider vinegar
1 1/2 teaspoons Vermont honey
1 teaspoon chopped fresh thyme
3/4 cup extra-virgin olive oil
1 Northern Spy apple, peeled, cored, and
    finely diced
Kosher salt and freshly ground black pepper

Blinis

1 cup all-purpose flour
2 teaspoons baking powder
Pinch salt
1 cup whole milk
1 large egg, lightly beaten
1 teaspoon olive oil
2/3 cup cooked wild rice
1 1/2 teaspoons chopped fresh thyme

Cabbage

4 tablespoons (2 ounces) unsalted butter
1 head savoy cabbage, leaves torn into
    2-inch pieces
1 tablespoon chopped fresh sage
Extra-virgin olive oil
Kosher salt and freshly ground black pepper
2/3 cup pistachio nuts, toasted

1. To make the veal: Preheat the oven to 300 degrees. Season the veal shoulder with salt and pepper to taste. Heat the oil in a large Dutch oven over medium-high heat until hot but not smoking. Add the veal and brown on all sides, about 4 minutes per side. Add the wine, garlic, thyme, and bay leaf. Add enough stock to cover the veal. Remove from heat, cover and transfer to oven. Cook, turning the veal halfway through cooking, until the meat is fork-tender, 4 to 5 hours.

2. To make the vinaigrette: Meanwhile, whisk together the vinegar, honey, and thyme in a small bowl. Slowly whisk in the oil until well combined. Stir in the apple and season with salt and pepper to taste. Set aside.

3. To make the blinis: When the veal is almost done, whisk together the flour, baking powder, and salt in a medium bowl. Make a well in the center of the dry ingredients, pour in the milk,

egg, and oil, and stir until just combined. Fold in the wild rice and thyme. Lightly grease a griddle or large skillet with cooking spray and heat over medium heat. For each blini, ladle 1/4 cup batter onto the prepared griddle and cook on one side until bubbles begin to form, about 3 minutes. Flip the blinis and cook until golden brown, about 2 minutes. Transfer to a platter and keep warm.

4. To make the cabbage: Melt the butter in a large skillet over medium heat. Add the cabbage and cook, stirring frequently, until tender and golden brown, 12 to 15 minutes. Add the sage and gently stir to combine. Toss with oil and season with salt and pepper to taste.

5. Cut the veal into medallions or pull apart in pieces. Place two or three blinis on each plate and top with the cabbage. Arrange the veal over the cabbage, sprinkle the pistachio nuts around the plates and drizzle the vinaigrette over the cabbage. Serve.

Twin Farms

LONGVIEW FARM

Longview Farm is a sheep farm located in Pownal, in the southwest corner of Vermont. The owners, Chris and Shannon Barsotti, aim to provide healthy food for their family and community, and to enhance the fertility and beauty of the land. The couple came to farming because of their desire to be closer to life's natural cycles and the source of their food. In return for all that their animals give them, the Barsottis strive to keep these creatures as healthy and content as they can be. They are committed to using sustainable agricultural practices, raising their lambs exclusively on pasture, as nature intended.

Roasted Leg of Grass-Fed Lamb

SERVES 8, WITH LEFTOVERS

This is one of Chris and Shannon's favorite recipes, a perfect dish for a large gathering of family and friends. A leg of lamb will yield more than enough meat for eight servings, but leftovers can be used to make Curried Lamb Tacos (page 177). Fresh Turkish bay leaves have a mild and complex flavor and are subtly sweet; they enhance the flavor of the roast and add a wonderful depth of flavor. If you can't find fresh bay leaves, you can substitute 20 to 24 dried bay leaves.

1 (9- to 10-pound) bone-in leg of lamb, preferably grass-fed, trimmed

5–6 garlic cloves, thinly sliced

1/4 cup extra-virgin olive oil

3 tablespoons fresh lemon juice

1/4 cup chopped fresh rosemary, plus sprigs for garnish

2 tablespoons chopped fresh thyme

Kosher salt and freshly ground black pepper

5 baking potatoes, peeled and quartered

10–12 fresh Turkish bay leaves

1 large sweet onion, cut into 8 wedges

1 cup beef stock

1/4 cup red wine

1. Preheat the oven to 500 degrees.

2. Using a sharp knife, make 1-inch slits all over the meat and insert garlic slices into the slits. In a small bowl, combine the oil, lemon juice, rosemary, and thyme. Rub the mixture evenly over the surface of the lamb and season with salt and pepper to taste. Place the lamb in a roasting pan and roast for 1 hour.

3. Meanwhile, place the potatoes in a large saucepan, cover with salted water by 1 inch, and bring to a boil. Cook the potatoes for 5 to 6 minutes, then drain and set aside.

4. Reduce the oven temperature to 350 degrees. Place the bay leaves on top of the roast, arrange the potatoes and onion wedges around it, and add the stock and wine to the pan. Roast until the internal temperature of the meat reaches 140 degrees (for medium-rare) and the potatoes are browned, crisp, and fork-tender, 1 1/2 to 2 hours. Baste the lamb and potatoes occasionally with pan juices and turn the potatoes once while roasting.

5. Transfer the lamb to a carving board and let rest for 15 minutes. Transfer the potatoes and onions to a platter and season with salt and pepper to taste. Pour the pan juices into a small saucepan, scraping the bits from the bottom of the roasting pan, and bring to a simmer over medium heat. Season with salt and pepper to taste.

6. Carve the lamb into thin slices and arrange on a platter with the potatoes and onion wedges. Drizzle with some of the pan juices and garnish with rosemary sprigs. Serve along with the remaining pan juices.

Longview Farm

Leftover Roast Leg of Lamb Tacos

SERVES 6

Manchego is a sheep's milk cheese made in the La Mancha region of Spain. It has a creamy texture with a slightly piquant taste. You can substitute shredded Monterey Jack, cheddar, or mozzarella. In addition to the cheese, serve these tacos with an assortment of toppings, such as shredded lettuce, black beans, fresh salsa, and cilantro.

2 tablespoons olive oil
3/4 cup diced red onion
Zest of 1 lime plus 2 tablespoons juice
3 garlic cloves, minced
6 mint leaves, thinly sliced
1 1/2 teaspoons curry powder
1/4 teaspoon ground cumin
3 cups shredded cooked lamb
Kosher salt and freshly ground black pepper
6 (8-inch) whole-wheat tortillas, warmed
Shredded Manchego cheese (optional)

Heat the oil in a medium skillet over medium heat. Add the onion, lime zest and juice, garlic, mint, curry powder, and cumin and cook until the onions are soft. Add the lamb and cook until heated through. Season with salt and pepper to taste. Spoon the lamb filling into the tortillas and sprinkle with shredded Manchego, if desired. Serve with an assortment of toppings.

Longview Farm

Blackberry-Blueberry Jam

MAKES 10 HALF-PINT JARS

Pomona's Universal Pectin (an all-natural pectin) is available in most natural foods stores. Each box of pectin contains a packet of calcium powder and directions for making calcium water, which you will need for this recipe. If possible, use organic blueberries, blackberries, and lemons for this jam. Unopened, the jam will last up to nine months. After opening, it should be refrigerated and used within three weeks.

1 3/4 cups organic cane sugar
4 teaspoons Pomona's Universal Pectin
4 pints blueberries
2 pints blackberries
1/2 cup fresh lemon juice (3 lemons)
4 teaspoons calcium water

1. Wash ten 1/2-pint glass jam jars and lids. Place the jars in two large pots, such as stockpots or canning pots, and cover with water. Bring to a boil, then reduce the heat to the lowest setting, letting the jars and lids remain in hot water until ready to use.

2. In a small bowl, stir together the sugar and pectin. Place the blueberries and blackberries in a blender and crush.

3. Transfer the berries to a large saucepan, add the lemon juice and calcium water, and bring to a boil over medium-high heat, stirring constantly. Stir in the sugar-pectin mixture and return to a boil for about 2 minutes, stirring constantly. Remove from the heat and skim off any foam.

4. Remove the jars from the hot water and let air-dry. Carefully ladle the hot jam into the hot glass jars, leaving 1/4-inch space at top. Remove any air bubbles and place the hot (dried) lids on the jars and twist as tightly as possible when closing. Arrange the jars in a single layer in the two pots, cover them with hot water, and bring to a boil. Boil for 12 minutes, then immediately remove the jars and set them on a cooling rack or towel. (As the jars cool, the lids will become visibly concave; often there is an audible pop when they seal.) Let sit for at least 12 hours before moving or serving so that the jam will have time to set.

Sunshine Valley Berry Farm

THE MAD TACO

Joey Nagy felt there was a culinary void in the state of Vermont—the lack of good Mexican food. To remedy the situation, he and his partners, the folks behind the Three Penny Taproom in Montpelier, opened not one, but two restaurants (in Waitsfield and Montpelier), both named the Mad Taco. Both restaurants make everything but the cheese and the tortillas from scratch. They also focus on creating relationships with neighboring farms, sourcing as many of their ingredients locally as possible. One great example is the delicious pork that accounts for a large portion of their menu. Every month, the restaurants buy whole pigs from local farms and use the meat to create myriad specials and staple dishes. To complement the pork and other Mexican fare, their tap list always includes a choice of beers from Lawson's Finest Liquids, in nearby Warren.

Habanero Carrot Hot Sauce

MAKES 2 1/2 CUPS

At the Mad Taco, this hot sauce is used with everything. The sweetness from the carrots and onion balances the heat from the habanero peppers. This hot sauce is not for faint palates! It is fiery hot with hints of citrus and tropical fruit that explode in your mouth. Cutting back on the number of habanero peppers can reduce the spiciness to your preferred level.

1 1/2 teaspoons vegetable oil
1 medium Spanish onion, diced
12 habanero peppers, halved, stemmed, and seeded
1 cup diced carrots (about 2 medium)
3 garlic cloves, chopped
1/2 cup white wine vinegar
1 cup water, plus extra as needed
Salt

Heat the oil in a medium saucepan over medium heat. Add the onion and cook, stirring occasionally, until golden brown, about 15 minutes. Increase the heat to medium-high and add the peppers, carrots, garlic, vinegar, and water. Cook, stirring frequently, until tender, about 10 minutes. Transfer to a blender and blend until smooth. Season with salt to taste. The sauce should be as thick as ketchup; if it is too thick, adjust the consistency with additional water.

The Mad Taco

Orange-Basil Dipping Sauce

MAKES 1 CUP

This versatile dipping sauce is bright and lively with strong citrus flavors, as well as a nice (but not overpowering) zip from the Sriracha hot chili sauce. It's perfect with Beer-Battered Fiddleheads (page 88). For a spicier dipping sauce, increase the amount of hot chili sauce to suit your personal taste.

1 cup mayonnaise
2 tablespoons plain yogurt
Finely grated zest and juice from 1 orange
2 tablespoons chopped fresh basil
1/2 teaspoon Sriracha or other hot chili sauce
Kosher salt and freshly ground black pepper

In a medium bowl, whisk together the mayonnaise, yogurt, orange zest and juice, basil and hot sauce. Season with salt and pepper to taste.

Fiddlehead Brewery

Spicy Mayo

MAKES ABOUT 1 1/2 CUPS

With its creamy texture and "big kick" flavors, this mayonnaise pairs perfectly with light and succulent Hush Puppies (page 29). As with any recipe using raw eggs, to avoid foodborne illness, make sure you use only fresh, clean, properly refrigerated eggs with intact shells.

2 large egg yolks
2 tablespoons fresh lemon juice
2 teaspoons whole-grain mustard
1 teaspoon Dijon mustard
1 teaspoon New Mexico chile powder
Kosher salt
1 cup safflower oil
1 shallot, minced
2 tablespoons minced pickled jalapeños

Process the egg yolks, lemon juice, whole-grain mustard, Dijon mustard, chile powder, and 1 teaspoon salt in a food processor. With the processor running, slowly add the oil in a steady stream until well blended. Add the shallot and pickled jalapeños and blend for another 2 to 3 seconds. Pour into a bowl and season with salt to taste. Cover and refrigerate until ready to use.

The Pitcher Inn

DANA FOREST FARM

For the Laskovski family, Dana Forest Farm began as an "off the grid" venture for a simple and sustainable life. It evolved into the unearthing of an old farmstead, edible landscapes, a working forest, and certified organic shiitake mushrooms. The farm remains simple and is still off the grid. The family's mission is to manage their forest sustainably while providing customers with the healthiest, best-tasting shiitakes in the world.

The farm is located in the Dana Forest in Waitsfield. The Laskovskis envision their operation as a farm in the woods, where they cultivate not only shiitakes, but also ginseng, nut trees, and fruit trees. They are inspired by the legendary back-to-the-land couple Helen and Scott Nearing, who called their own property "Forest Farm." Dana Forest Farm is the culmination of many ideas that solidified into just a few words. It represents the Laskovskis' connection to the past, their feelings about the present, and their vision of farming for the future.

Shiitake Bits

MAKES 3/4 CUP

These shiitake bits are very similar to smoky bacon bits. They are crisp and crunchy, with a burst of earthy flavor. You can sprinkle them on salads, soups or in dips. They may be stored in a sealed container at room temperature for up to a week.

8 ounces shiitake mushrooms, trimmed and
    sliced 1/8 inch thick
2 tablespoons olive oil
Kosher salt and freshly ground black pepper

1. Preheat the oven to 375 degrees. Lightly oil a baking sheet and set aside.

2. Combine the mushrooms and oil in a bowl, and gently toss to coat. Spread the mushrooms out in a single layer on the prepared baking sheet and sprinkle with salt and pepper. Bake until the mushrooms are evenly brown and just crisp, about 40 minutes. Let cool slightly and season with additional salt and pepper, if desired. Serve.

Dana Forest Farm

Autumn Spice Crème Anglaise

MAKES 1 3/4 CUPS

This is a rich, silky smooth, thick custard sauce. It is the perfect complement to Spiced Cider Semifreddo (page 225), Apple Cider Caramel Sauce (page 135), and Buttermilk Doughnuts (page 32).

1 cup whole milk
1 cup heavy cream
1/2 cup granulated sugar
1/2 teaspoon salt
4 large egg yolks
1 1/2 teaspoons vanilla extract
1 teaspoon ground cinnamon
1/4 teaspoon grated nutmeg
1/4 teaspoon ground allspice
1/4 teaspoon ground cloves

1. Fill a large bowl with ice water and set aside.

2. Combine the milk, cream, 1/4 cup of the sugar, and the salt in a heavy-bottomed medium saucepan and bring to a boil over medium-high heat. Remove from the heat.

3. In a medium bowl whisk together the egg yolks, remaining 1/4 cup sugar, and vanilla. Whisking constantly, add the milk mixture to the yolk mixture in a slow, steady stream. Return the custard to the saucepan and cook over low heat until thick enough to coat the back of a wooden spoon, about 5 minutes.

4. Strain the sauce into a bowl and stir in the cinnamon, nutmeg, allspice, and cloves. Set the bowl in the ice bath to cool completely. Serve.

The Reluctant Panther Inn and Restaurant

THE VERMONT CRANBERRY COMPANY

The Vermont Cranberry Company, located in Fletcher, is the first commercial grower of cranberries in Vermont. Bob Lesnikoski, essentially a self-taught grower, found his niche growing cranberries back in 1996. Bob was a logging contractor who was looking for another profession, specifically something hands-on involving food. At that time, the cranberry industry was expanding from Massachusetts to Maine. During his job transition, Bob decided to meet some of the growers in Maine to see if the berries would be a good fit for his property. After speaking with him, he decided to give the fruit a try. It wasn't long before he was selling his berries to local restaurants and at nearby farmers' markets.

Today, his company continues to be successful with help from his wife, Elizabeth, and their three children who assist with growing, harvesting, and meticulously hand-sorting their premium berries for color and size. The whole family packs the fruit almost every day. Then Bob, better known to Vermont locals as "Cranberry Bob," delivers them throughout Vermont. They are pretty tired by the time the holiday season rolls around. However, it is rewarding for the Lesnikoski family to sit down at the table during their Thanksgiving meal and think about all the people throughout Vermont who are enjoying their cranberries.

On a little less than 3 acres, the company produces just over 20,000 pounds of cranberries annually from its three producing man-made bogs. The bulk of their sales are fresh fruit for the holiday season. They are small growers, so Bob can grow fruit using the cultural practices that were developed before chemical inputs became common—one example being hand weeding. The company's mission is to produce sustainably grown cranberries in Vermont.

One of the reasons Bob changed from the forest product industry to farming (particularly with a perennial fruit crop such as cranberries) is because it enables him to be personally invested in his property, cranberry beds, and fields. Bob shares, "If done right, these plants are going to outlive me and hopefully, a family member, or another young farmer, will continue my efforts. These cranberries will be my legacy, which is very important to me."

Vermont Cranberry Sauce

SERVES 4

If stored in the refrigerator, this sauce can be made up to one week prior to serving. Use more or less sugar depending on your tastes. For a slight twist, you can substitute Vermont maple syrup or honey for the sugar—the only difference is that the sauce may not gel as well.

3/4 cup Vermont apple cider
3/4 to 1 cup granulated or packed brown sugar
1/8 teaspoon salt
12 ounces fresh Vermont cranberries

Combine the cider, sugar, and salt in a medium saucepan and bring to a boil over medium-high heat, stirring often. Reduce the heat to a simmer and stir in the cranberries. Cook, uncovered, until the cranberries have popped and the liquid has slightly reduced, stirring occasionally, about 5 minutes. Let cool to room temperature. Transfer to a serving dish and serve, or refrigerate until needed.

Vermont Cranberry Company

Apple Cider Caramel Sauce

MAKES 1 1/2 CUPS

Serve this sauce with Buttermilk Doughnuts (page 32), Spiced Cider Semifreddo (page 225), and Autumn Spice Crème Anglaise (page 183).

2 cups Vermont apple cider
1/4 cup apple brandy
1/2 cup packed dark brown sugar
1 cinnamon stick
3 tablespoons (1 1/2 ounces) unsalted butter

Combine the cider and brandy in a medium saucepan and bring to a boil over high heat. Reduce the heat to medium, maintaining an easy boil, and add the sugar and cinnamon stick. Cook, stirring occasionally, until the sauce is thickened and reduced by half, 15 to 20 minutes. Transfer to a small bowl, stir in the butter, cover, and chill. Remove the cinnamon stick before serving.

The Reluctant Panther Inn and Restaurant

DRINKS

SUNSHINE VALLEY BERRY FARM

In 2007, Rob Meadows and Patricia Rydle were looking for both a change in career and a business they could work in together. When they heard that Blair's Berry Farm in Rochester was up for sale they decided that growing berries would be a good fit. The couple purchased the farm and renamed it Sunshine Valley Berry Farm. Today, they cultivate raspberries, blueberries, and blackberries and sell them pre-picked or pick-your-own. All of the berries at Sunshine Valley are certified organic.

Sunshine Smoothies

SERVES 4

These smoothies are best enjoyed right away; however, leftovers can be refrigerated for up to three days. If refrigerating, leave as little air at the top of the container as possible to reduce oxidation. You can also freeze this mixture. Add a little lemon or orange juice to the thawed smoothie before serving, to give it a fresh flavor.

1 large handful dandelion greens and flowers, stems removed and discarded

1 1/2 pints blueberries

1 cup spring water, plus extra as needed

3/4 cup fresh orange juice

1/4 cup fresh lemon juice

3/4 cup chopped mango

1/2 cup baby spinach

2 Medjool dates, pitted

1 tablespoon packed fresh mint leaves, plus extra for garnish

1 tablespoon shredded unsweetened coconut

1 tablespoon plain yogurt (optional)

1 1/2 teaspoons hulled hemp seed or maca powder (optional)

1. Soak the dandelion greens in a large bowl of cold water for about 30 minutes. Rinse and drain the greens; transfer to a blender.

2. Add the blueberries, water, orange juice, lemon juice, mango, spinach, dates, mint, coconut, yogurt, if using, and hemp seed, if using. Blend until smooth, adding extra water if needed. Serve, garnished with mint leaves.

Sunshine Valley Berry Farm

Banana and Marcona Almond Smoothies

SERVES 2

At the Bluebird Tavern, the emphasis is on slowing down, savoring, and enjoying a meal, but sometimes there is a need to get-up-and-go in the morning, as well. When the morning kitchen team were discovered whipping up some pretty amazing smoothies, it was decided to make them a fun addition to the brunch menu. The smoothie selection is changed every week. This is a great way to use up odds and ends and explore new flavor pairings. Marcona almonds, grown in Spain, are larger and sweeter than domestic almonds; if you can't find them, you can substitute California almonds.

2 large ripe bananas, preferably frozen, peeled and sliced

1 cup plain Greek-style yogurt

1/4 cup plain kefir

1/4 cup Marcona almonds, toasted and chopped

1 teaspoon grated orange zest plus 1 tablespoon juice

1 tablespoon pure Vermont maple syrup

2 tablespoons crushed ice

3 tablespoons whipped cream

Chinese five-spice powder

Blend the bananas, yogurt, kefir, almonds, orange zest and juice, maple syrup, and ice in a blender until smooth. Pour into two glasses and top with a dollop of whipped cream and a light sprinkle of Chinese five-spice powder. Serve immediately.

Bluebird Tavern

THE BLUEBIRD TAVERN

The Bluebird Tavern celebrates the tradition, spirit, and conviviality of the New England tavern, a place for the community to gather and share food and drink.

The Bluebird sources its ingredients from Vermont and New England farmers and producers as well as from neighbors and friends, who invest their passion in everything they produce. Buying products from within the community helps to ensure that its strong agricultural traditions continue to thrive.

Its menu is a modern interpretation of traditional New England tavern fare and is also influenced by the classic cuisines of France and Italy. The Bluebird cooks with the seasons, creating a strong connection with the landscape, as well as a sense of anticipation and excitement. During the harvest months, when fresh produce is abundant, they pickle and preserve the bounty for winter, creating a well-stocked pantry as New Englanders have done for generations.

Careful attention and great pride are taken in the selection of beverages for the tavern. Being in Vermont, they are fortunate to offer access to one of the most dynamic craft beer scenes in America today, and their wines come from producers whose vineyards have remained within their families for generations and who cultivate without harmful chemicals.

Berry Good Smoothies

SERVES 4

River Berry Farm is a family-owned organic small fruit and vegetable farm located on the Lamoille River in Fairfax. The small farm has been in operation since 1992. The owners, Jane Sorensen and David Marchant, and their children, Huck and Ada, along with a hardworking crew grow 50 acres of vegetables, 3 acres of strawberries and 1 1/2 acres of raspberries. The farm also consists of 18,000 square feet of greenhouse crops and is home to 100 organic chickens.

1 cup frozen strawberries, coarsely chopped
3/4 cup frozen raspberries or blackberries
2 cups skim milk or soy milk
1/2 cup plain or vanilla nonfat yogurt
2 tablespoons Vermont honey
Crushed ice (optional)

Place the strawberries, raspberries, milk, yogurt, and honey in a blender and purée until smooth. Divide the mixture among four tall glasses, add crushed ice, if desired, and serve.

River Berry Farm

DAILY CHOCOLATE

Daily Chocolate is a small, quaint chocolate shop located several steps below street level in the heart of Vergennes, the oldest city in Vermont. Against a backdrop of exposed brick and Panton stone is a dazzling display of handcrafted chocolates—cherry wine clusters, black rum caramels, coconut lime crèmes, classic almond bark, English toffee, fruity bark, coconut clusters and caramel pretzels—that call to mind a modern Willa Wonka's chocolate factory. The owners, Jen Roberts and Judd Markowski, focus on freshness and flavor and make their chocolates daily using local and organic ingredients.

Daily Chocolate's Hot Cocoa Mix

MAKES ABOUT 16 SERVINGS

This recipe makes a great inexpensive gift. Just scoop the cocoa mixture into an attractive container and tie with a decorative ribbon. Be sure to attach the Hot Cocoa recipe directions (step 2) below.

8 ounces dark chocolate (at least 70 percent cacao), coarsely chopped
3/4 cup granulated sugar
1 1/3 cups unsweetened natural cocoa powder, preferably organic
Pinch kosher salt

1. Process the chocolate in a food processor until finely ground. Add the sugar, cocoa powder, and salt and process until well combined.

Note: Store in an airtight container, or go on to step 2 to make Hot Cocoa.

2. For each serving, heat 1 cup milk until hot, but not boiling. Add 2 to 4 tablespoons cocoa mix, stirring until the chocolate is melted and smooth. Top with a dollop of whipped cream, chocolate shavings, or marshmallows, if desired.

Daily Chocolate

DESSERTS

SAXTON'S RIVER DISTILLERY

Part of Christian Stromberg's Lithuanian heritage is making a traditional spiced honey liqueur called Krupnikas, which is typically served at weddings and other celebrations. Making Krupnikas opened the door for Stromberg to create other liqueurs. Because he lives in Vermont, he began experimenting with maple syrup, and after numerous attempts he thought he had something. Others agreed.

At that time Stromberg and a friend were building a barn on his property in Brattleboro. The barn became the original distillery, which was launched in January of 2007. The company continues to grow, gaining new fans as they are introduced to a unique liqueur with European roots and a distinctly Vermont character.

Sapling Tiramisu

SERVES 6 TO 8

This tiramisu recipe has been in Christian Stromberg's mother-in-law's recipe file for three decades. The original recipe uses Marsala, but Stromberg makes it with Sapling Vermont Maple Liqueur. The liqueur has a lovely maple flavor, which is excellent for tiramisu because it complements the smooth and creamy custard-like layers of the dish. Stromberg uses Vermont Butter & Cheese mascarpone cheese in this dessert.

4 large eggs, separated
1/2 cup granulated sugar
1 (16-ounce) container mascarpone cheese
1/8 teaspoon salt
1 cup heavy cream, chilled
2 cups very strong brewed coffee or espresso, cooled
2–4 tablespoons Sapling Vermont or other maple liqueur
24 dried ladyfingers (savoiardi)
Unsweetened cocoa powder or shaved dark chocolate

1. Lightly grease a 9 x 13-inch baking dish and set aside.

2. Using an electric mixture, beat together the egg yolks and 6 tablespoons of the sugar until thick, about 4 minutes. Add the mascarpone and beat until smooth. In a separate bowl, beat together the egg whites and salt until soft peaks form. In a third bowl, beat together the heavy cream and remaining 2 tablespoons sugar until soft peaks form. Fold the cream into the mascarpone mixture and then fold in the beaten egg whites.

3. Combine the coffee and maple liqueur in a shallow bowl. Working with one at a time, quickly dip 12 ladyfingers in the coffee mixture, soaking for 2 to 3 seconds, and arrange half of the biscuits on in the prepared baking dish. Spread half of the mascarpone mixture evenly over the top. Repeat with the remaining ladyfingers and mascarpone mixture.

4. Cover the tiramisu with plastic wrap and refrigerate for at least 8 hours. Just before serving, dust with cocoa powder or shaved dark chocolate.

Saxton's River Distillery

VERMONT PEANUT BUTTER COMPANY

Chris Kaiser founded the Vermont Peanut Butter Company in 2009 with the goal of creating high-quality, locally made nut butters that are free from preservatives, hydrogenated oils, GMO's, palm fruit oils, and excess sugar and salt. He also wanted to incorporate social responsibility and community support in the company's practices.

All the peanuts that Vermont Peanut Butter Company uses are grown in the United States, on small farms; that way, Kaiser knows exactly where the nuts come from and how they are grown. The company has also taken a green pledge, they use recyclable (and BPA-free) containers, they pack all shipments in either newspaper or recycled shredded paper, and use alternative energy to power over 30 percent of the machines that they operate.

Chewy Peanut Butter Bars

MAKES 12

These chewy peanut butter bars are great on their own or served with a scoop of ice cream.

1 cup creamy peanut butter
1/3 cup unsalted butter, softened
2/3 cup granulated sugar
1/2 cup packed light brown sugar
2 large eggs, lightly beaten
1/2 teaspoon vanilla extract
1 cup all-purpose flour
1 teaspoon baking powder
1/4 teaspoon salt
1 cup semi-sweet chocolate chips

1. Preheat the oven to 350 degrees. Spray an 8-inch square baking pan with nonstick cooking spray, then line it with parchment paper. Set aside.

2. In a bowl of an electric mixer, cream together the peanut butter and butter until light and fluffy. Gradually add the sugars, eggs, and vanilla and mix until well combined.

3. In a separate bowl, stir together the flour, baking powder, and salt. Gradually add to the sugar mixture, stirring until just combined. (The batter will appear wet and slightly oily.) Fold in the chocolate chips.

4. With a rubber spatula, scrape the batter into the prepared pan and distribute evenly. Bake, rotating the pan halfway through baking, until golden brown and the edges start to pull away from the sides of pan, about 30 minutes. Let cool completely on a cooling rack before cutting into bars.

Brock Miller, Production Manager of the Vermont Peanut Butter Company

OSBORNE FAMILY MAPLE

Osborne Family Maple, in the remote Northeast Kingdom town of Ferdinand, where moose outnumber people three to one, dates back to the late 1930s. Four generations of Osbornes have patiently managed the land, resulting in the 4,000-tap sugarbush that they have today. Certified organic maple producers, the Osborne family manages their woods to promote biodiversity as well as sap production, because a healthy forest ecosystem is much less susceptible to nonnative pests and invasive plants. They approach their recipes in much the same way, using fresh, local ingredients and pure Vermont maple syrup to bring new life to traditional recipes.

Maple Bars

MAKES 16 BARS

These chewy, sweet bars are a treat served on their own or with maple or vanilla ice cream.

Crust

1 cup plus 1 tablespoon all-purpose flour
1/3 cup packed light brown sugar
8 tablespoons (4 ounces) butter

Maple Filling

1 cup pure Vermont maple syrup
3/4 cup packed light brown sugar
3 large eggs, lightly beaten
2 tablespoons all-purpose flour
1/2 teaspoon vanilla extract
1 1/2 cups unsweetened shredded coconut
1/2 cup chopped pecans

1. To make the crust: Preheat the oven to 425 degrees. Place the flour and sugar in a medium bowl. Blend in the butter using a pastry cutter or your fingers, until the mixture begins to form pea-sized pieces. Press into a 9-inch square baking pan. Bake for 5 minutes.

2. To make the maple filling: Meanwhile, stir the maple syrup and sugar together in a medium saucepan over medium heat until the sugar has dissolved. Let cool, then whisk in the eggs, flour, and vanilla. Stir in the coconut. Pour the filling over the crust and sprinkle the pecans evenly over the top.

3. Bake for 10 minutes, then reduce the heat to 350 degrees and continue to bake until golden brown, about 20 minutes longer. Let cool in the pan for 15 minutes before cutting.

Osborne Family Maple

Cheryl's Organic Oatmeal and Chocolate Chip Cookies

MAKES 3 DOZEN COOKIES

This original oatmeal and chocolate chip cookie recipe was passed down to Cheryl from her mother. Over the years, she has tweaked the recipe a bit. She uses organic ingredients wherever she can in this recipe, including King Arthur organic flour, and her own butter. The cookies are chewy, sweet and not too chocolaty. The cherries add a nice tang and pair very well with the nuts. Try substituting dried cranberries for the cherries, for a sweeter alternative.

2 cups all-purpose flour

1 teaspoon baking soda

1 teaspoon baking powder

1 teaspoon salt

16 tablespoons (8 ounces) unsalted butter, room temperature

1 cup packed dark brown sugar

1 cup granulated sugar

2 large eggs

1 teaspoon vanilla extract

1 cup quick oats

1 cup chocolate chips

2/3 cup chopped dried cherries

1/2 cup chopped pecans or walnuts (optional)

1. Preheat the oven to 350 degrees. Line two baking sheets with parchment paper or spray with nonstick cooking spray; set aside. Sift together the flour, baking soda, baking powder, and salt.

2. With an electric mixer, cream together the butter, brown sugar, and granulated sugar, scraping down the sides and bottom of the bowl as necessary, until light and fluffy, 3 to 4 minutes. Add the eggs one at a time, beating until just combined. Add the vanilla and beat well until combined, scraping down the sides of the bowl as needed.

3. Add the flour mixture to the egg mixture and stir until just combined. The batter will be stiff. Stir in the oats, chocolate chips, dried cherries, and nuts, if using.

4. Using a 2-inch diameter ice cream scoop, drop the dough onto the prepared baking sheets. Bake until the edges are light golden brown but cookies are still soft in the center, 12 to 14 minutes. Let the cookies cool on the baking sheets about 3 minutes before transferring them to a cooling rack. Repeat with the remaining dough.

Kimball Brook Farm

Dunc's Backwoods Rum Cake

SERVES 8 TO 10

Dunc's Mill, in Barnet, is the oldest continuously operating distillery in Vermont. Short for Duncan's Idea Mill, LLC, it was the original home of Vermont Spirits and the birthplace of Vermont Spirits Gold Vodka. Duncan Holaday, founder and creator of Vermont Spirits, has now turned his attention to rum, adding local flavors of elderflowers and his own maple sap. Dunc's Mill Backwoods Reserve Rum is made from organic cane sugar and fair trade molasses. It is made from start to finish, from fermenter to still and barrel to bottle at the distillery.

This moist, nutty cake is pretty served with local berries or fresh peach slices.

3 cups unbleached all-purpose flour
1 teaspoon baking powder
1/2 teaspoon salt
1/2 cup cream or whole milk
1/2 cup rum, preferably Dunc's Mill Backwoods
16 tablespoons (8 ounces) unsalted butter, softened
3 cups granulated sugar
5 large eggs, lightly beaten

1. Preheat the oven to 350 degrees. Coat a 10-inch Bundt or tube pan with nonstick cooking spray and set aside. Whisk together the flour, baking powder, and salt in a medium bowl. In a separate bowl, combine the cream and rum.

2. Using an electric mixer, beat the butter until fluffy. Gradually add the sugar and eggs and beat until well combined.

3. While the mixer is running, alternately add the flour and rum mixture to the egg mixture and mix until smooth. Transfer to the prepared pan and bake until a toothpick inserted in the cake comes out clean, about 1 hour. Let the cake cool in the pan on a cooling rack for 30 minutes, then turn the cake out onto the rack and let cool completely before serving.

Dunc's Mill

SCOTT FARM

The Scott Farm Dummerston has a recorded history dating back to 1791, when George Washington was serving his first term as president. The farm consists of 571 acres and 23 buildings, all of which are listed on the National Register of Historic Places. When the Landmark Trust USA, a Vermont nonprofit, took over the farm in 1995, many of the buildings had fallen into disrepair and the orchard was growing a single variety of apple. This apple, McIntosh, was conventionally sprayed and sold on the wholesale market. The trust, with the help of orchardist Ezekiel Goodband, transformed the orchard into one that contained 90 different varieties of apples, all ecologically grown and marketed both locally and regionally. The farm also grows peaches, plums, nectarines, pears, berries, grapes, cherries, and hard-to-find fruits such as quince, medlars, and gooseberries. The Scott Farm's buildings have been thoughtfully repaired and upgraded so that they are beautifully preserved and energy-efficient. The farm hosts educational programs, workshops, and weddings. Two of its historic houses have been authentically restored and are available for short-term holiday rental.

Applesauce Cake

SERVES 12 TO 15

Although you can use store-bought applesauce for this cake, homemade makes it really special. Scott Farm uses a combination of Bramley's Seedling, Reine des Reinettes, Rhode Island Greening, Ribston Pippin and Sheep's Nose in their applesauce. If you can't find those varieties, any of these would make a lovely applesauce: McIntosh, Cortland, Red Astrakan, Gala, Gravenstein, or Paula Red.

2 cups all-purpose flour
1 cup granulated sugar
1 teaspoon salt
1 1/2 teaspoons baking powder
3/4 teaspoon baking soda
1/2 teaspoon ground cinnamon
1/8 teaspoon ground cloves
1/8 teaspoon grated nutmeg
2 large eggs
4 tablespoons (2 ounces) unsalted butter, softened
2 cups applesauce, preferably homemade
1/2 teaspoon vanilla extract
Confectioners' sugar

1. Preheat the oven to 375 degrees. Spray a 9 x 13-inch baking pan with nonstick cooking spray and set aside. Sift together the flour, sugar, salt, baking powder, baking soda, cinnamon, cloves, and nutmeg.

2. Using an electric mixer, beat together the eggs, butter, applesauce, and vanilla until smooth. Fold in the flour mixture until just combined, being careful not to overmix.

3. Pour the batter into the pan and spread
   evenly. Bake until a toothpick inserted into the
   center comes out clean, about 25 minutes.
   Set the cake pan on a cooling rack and let
   cool completely. Cut into squares, dust with
   confectioners' sugar, and serve.

Scott Farm

Country Apple Cake

SERVES 6 TO 8

Kelly Carlin started working for Scott Farm as an office manager in 2002. At the time, Kelly's knowledge of apples was limited to the six or so varieties that are found in most local supermarkets. Her idea of an apple dessert was confined to an apple crisp, and pies were a scary endeavor at best. Over the years she has learned that apples can have an amazing variety of colors, textures, shapes and tastes. Kelly has discovered that the best thing you can do with an apple recipe is to let the fruit speak for itself. This recipe for apple cake is a delicious example. For the best flavor, use a few varieties of apple in this cake. Good choices include the French heirlooms Calville Blanc d'Hiver, a 15th-century apple that has a vanilla-like flavor and a wonderful texture when cooked, and Reine des Reinettes, a juicy apple from the 1700s that has a high sugar content balanced with acidity. This moist, dense light caramel color cake is great served as a dessert with ice cream or as a quick breakfast treat.

3 cups all-purpose flour
1 tablespoon baking powder
1 teaspoon ground cinnamon
1/2 teaspoon salt
1 cup vegetable oil
2 cups granulated sugar
4 large eggs
2 1/2 teaspoons vanilla extract
4 apples, cored and chopped into 1-inch pieces

1. Center a rack in the oven and preheat to 350 degrees. Spray a 12-cup Bundt or tube pan with nonstick cooking spray and set aside. In a large bowl sift together the flour, baking powder, cinnamon, and salt.

2. Using an electric mixer, cream together the oil, sugar, eggs, and vanilla, scraping down the sides of the bowl as needed. Add the flour mixture and beat until smooth.

3. Pour half of the batter into the prepared pan and layer half of the apples on top. Repeat with the remaining batter and apples. Bake until a toothpick inserted in the center of the cake comes out clean, about 1 1/4 hours.

4. Let the cake cool in the pan for about 15 minutes, then invert onto a cooling rack and let cool completely. Reinvert onto a serving plate and serve.

Scott Farm

Chocolate Zucchini Cake

MAKES 15 TO 20 PIECES

This cake recipe, courtesy of Pomykala Farm employees Hillary and Gaelan Chutter-Ames, is a great way to use that extra mid-summer zucchini. The zucchini keeps the cake nice and moist. It is a sure hit for coffee breaks and a terrific snack for children, who will never suspect that it contains vegetables.

2 1/2 cups all-purpose flour

1/4 cup unsweetened cocoa

1 teaspoon baking soda

1/2 teaspoon baking powder

1/2 teaspoon ground cinnamon

1/2 teaspoon ground cloves

8 tablespoons (4 ounces) unsalted butter, softened

1 3/4 cups granulated sugar

1/2 cup vegetable or canola oil

1/2 cup buttermilk

2 large eggs, lightly beaten

1 teaspoon vanilla extract

2 1/4 cups packed, grated zucchini

1/3 cup chocolate chips

1. Preheat the oven to 325 degrees. Spray a 9 x 13-inch pan with nonstick cooking spray and set aside. Whisk together the flour, cocoa, baking soda, baking powder, cinnamon, and cloves.

2. Using an electric mixer, beat the butter, sugar, oil, buttermilk, eggs, and vanilla for 3 minutes, scraping down the sides of the bowl as needed. Add the flour mixture and beat until smooth. Fold in the zucchini and pour the batter into the prepared pan.

3. Sprinkle the chocolate chips evenly over the top. Bake the cake until a toothpick inserted in the center comes out clean, 45 to 50 minutes.

4. Let the cake cool in the pan for 15 minutes, then invert onto a cooling rack and let cool completely before serving.

Hillary and Gaelan Chutter-Ames of Pomykala Farm

THE BAKERY AT THE FARMHOUSE KITCHEN

Located in Burlington, the Bakery at the Farmhouse Kitchen is the home of the original buttercrunch cake. Emily Conn, the bakery's owner, models these buttery, moist cakes with their nice contrasting buttercrunch topping after an old family recipe. The idea for an almond buttercrunch cake–centric bakery originated when Conn's family and friends continuously requested (and, at times, begged for) the cake, which was the highlight of many special occasions and celebrations. The flavor of the cake varies and is adaptable to Vermont's seasonal bounty.

Winter Pudding with Caramelized Cranberries

SERVES 8

Note that this recipe makes more cranberry sauce than you will need in the cake; save the extra cranberries and serve over ice cream or pancakes. Be sure not to overmix the batter in step 3 or the pudding will not rise as much. In the summer, this recipe works well with sour cherries.

2 cups granulated sugar
2 tablespoons water
3 cups fresh cranberries
8 tablespoons (4 ounces) unsalted butter
3/4 cup all-purpose flour
2 teaspoons baking powder
Pinch salt
3/4 cup milk
1/2 teaspoon vanilla extract

1. Preheat the oven to 350 degrees.

2. Combine 1 cup of the sugar and the water in a medium skillet over medium-low heat and stir until the sugar begins to dissolve. Add the cranberries and continue to cook, stirring often, until they soften and begin to pop, about 10 minutes. Set aside.

3. Melt the butter in a 10-inch cast-iron skillet in the oven. Sift the remaining 1 cup sugar, the flour, baking powder, and salt into a medium bowl. Add the milk and vanilla, stirring until almost combined. Do not overmix.

3. When the butter has melted, carefully remove the pan from the oven. Pour the batter into the middle of the pan. As you pour, quickly tilt the pan in all directions to spread the batter evenly across the bottom of the pan. Pour 2 cups of the cranberries in the middle of the dough. Do not mix the berries into the batter. Carefully return the pan to the oven and bake until the fruit starts to bubble and the edges are nicely browned, 45 minutes to 1 hour. Let cool slightly, then serve.

The Bakery at the Farmhouse Kitchen

No-Bake Vanilla Bean Cheesecake

SERVES 6

This rich cheesecake is both simple and delicious. It has no crust, requires no baking, and the vanilla bean imbues it with a luscious flavor. Angela loves this recipe so much that she used to sell the little cheesecakes at the West River Farmers' Market in Londonderry. It is inspired by a no-bake cheesecake in *Instant Gratification*, by Lauren Chattman, which is Angela's bible for simple, quick desserts. Angela uses Mettowee cheese, a fresh, creamy, pasteurized goat's milk chevre named for the Mettowee River Valley, in this cheesecake, but you can substitute another mild, fresh goat cheese, or cream cheese. For a delightful topping, slice some berries or stone fruit, such as peaches or plums, and soak them in a bit of sugar.

1/2 teaspoon unflavored gelatin
2 tablespoons water
1/2 vanilla bean
1 pound Mettowee cheese
6 tablespoons heavy cream
2/3 cup granulated sugar

1. Spray a 6-inch springform pan with nonstick cooking spray and set aside. Place the gelatin in a small heatproof bowl. Add the water and mix until well combined; let stand for 3 minutes.

2. Meanwhile, pour 1 inch of water into a small saucepan and bring to a simmer over medium heat. Place the bowl with the gelatin over (but not touching) the simmering water and stir just until the gelatin is completely dissolved, about 2 minutes (do not overheat the gelatin). Let cool.

3. Place the vanilla bean on a work surface and split it in half lengthwise using a paring knife. Scrape the seeds into a large bowl and add the Mettowee, heavy cream, and sugar.

4. Using an electric mixer, beat the cheese mixture until light and fluffy, about 3 minutes, scraping down the sides of the bowl as needed. Beat in the gelatin mixture until well blended, scraping down the bowl. Scrape the batter into the springform pan and smooth the top with a rubber spatula. Cover with plastic wrap and refrigerate until firm, 6 hours or overnight.

5. To unmold, run a hot knife around the edge of the pan to loosen, and gently release the sides of the pan. Set the cake, supported by the springform base, on a cake plate and serve. (The cheesecake will keep, covered and refrigerated, up to four days.)

Angela Miller of Consider Bardwell Farm

Vermont Spirited Apple Ice Cream

MAKES 1 QUART

This recipe takes a bit of advance planning; make both the apple mixture and ice cream mixture the day before you plan to serve the ice cream.

Vermont Spirited Apples

3 cups peeled, cored, and diced Granny Smith apples (3 large or 4 medium apples)
1/2 cup vodka
2 tablespoons pure Vermont maple syrup
Pinch ground cinnamon
Pinch salt

Ice Cream

2 cups whole milk
3 large eggs
1/2 cup plus 1 tablespoon pure Vermont maple syrup
3 tablespoons sugar
2 cups heavy cream

1. To make the Vermont Spirited Apples: Preheat the oven to 350 degrees. Butter a 1-quart casserole dish, then add the apples, 2 tablespoons of the vodka, the maple syrup, cinnamon, and salt. Stir to combine. Cover the casserole dish and bake until the apples are very tender, 30 to 35 minutes. Let cool to room temperature, then add the remaining 6 tablespoons vodka and refrigerate overnight.

2. To make the ice cream: Beat the milk and eggs together in a large saucepan. Add the maple syrup and sugar. Cook over low heat, stirring constantly, until the mixture is thickened and coats a wooden spoon, about 10 minutes. (The mixture should be just beginning to boil.) Let cool and then stir in the heavy cream. Refrigerate overnight.

3. Pour the ice cream mixture into an ice cream machine and freeze according to the manufacturer's directions. When the batter is nearly frozen, add the apple mixture and continue processing until thoroughly mixed and firm. Transfer the ice cream to a container and freeze.

Edward F. Nesta and Debra C. Argen of Luxury Experience for Vermont Spirits

VERMONT SPIRITS

Vermont Spirits vodkas are hand-crafted in Quechee. Established in 1999, the company has made steady strides over the years, and their vodkas are now available throughout the United States and western Canada. While the business has grown, their approach to distilling has remained unchanged. Every stage in the production process is engineered in-house with hand-built stills, frequently employing simple gravity to transfer the evolving spirits between stages of production. The distiller, Harry Gorman, monitors each batch from start to finish, before he deems the product ready for bottling and shipment to a growing network of wholesalers.

The process of making Vermont Gold vodka begins with pure maple, distilled spring water and a mixture of nutrients designed to coax out the complex sugars of the maple sap. Next, temperature control and time are used to create the ideal environment for each fermentation. Vermont Spirits vodkas are triple-distilled using only local spring water, receiving a very light charcoal filtration at the end of each cycle. Only the techniques of artisan distilling, constant vigilance, and highly accurate, laboratory-quality stills allow the fermentation of the unique characteristics of maple to come through.

The company uses fractionating column stills in their batch-distilling process. A fractionating column distillation is the most accurate way to isolate and separate impurities, leaving the most flavorful and smoothest alcohol from the "heart of the run." By combining this technology with the artisan techniques of batch distillation, they are able to take the purification to a new level. The result is a smoother, distinctly American-style vodka.

Distiller Harry Gorman

Luxury Experience's Apple Pie with Tipsy Raisins

SERVES 8

The raisins need to soak in vodka overnight, so be sure to start this step the day before you plan to serve the pie. You can enjoy this apple pie on its own or, for a decadent treat, serve it on a pool of Maple Sauce (recipe follows) and top it with a scoop of Vermont Spirited Apple Ice Cream (page 204).

Pie Filling

1/4 cup raisins

2 tablespoons vodka

4 Granny Smith apples, cored, peeled, and sliced

3 tablespoons pure Vermont maple syrup

Pastry

2 1/2 cups unbleached all-purpose flour

2 tablespoons granulated sugar

1 teaspoon salt

12 tablespoons (6 ounces) unsalted butter, cut into cubes and chilled

1/2 cup vegetable shortening, cut into cubes and chilled

6–8 tablespoons vodka, chilled

Cinnamon sugar, for sprinkling the pastry leaves

1. To make the filling: Place the raisins and vodka in a jar. Put the lid on the jar and shake to coat the raisins with the vodka. Let sit for several hours or overnight.

2. Preheat the oven to 350 degrees. Toss the apples with the maple syrup and raisins and set aside.

3. To make the pastry: Process the flour, sugar, and salt in a food processor to blend. Add the butter and shortening, a few pieces at a time, and pulse just to combine. Add 6 tablespoons of the chilled vodka and pulse until the dough starts to hold together. If the dough is too crumbly, add the remaining 2 tablespoons vodka as needed. Do not overprocess.

4. Divide the dough in half and roll one half out between sheets of parchment paper to form a 12-inch round. Carefully transfer the dough to a 9-inch pie plate, spoon the filling into the crust, and smooth the top. Roll the remaining dough into a 12-inch round and place on the filling. Trim any excess dough from the crusts and then crimp together to seal.

5. Roll the leftover dough out 1/8 inch thick and use a leaf cookie cutter to cut shapes from the dough. Place the leaves on a baking sheet, and sprinkle them with cinnamon sugar. Bake the pie and pastry leaves until the pastry is golden brown, 35 to 40 minutes. Let the pie cool slightly, then serve with the pastry leaves.

Edward F. Nesta and Debra C. Argen of Luxury Experience for Vermont Spirits

Maple Sauce

MAKES 1 CUP

1/2 cup sweetened condensed milk
1/2 cup pure Vermont maple syrup

Stir together the milk and maple syrup in a microwave-safe bowl. Microwave for 1 minute; watch carefully so the mixture does not boil over. Let cool slightly before serving.

Edward F. Nesta and Debra C. Argen of Luxury Experience for Vermont Spirits

Bayley Hazen Blue Cheese Cake with Hazelnut Crust and Poached Pears

SERVES 12

This cheesecake was inspired by the incredible variety of artisan cheeses made in Vermont. Jasper Hill Farm's Bayley Hazen Blue was chosen for its slightly crumbly, dense texture and balanced, nutty flavor. A blue cheese cheesecake isn't your typical restaurant fare, nor is it something you might think to make at home, but it is well worth trying. The hazelnuts and pears complement the blue cheese filling perfectly. This makes an unusual savory dessert or, cut into smaller portions, an elegant appetizer.

Cheesecake

1 cup ground hazelnuts

1 cup graham cracker crumbs

4 tablespoons (2 ounces) unsalted butter, melted

12 ounces cream cheese, softened

12 ounces Bayley Hazen Blue cheese, room temperature

4 large eggs, lightly beaten

1 cup heavy cream

1/4 cup Worcestershire sauce

2 tablespoons Tabasco sauce

1/2 teaspoon salt

2 teaspoons freshly ground black pepper

Poached Pears

2 cups port wine

2 tablespoons granulated sugar

2 firm Bartlett or Bosc pears, peeled, cored, and quartered

1. To make the cheesecake: Preheat the oven to 350 degrees. Stir together the hazelnuts, graham cracker crumbs, and butter. Press gently into the bottom of a 9-inch springform pan. Set aside.

2. With an electric mixer, beat together the cream cheese, blue cheese, eggs, cream, Worcestershire sauce, Tabasco sauce, salt, and pepper until smooth, scraping down the sides of the bowl as needed. Spread the cheese filling evenly over the crust and smooth the top with a rubber spatula. Set the springform pan in a roasting pan and add enough hot water to come halfway up the sides of the springform pan. Bake for 50 minutes. Remove from the water bath and let cool to room temperature, then cover with plastic wrap and refrigerate for 8 hours or overnight.

3. To make the poached pears: Combine the port wine and sugar in a medium saucepan and bring to a boil over medium-high heat. Reduce the heat to medium-low, add the pears, cover, and cook until the pears are tender, 12 to 15 minutes. Transfer the pears to a plate and refrigerate. Increase the heat to medium-high and reduce the poaching liquid by half, about 10 minutes. Pour the liquid into a heatproof container and refrigerate for at least 30 minutes, or until ready to serve.

4. To unmold the cheesecake, run a hot knife around the edge of the pan to loosen, and gently release the sides of the pan. Set the cake, supported by the springform base, on a cake plate. Slice each pear quarter lengthwise into 3 thin slices and arrange the slices in a circular fan design on top of the cake. Cut the cheesecake into wedges, spoon a little of the reserved poaching liquid around each piece, and serve.

West Mountain Inn

POORHOUSE PIES

Jamie and Paula Eisenberg opened Poorhouse Pies, located in Underhill, during the summer of 2009. Poorhouse Pies offers house-baked goods and specializes in making traditional, as well as inventive, pies. They use local ingredients whenever possible.

Raisin Hell Pie

SERVES 8

This pie was created when the Eisenbergs started researching pies that were made with raisins. After testing a recipe for a "Funeral Pie" (made to be taken to wakes) they found the end result to be too rich. Thinking that the pie wouldn't be very popular—especially with that name—the two decided to balance the richness of its raisin filling with the sour combo of cherries and cranberries. Topping it with oat streusel seemed a natural match. It is a perfect fit for the Thanksgiving through Christmas season . . . in other words, it's a Raisin Hell for the Holidays pie! Serve this pie with a dollop of whipped cream or a scoop of ice cream, if you like.

Crust

1 cup all-purpose flour, plus extra for rolling
1/4 teaspoon salt
2 tablespoons (1 ounce) unsalted butter, cut into small cubes and chilled
1 1/2 tablespoons shortening
3 tablespoons ice-cold water

Raisin Filling

1 cup raisins
1/2 cup water
1/4 cup granulated sugar
1/4 cup packed light brown sugar
1 tablespoon fresh lemon juice
1/2 teaspoon ground cinnamon
1/8 teaspoon salt
2 tablespoons cornstarch
1/4 cup water

Cherry-Cranberry Filling

2 cups frozen cherries

2 cups frozen whole cranberries

1/2 cup granulated sugar

1/2 teaspoon lemon zest

2 tablespoons cornstarch

1/4 cup water

Streusel Topping

1/2 cup oats

1/2 cup all-purpose flour

1/4 cup granulated sugar

1/4 cup packed light brown sugar

1/2 teaspoon ground cinnamon

1/8 teaspoon salt

6 tablespoons (3 ounces) unsalted butter,
    cut into small cubes and chilled

1. To make the crust: Combine the flour and salt in a large bowl. With a pastry blender, cut the butter and shortening into the flour until just crumbly. Add the water, 1 tablespoon at a time, and mix until the dough just comes together. Turn the dough out onto a lightly floured surface and form into a disk. Wrap in plastic wrap and refrigerate for at least 1 hour.

2. To make the raisin filling: While the dough chills, combine the raisins, water, granulated sugar, brown sugar, lemon juice, cinnamon, and salt in a small saucepan. Bring to a simmer over medium heat. In a small bowl, whisk the cornstarch and water together. Whisk into the raisin mixture, bring to a boil over medium-high heat, and cook for 2 minutes, stirring frequently. Set aside to cool.

3. To make the cherry-cranberry filling: Combine the cherries, cranberries, sugar, and lemon zest in a small saucepan. Bring to a simmer over medium heat. In a small bowl, whisk the cornstarch and water together. Whisk into the cherry mixture, bring to a boil over medium-high heat, and cook for 2 minutes, stirring frequently. Set aside to cool.

4. To make the streusel topping: Process the oats in a food processor until coarsely ground, then transfer to a medium bowl. Place the flour, granulated sugar, brown sugar, cinnamon,

and salt in the empty food processor bowl and pulse to blend, then add the butter and pulse until crumbly. Transfer to the bowl with the oats. Rub the mixture together with your fingertips until large lumps form. Refrigerate until the streusel is firm, about 30 minutes.

5. Meanwhile, on a lightly floured surface, roll the dough out into a 12-inch round. Transfer to a 9-inch pie plate, trim the excess dough, leaving a 1/2-inch overhang, and crimp the edges. Place the crust in the refrigerator and chill for at least 30 minutes.

6. Preheat the oven to 375 degrees. Spread the raisin filling evenly over the bottom of the chilled crust, then spread the cherry-cranberry filling over the raisin filling and top with the streusel. Place the pie on a baking sheet and bake for 30 minutes. Rotate the baking sheet and bake until the pie is light golden brown and the filling is bubbling, 15 to 20 minutes.

7. Transfer the pie to a cooling rack and let cool completely before serving.

Poorhouse Pies

Maple Apple Pie

SERVES 8

This apple pie recipe has been made countless times at Ledgenear Farm and lovingly shared with family and friends. The Coes think that it is the perfect combination of lemon, maple syrup, and apples. The recipe is a great example of how maple syrup can be used as a sugar substitute in baking. Serve the pie with a dollop of whipped cream or a scoop of maple or vanilla ice cream, if desired.

Crust

2 cups all-purpose flour

2 teaspoons salt

16 tablespoons (8 ounces) unsalted butter

1/3 cup water

1 teaspoon granulated sugar

Filling

8 Cortland or McIntosh apples, peeled, cored, and cut into chunks

1 tablespoon all-purpose flour

3/4 cup pure Vermont maple syrup, or to taste

1 teaspoon fresh lemon juice

1/2 teaspoon ground cinnamon

1/4 teaspoon grated nutmeg

Coarse sugar, as needed

1. To make the crust. Preheat the oven to 375 degrees. Combine the flour, sugar, and salt in a large bowl. With a pastry cutter or your fingers, cut the butter into the flour until the mixture begins to form pea-sized pieces. Add the water, 1 tablespoon at a time, and mix until the dough just comes together. Do not overmix. Turn the dough out onto a lightly floured work surface and form into two disks. Roll one disk

into a 12-inch round. Transfer to a 9-inch pie plate and trim the excess dough, leaving 1/2-inch overhang.

2. To make the filling: Combine the apples and flour in a large bowl. Pour the apples into the crust and drizzle with the maple syrup and lemon juice. Sprinkle the cinnamon and nutmeg over the top

3. Roll the second disk of dough out to a 12-inch round and place it over the apple filling. Trim the excess dough along the edge, leaving 1/2-inch overhang. Fold the edges of the dough under, then crimp to seal. Cut slits in the top crust and sprinkle with coarse sugar.

4. Place the pie on a baking sheet and bake until the apples are tender and the filling is bubbling, about 1 1/4 hours. (If necessary, cover the perimeter of the crust with a foil collar to prevent it from overbrowning.) Transfer the pie to a cooling rack and let cool completely before serving.

Ledgenear Farm

LEDGENEAR FARM

Ledgenear Farm is located on a hilltop in Vermont's Northeast Kingdom. Its homestead dates back to the 1850s. Hardscrabble but beautiful, the farm has provided for multiple generations growing field crops, herding sheep, milking cows, and producing maple syrup. James Coe was born on the farm. After 12 years of running an architectural firm in Portland, Oregon, James returned with his wife, Nella, and their children to pursue a sustainable agrarian future. On roughly 250 acres, the Coes currently tap about 1,000 maple trees and plan to expand to as many as 3,000 over the next few years.

Maple Pecan Pie

SERVES 8

This recipe has been in Poorhouse Pies' archives for years. It is a moist and nutty pie that is not too sweet and is full of maple flavor. The Eisenbergs shared this recipe with a friend who needed to bake something for a local maple cooking contest; it won first prize. Use a full-flavored maple syrup, such as grade A dark amber or grade B, in this pie.

Crust

1 cup all-purpose flour plus extra for rolling
1/4 teaspoon salt
2 tablespoons (1 ounce) unsalted butter, cut into small cubes and chilled
1 1/2 tablespoons shortening
3 tablespoons ice water

Maple Filling

3 large eggs, lightly beaten
3/4 cup packed light brown sugar
1/4 cup granulated sugar
1 cup pure Vermont maple syrup
3 tablespoons (1 1/2 ounces) unsalted butter, melted and slightly cooled
1 tablespoon all-purpose flour
1/4 teaspoon salt
1 teaspoon vanilla extract
1/8 teaspoon grated orange zest (optional)
1 3/4 cups pecan halves
Whipped cream or vanilla or coffee ice cream (optional)

1. To make the crust: Combine the flour and salt in a large bowl. With a pastry blender, cut the butter and shortening into the flour until just crumbly. Add the water, 1 tablespoon at a time, and mix until the dough just comes together. Turn the dough out onto a lightly floured surface and form into a disk. Wrap the disk in plastic wrap and refrigerator for at least 1 hour.

2. On a lightly floured surface, roll the disk of dough out into a 12-inch round. Transfer to a 9-inch pie plate, trim the excess dough, leaving a 1/2-inch overhang, and crimp the edges. Place the crust in the refrigerator and chill for at least 30 minutes.

3. To make the maple filling: Whisk together the eggs, sugars, maple syrup, butter, flour, salt, vanilla, and orange zest, if using, until smooth.

4. Preheat the oven to 375 degrees. Evenly line the bottom of pie crust with the pecans. Pour the mixture over the nuts and rake with a fork to evenly distribute. Place the pie on a baking sheet and bake for 25 minutes. Rotate the baking sheet and bake until the pie is puffy and beginning to crack on the surface, about 25 minutes longer. (If necessary, cover the perimeter of the crust with a foil collar to prevent it from overbrowning.)

5. Transfer the pie to a cooling rack and let cool completely. Serve with a dollop of whipped cream or a scoop of ice cream, if desired.

Poorhouse Pies

CAPITAL CITY FARMERS MARKET

As one of the oldest farmers' markets in Vermont, the Capital City Farmers Market in Montpelier offers customers a wide variety of fresh fruits and vegetables, cheeses, meats, honey, maple syrup, spirits, wild edibles, plants, and cut flowers, as well as prepared foods and crafts—every season, all year long. To highlight and promote the region's local farms, the market requires that all food vendors use at least three local farm ingredients in their products and post signs listing the farms that their ingredients came from.

Customers can learn how to use the fresh foods they buy from the market's farmers at the many demonstrations hosted during the year, which are in partnership with local chefs and the New England Culinary Institute. With 52 vendors at its outdoor market, and over 30 at its indoor location, there's always something new and exciting to try at the market.

Maple Roast Pumpkin Pie

SERVES 8

It had never occurred to Claire Fitts, the owner of Butterfly Bakery, to use fresh pumpkin in baked goods when canned was so widely used, but a few years ago a friend of hers received a pumpkin from her CSA. They stared at the gourd-like squash for a while and then decided to give pie a try before the pumpkin went bad (with little hope for success). The results were amazing. Fitts has never gone back to using canned pumpkin for anything since.

This recipe produces more purée than you will need for the pie. You can store the remaining pumpkin purée in an airtight container in the refrigerator for up to five days or in the freezer for several months. In a pinch, you can substitute 1 1/2 cups of organic canned purée (just be sure not to use pie filling, which is spiced and sweetened). Serve the pie with vanilla or maple ice cream, or a dollop of whipped cream.

1 pie pumpkin (3 to 4 pounds)
3 large eggs, lightly beaten
2/3 cup pure Vermont maple syrup
1 1/2 teaspoons vanilla extract
1 teaspoon ground cinnamon
1/2 teaspoon ground ginger
1/4 teaspoon ground cloves
1 (9-inch) unbaked pie shell

1. Preheat the oven to 450 degrees. Lightly grease a baking sheet and set aside.

2. Cut the pumpkin in half lengthwise; scoop out the seeds and strings and discard them. Place the pumpkin, open side down, on the prepared baking sheet. Roast until fork-tender, about 40 minutes. Set aside to cool. When the pumpkin is cool enough to handle, scoop

out the flesh, transfer to a food processor, and process until smooth.

3. Reduce the oven temperature to 350 degrees. In a large bowl, whisk together 1 1/2 cups of the pumpkin purée, the eggs, maple syrup, vanilla, cinnamon, ginger and cloves until smooth. Pour the mixture into the pie shell and bake for 30 minutes. Rotate the pie and bake, until a knife inserted into the center comes out clean, about 30 minutes. Let cool slightly; serve warm or at room temperature.

Claire Fitts of Butterfly Bakery for the Capital City Farmers Market

CEDAR CIRCLE FARM & EDUCATION CENTER

Located in East Thetford, Cedar Circle Farm & Education Center is a certified organic vegetable and berry farm, overlooking the Connecticut River. The Vermont Land Trust conserved the farm in 1990. In addition to the farm's 40 acres of cropland, 6 greenhouses and 5 hoophouses, Cedar Circle also offers a farm stand, coffee shop, licensed commercial kitchen and an agricultural education center. The goal of the education center is four-fold: to raise public awareness about the importance of locally grown, organic produce; to train young and aspiring farmers; to increase access to organically grown produce in low-income communities; and to create models for farm-appropriate alternative energy strategies. Additionally, the farm hosts dinners, festivals, tastings and more throughout the season to inspire the public to support and delight in locally grown organic food.

Butternut Apple Crisp

SERVES 8

At the 2011 Pumpkin Festival the farm was eager to get away from the heavy, cloying desserts most often seen in autumn. The farm's stores were bursting with winter squash and bushels of apples that looked so good side by side, they decided to pair them in this twist on a classic crisp. At the farm, they get their apples from Champlain Orchards, in Shoreham, or from their own trees. This recipe works well if you use a mixture of firm, tart apples, such as Granny Smith, and apples that soften when cooked, such as MacIntosh.

Topping

1 cup raw whole almonds

3/4 cup all-purpose flour

1/2 cup packed light brown sugar

1/2 cup granulated sugar

3/4 teaspoon ground cinnamon

1/2 teaspoon grated nutmeg

12 tablespoons (6 ounces) unsalted butter, cut into 1/2-inch pieces

Filling

3/4 cup granulated sugar

1/4 cup packed light brown sugar

Zest and juice from 1 lemon

1 teaspoon vanilla extract

1 teaspoon tapioca starch

1 teaspoon ground cinnamon

1/2 teaspoon grated nutmeg

1/2 teaspoon ground ginger

1 1/2 pounds butternut squash (1 small), peeled, seeded and cut into 1/8-inch slices (4 cups)

6 large apples, peeled, cored, and cut into 1/8-inch slices

Vanilla ice cream, for serving

1. To make the topping: Preheat the oven to 200 degrees. Place the almonds in a single layer on a baking sheet and toast, stirring occasionally, until golden brown, about 40 minutes. Set aside to cool.

2. To make the filling: Increase the oven temperature to 375 degrees. Lightly grease a 9 x 13-inch baking dish and set aside.

3. Combine the granulated sugar, brown sugar, lemon zest and juice, vanilla, tapioca starch, cinnamon, nutmeg, and ginger in a large bowl. Add the squash and apples and toss to coat. Spoon into prepared baking dish. Cover and bake until the squash is fork-tender, about 30 minutes.

4. Meanwhile, process the almonds in a food processor until coarsely ground. Add the flour, sugars, cinnamon, nutmeg, and salt and pulse to blend. Add the butter and pulse until crumbly.

5. Stir the filling and sprinkle the topping evenly over the top. Bake uncovered until the crisp is light golden brown and bubbling, about 30 minutes.

6. Cool the crisp slightly, allowing the juices to be absorbed, and serve with ice cream, if desired.

Alison Baker of Cedar Circle Farm

Note: If you use a mandoline, preparation for this dish is very quick and easy. Otherwise, slicing up the squash and apples takes some time, but larger pieces will work just as well.

SIMON PEARCE

Prior to opening the workshop, Simon Pearce developed his design aesthetic and honed his skills working at Shanagarry Pottery, which was owned by his parents. Pearce then gained glassblowing experience working in European glass houses, traveling the world, and studying at the Royal College of Art in London. Pearce opened his first glassblowing workshop in Kilkenny, Ireland.

Seeking independence from European business constraints and high energy costs, Pearce moved his operation to Quechee, Vermont, where he completed the restoration of a historic woolen mill. The Ottaquechee River provides hydroelectric power for the glass furnaces along with electricity for the entire facility. Today, visitors to The Mill can view the hydroelectric turbine, interact with the teams of glassblowers, watch potters at work, shop in the retail store and enjoy a meal in the restaurant.

Warm Apple Crisp with Hazelnut Crumble

SERVES 10 TO 12

In autumn look for firm, local, organic apples for this easy recipe. Calvados is a very nice alternative to domestic applejack. Handmade in their Windsor, Vermont, pottery factory, Simon Pearce's Brookfield Bakeware is the perfect choice for cooking and serving this flavorful crisp.

Apple Filling

Grated zest and juice of 1 lemon
1/2 cup Vermont apple cider
1/2 cup granulated sugar
1/8 teaspoon ground cinnamon
1/8 teaspoon grated nutmeg
4 tablespoons (2 ounces) unsalted butter, melted
1 ounce apple brandy, such as Apple Jack (optional)
12 large Granny Smith apples (3 1/4 to 3 1/2 pounds), peeled, cored and cut into 1/4-inch-thick slices

Hazelnut Crumble Topping

1 cup all-purpose flour
1 cup whole-wheat flour
1 cup packed light brown sugar
1 teaspoon ground cinnamon
16 tablespoons (8 ounces) unsalted butter, cut into pieces and chilled
1 cup hazelnuts, toasted and coarsely chopped
1 pint vanilla ice cream (optional)

1. Preheat the oven to 350 degrees. Butter a 9 x 13-inch baking dish or other shallow 2-quart baking dish. Set aside.

2. To make the apple filling: Combine the lemon zest and juice, cider, sugar, cinnamon, nutmeg, butter and brandy, if desired, in a large bowl. Add the apples and toss to coat. Set aside.

3. To make the hazelnut crumble topping: In a medium bowl combine the all-purpose flour, whole-wheat flour, sugar, and cinnamon. Using your fingers, work in the butter until the mixture is crumbly and forms pea-sized lumps. Add the hazelnuts; mix until evenly distributed.

4. Spread the apple mixture in the bottom of the prepared baking dish. Sprinkle the hazelnut crumble evenly over the apples. Bake for 25 minutes, rotate the dish and bake until the top is crisp and golden brown, about 25 more minutes. Let cool for 10 minutes; serve warm with scoops of vanilla ice cream, if desired.

Simon Pearce

THE SILVER FORK RESTAURANT

The Silver Fork is a small, elegant six-table restaurant in Manchester Center that showcases the award-winning cooking skills of Chef Mark French. When he was younger, French trained with a German chef, then worked with international chefs for 10 years, and later lived and cooked in Puerto Rico for 13 years. It is obvious that he incorporates all of these amazing experiences into his cooking style. His international menu is always in "movement" with an emphasis on flavor, freshness and inspiration. The restaurant offers a full bar and a large selection of wines by the glass that change as frequently as the menu, and are all dedicated to enhancing each meal. With a strong belief in friends, fun, and flavor, the Silver Fork is a unique dining experience.

Bread Pudding Soufflés with Coconut Vanilla Crème Anglaise

SERVES 8

Mark French developed this recipe at the last minute for group of patrons who were eating at the restaurant. He created the dish using only ingredients that were available in his kitchen at the time. Note that you will need a total of 14 eggs for this recipe; reserve two of the leftover whites from the crème anglaise to use in the soufflés.

Crème Anglaise

1 vanilla bean
2 cups heavy cream
2 cups whole milk
1 can cream of coconut, such as Coco Lopez
6 tablespoons granulated sugar
8 large egg yolks, beaten
2 tablespoons cornstarch

Soufflés

Unsalted butter, for soufflé cups
Granulated sugar, for soufflé cups
2 (14-ounce) cans sweetened condensed milk
2 cups milk
6 large eggs, separated, plus 2 large egg whites
1 1/2 teaspoons vanilla extract
1 teaspoon ground cinnamon
1 pound (1 loaf) bread, such as challah,
    cut into 1/2-inch cubes
4 bananas, sliced
1 cup raisins
1/2 cup sliced almonds
Confectioners' sugar

1. To make the crème anglaise: Place the vanilla bean on a work surface and split it in half lengthwise using a paring knife. Scrape the seeds into a large saucepan and add the cream, milk, cream of coconut, and sugar. Bring to a simmer over medium heat.

2. Combine the egg yolks and cornstarch in a large bowl and whisk until pale yellow. While whisking, add 1/4 cup of the warm cream mixture. Slowly add the remaining cream, then return the mixture to the saucepan and simmer gently, stirring often, for 15 minutes. Strain the mixture through a fine-mesh strainer and refrigerate until ready to serve.

3. To make the soufflés: Preheat the oven to 350 degrees. Coat eight 8-ounce soufflé cups or soup cups with butter. Line each cup with granulated sugar and discard any excess.

4. In a large bowl, whisk together the condensed milk, milk, egg yolks, vanilla, and cinnamon. Add the bread, bananas, raisins, and almonds and toss to coat. Beat the egg whites until stiff peaks form and gently fold into the bread mixture.

5. Divide the soufflé mixture among the cups.

6. Bake the soufflés, uncovered, until set and the bread is puffed and lightly browned, 20 to 25 minutes. Unmold the soufflés onto dessert plates, pour some of the crème anglaise on and around each soufflé, dust with confectioners' sugar, and serve.

The Silver Fork

NEWHALL FARM

Located at an elevation of nearly 1800 feet in the Vermont "Alps," Newhall Farm raises heritage breeds in a sustainable, free-range environment without growth hormones or antibiotics, and with only organic sprays used in their orchards.

Under the direction of Linda and Ted Fondulas, Newhall Farm is committed to producing only the highest quality natural foods by means of skilled animal husbandry and fostering responsible stewardship of the land.

The husband-and-wife team have developed numerous products for the farm, including, of course, a savory Vermont taste-of-place maple syrup made the old-fashioned way, using free-run sap that is wood-fired and wood filtered; newly developed ice cider; grass-fed beef; Berkshire pork; and pastured lamb. They also raise and thereby help conserve Vermont's only heritage breed of cattle, the Randall.

Newhall Farm Pumpkin Custard

SERVES 6

The custard preparation came about during the fall when Ted and Linda Fondulas were looking for a new seasonal dessert. Lucy Allen, their pastry chef at the time when the couple owned Hemingway's Restaurant, worked out this recipe using fresh pumpkin. Any sugar pumpkin, such as Baby Pam, will work well in this recipe. You will need an electric juicer, such as a Vitamix, for this recipe.

2 (3-pound) baking pumpkins
4 cups half-and-half
1-inch cinnamon stick
2 allspice berries
1-inch vanilla bean
1 teaspoon grated orange zest
1/2 cup whole milk, or as needed
4 large eggs plus 3 large egg yolks
6 tablespoons granulated sugar

1. Preheat the oven to 325 degrees. Spray six 6-ounce ramekins with nonstick cooking spray and set aside.

2. Cut the pumpkins in half lengthwise; remove and discard the seeds and strings. Peel the pumpkins, cut them into chunks, and juice them with an electric juicer. Reserve the pulp. Place the pumpkin juice in a medium saucepan over medium heat, and reduce to 1/2 cup, about 5 minutes. Pour the reduced juice over the reserved pumpkin pulp.

3. In a separate medium saucepan, bring the half-and-half, cinnamon stick, allspice berries, vanilla bean, and orange zest to a simmer over medium-high heat. Pour the mixture over the

pumpkin pulp and juice and let stand for
20 minutes.

4. Strain the half-and-half and pumpkin mixture
   through a fine-mesh strainer into a bowl,
   pressing firmly to get as much liquid into
   the bowl as possible, then strain again into a
   4-cup liquid measuring cup. (Straining twice
   is important to remove the starch from the
   pumpkin.) Add enough whole milk to equal
   3 cups. Return the pumpkin mixture to the
   saucepan and bring to a simmer over medium
   heat. Let cool.

5. Whisk together the eggs, yolks, and sugar in
   a medium bowl. Add the pumpkin cream a
   little at a time, whisking continually. Ladle the
   mixture into the prepared ramekins. Place
   the ramekins in a small roasting pan and add
   enough water to the roasting pan to come
   halfway up the sides of the ramekins.

6. Bake until the custards are set but still wiggly
   in the center, 35 to 40 minutes. Remove the
   ramekins from the roasting pan and refrigerate
   overnight before serving.

Newhall Farm

Panna Cotta with Maple Aspic

SERVES 6

A rich panna cotta is topped with a light maple aspic layer and subtly flavored with Vermont White and Vermont Gold Vodka, produced by Vermont Spirits. It is truly a serendipitous union; vodkas distilled from the fermentation of milk sugar and maple sap and their natural counterparts, cream and maple syrup. To make a lighter version you may substitute milk or half-and-half for up to 1 cup of the cream.

Panna Cotta

1/2 cup whole milk

1 packet (about 2 1/2 teaspoons) unflavored gelatin

2 cups heavy cream

1/2 cup Vermont White vodka

1/2 cup granulated sugar

2 teaspoons vanilla extract

Maple Aspic

1/4 cup water

1 teaspoon unflavored gelatin

1/2 cup pure Vermont maple syrup

1/4 cup Vermont Gold vodka

1. To make the panna cotta: Combine the milk and gelatin in a small bowl. Let sit for 10 minutes.

2. Meanwhile, heat the cream, vodka, and sugar in a large saucepan over medium heat until the mixture almost comes to a boil, stirring until the sugar is dissolved. Add the gelatin mixture and vanilla and gently whisk over low heat until the gelatin is dissolved.

3. Strain the mixture into a heatproof container with a spout and fill six martini glasses about two-thirds full. Transfer to the refrigerator.

4. To make the maple aspic: When the panna cotta has begun to set (after about 30 minutes), combine the water and gelatin in a small bowl. Let sit for 10 minutes.

5. Meanwhile, warm the maple syrup and vodka in a small saucepan over low heat until simmering. Add the gelatin mix and gently whisk until the gelatin has dissolved. Let the mixture cool slightly, then strain it into a container with a spout and let cool completely.

6. Make sure the panna cotta has set enough (jiggle it slightly; it should be firm), then slowly pour the cooled maple mixture over it. Refrigerate for several hours or overnight before serving.

Vanna Guldenschuh for Vermont Spirits

Spiced Cider Semifreddo

SERVES 6

The semifreddo has a texture similar to a frozen mousse, with the rich flavors of fall. It tastes great with Buttermilk Doughnuts (page 32), Autumn Spice Crème Anglaise (page 183), and a drizzle of Apple Cider Caramel Sauce (page 185). Vanilla bean paste is available at specialty food stores or online at www.kingarthurflour.com.

3 large yolks

2 large eggs, separated

10 tablespoons granulated sugar

1 1/2 teaspoons vanilla bean paste

1 cup Vermont apple cider

1 teaspoon ground cinnamon

1/4 teaspoon grated nutmeg

1/4 teaspoon ground allspice

1/4 teaspoon ground cloves

1/2 cup heavy cream, plus extra for whipping

1. Using an electric mixer, beat the egg yolks, 1/4 cup of the sugar, and the vanilla bean paste, scraping down the sides and bottom of the bowl, until the yolks are pale yellow and have tripled in volume, about 12 minutes.

2. Meanwhile, fill a large bowl with ice water and set aside.

3. In a small saucepan, bring the apple cider to a simmer and cook until reduced to 1/2 cup. Let cool completely.

4. Combine the cinnamon, nutmeg, allspice, and cloves in a small bowl. Stir the spices and 6 tablespoons of the reduced cider into the egg yolk mixture. Transfer the egg yolk mixture to a bowl and place in the prepared ice bath.

5. Whip the heavy cream with 3 tablespoons sugar until stiff peaks form. Fold into the yolk mixture.

6. In a separate bowl, whip the reserved egg whites until frothy. While whipping, gradually add the remaining 3 tablespoons sugar until stiff peaks form. Fold the egg whites into the egg yolk mixture.

7. Divide the mixture equally into six 1-cup ramekins, filling each about two-thirds full. Cover with plastic wrap and freeze for at least 6 hours or overnight. Whip extra cream, top each ramekin with a dollop of whipped cream, and serve.

The Reluctant Panther Inn and Restaurant

DARBY FARM

Darby Farm, in Alburgh, is a diversified, certified organic family-run operation, which produces strawberries, vegetables, honey, and grains. The farm has been in the Darby family for over 200 years. Heather Darby, a member of the seventh generation of this Vermont farming family, operates the farm with her husband, Ron Hermann. They offer CSA shares in the summertime, along with a farm stand, which is open from May to October.

In 2007, Darby started an apiary on the farm. Her goal was to carry on the legacy of her great grandfather, Aubrey Darby, who was once a prominent beekeeper in Vermont. Today, she has 15 hives, which offer her a great deal of pleasure and relaxation, as well as sweet rewards.

Honey Ice Cream with Fresh Strawberries

SERVES 6

You can adjust the intensity of the honey flavor by modifying the amount used. The sliced strawberries provide a bright counterpoint to the honey's sweetness, but you can omit them, allowing the velvety smooth ice cream to stand on its own.

1 cup whole milk
4 large egg yolks
1/2–3/4 cup Vermont honey
3 cups heavy cream
2 cups sliced strawberries

1. Heat the milk in a medium saucepan over medium-low heat until it just starts to simmer.

2. While the milk is heating, whisk the egg yolks in a medium bowl. Gradually add the hot milk to the egg yolks and whisk to combine. Gently stir in the honey.

3. Return the mixture to the saucepan and cook over medium-low heat, stirring constantly, until the mixture thickens and coats a wooden spoon.

4. Add the heavy cream and stir to combine. Strain the mixture through a fine-mesh strainer into a clean container. Cover with plastic wrap, pressing the plastic directly onto the surface of the mixture, and refrigerate overnight.

5. Pour the ice cream mixture into an ice cream maker and freeze according to the manufacturer's directions. Scoop the ice cream into bowls and top each serving with 1/3 cup sliced strawberries.

Darby Farm

Vermont Maple Ice Cream

SERVES 6 TO 8

This rich and creamy ice cream has a beautiful, delicate maple flavor.

4 cups half-and-half
10 large egg yolks
6 tablespoons granulated sugar
1 1/2 cups grade B Vermont maple syrup
1 cup heavy cream

1. Heat the half-and-half in a medium saucepan over low heat until it just starts to simmer.

2. While the half-and-half is heating, whisk together the egg yolks and sugar in a medium bowl until slightly thickened and pale yellow in color. Gradually add the hot half-and-half to the egg yolk mixture and whisk to combine. Gently stir in the maple syrup.

3. Return the mixture to the saucepan and cook over medium-low heat, stirring constantly, until the mixture thickens and coats a wooden spoon. Do not bring mixture to a boil.

4. Add the heavy cream and stir to combine. Strain the mixture through a fine-mesh strainer into a clean container. Cover with plastic wrap, pressing it directly onto the surface of the mixture, and refrigerate overnight.

5. Pour the ice cream mixture into an ice cream maker and freeze according to the manufacturer's directions. Serve.

Jim Gioia and the Warren Store

Maple Crème Brûlée

SERVES 4

The flavor of pure Vermont maple syrup is highlighted in this silky, creamy custard.

2 cups heavy cream
1/2 teaspoon vanilla extract
3 large eggs plus 1 medium egg, lightly beaten
1/4 cup pure Vermont maple syrup, preferably Grade B
2 tablespoons raw cane or turbinado sugar

1. Preheat the oven to 325 degrees.

2. Bring the heavy cream and vanilla to a simmer in a medium saucepan over medium-high heat. Let cool to lukewarm.

3. In a medium bowl, whisk together the eggs and maple syrup. Add the warm cream a little at a time, whisking continually. Ladle into four 8-ounce broiler-safe ramekins. Place the ramekins in a small roasting pan and add enough water to the roasting pan to come halfway up the sides of the ramekins. Bake until the custard is set but still wiggling in the center, about 40 minutes. Remove the ramekins from the roasting pan and refrigerate for at least 2 hours or up to 3 days.

4. Adjust an oven rack to the top position and heat the broiler. Place the ramekins on a baking sheet and sprinkle the custards with the sugar. Broil until the sugar caramelizes. Serve immediately.

Osborne Family Maple

DIRECTORY

Vermont Farm Table Cookbook Directory

A

Amee Farm
4268 Route 100 Pittsfield, VT 05762
E-mail: leeann@riversidefarmvermont.com
Telephone: 802-746-8934
Fax: 802-746-9093
Web site: www.ameefarmstand.com and
www.ameefarm.com
Amee Farm Lemon Lavender Dressing

American Flatbread
Lareau Farm
46 Lareau Road
Waitsfield, VT 05673
E-mail: George@americanflatbread.com
Telephone: 802-496-8856
Web site: www.americanflatbread.com
Harvest Flatbread

Arcana Gardens & Greenhouses
175 Schillhammer Road
Jericho, VT 05465-3045
E-mail: farm@arcana.ws
Telephone: 802-899-5123
Web site: www.arcana.ws
Celeriac, Fennel, and Leek Chowder
Baked in Winter Squash

Ariel's Restaurant
P.O. Box 468
29 Stone Road
Brookfield, VT 05036
E-mail: arielsrestaurant@yahoo.com
Telephone: 802-276-3939
Web site: www.arielsrestaurant.com
Mediterranean Couscous Pilaf
Moroccan-Style Chicken with Apricots and Almonds
Ramp and Potato Soup with Roasted Ramp
Dumplings and Pea Shoots
Ramp Dumplings
Ricotta Gnocchi
Simple Ricotta Cheese

B

The Bakery at the Farmhouse Kitchen
"Home of the Original Almond Buttercrunch Cake"
E-mail: info@almondcakesvt.com
Telephone: 802-862-5524
Web site: www.thebakeryatthefarmhousekitchen.com
Winter Pudding with Caramelized Cranberries

Bella Farm, LLC
P.O. Box 107
Monkton, VT 05469
E-mail: bellapesto@gmail.com
Telephone: 802-373-1875
Web site: www.bellapesto.com
Sage and Cherry Tomato Polenta

The Belted Cow Bistro
4 Park Street
Essex Junction, VT 05452-3628
E-mail: beltedcowbistro@hotmail.com
Telephone: 802-316-3883
Web site: www.beltedcowvt.com
Butternut Squash Soup with Smoky Bacon and
Maple Syrup
Pasta with Veal and Pancetta Bolognese

Black Krim Tavern
21 Merchants Row
Randolph, VT 05060
E-mail: blackkrimtavern@gmail.com
Telephone: 802-728-6776
Roasted Chicken with Chilled Heirloom Tomato Purée
and Scallion Rice Cakes Topped with Crispy Kale
Turnip Greens and Red Leaf Lettuce with Roasted
Onions, Toasted Corn Kernels, and Basil Vinaigrette

Bluebird Tavern
86 St. Paul Street
Burlington, VT 05401
E-mail: eat@bluebirdvermont.com
Telephone: 802-540-1786
Web site: www.bluebirdtavern.com
Banana and Marcona Almond Smoothies
Mussels with Brown Beans and Hard Cola

Blue Ledge Farm
2001 Old Jerusalem Road
Leicester, VT 05769
E-mail: blueledge@hotmail.com
Telephone: 802-247-0095

Web site: www.blueledgefarm.com
Pasta with Goat Cheese and Roasted Tomatoes

Boyden Valley Winery
64 Vermont Route 104
Cambridge, VT 05444
E-mail: info@boydenvalley.com
Telephone: 802-644-8151
Fax: 802-644-8212
Web site: www.boydenvalley.com
Pork Tenderloin with Cassis and Soy Sauce Reduction

Burlington Country Club
568 South Prospect Street
Burlington, VT 05401
Telephone: 802-864-4683 X 113
E-mail: David.Merrill@BurlingtonCountryClub.org
Fax: 802-860-0457
Web site: www.burlingtoncountryclub.org
Coq au Vin

Burlington Farmers' Market
P.O. Box 1333
Burlington, VT 05402
E-mail: info@burlingtonfarmersmarket.org
Telephone: 802-310-5172
Web site: www.burlingtonfarmersmarket.org
Pickled Cucumber and Sweet Onion Salad
Zucchini Spread

Butterfly Bakery of Vermont
87 Barre Street
Montpelier, VT 05602
E-mail: claire@butterflybakeryvt.com
Telephone: 802-310-1725
Web site: www.butterflybakeryvt.com
Maple Roast Pumpkin Pie

Butterworks Farm
421 Trumpass Road
Westfield, VT 05874
E-mail: jack@butterworksfarm.com
Telephone: 802-744-6855
Web site: www.butterworksfarm.com
Maple Cornbread

C
Capital City Farmers Market
P.O. Box 515
Montpelier, VT 05601

E-mail: manager@montpelierfarmersmarket.com
Telephone: 802-223-2958
Web site: www.montpelierfarmersmarket.com
Maple Roast Pumpkin Pie
Creamy Camembert Cheese and Potato Soup with
Black Pepper Croutons
Lemon Ginger Roast Chicken with Brown Rice Soup

Carpenter & Main Restaurant
326 Main Street
P.O. Box 1623
Norwich, VT 05055
E-mail: brucemacleod1961@yahoo.com
Telephone: 802-649-2922
Web site: www.carpenterandmain.com
Tarentaise Bread Pudding

Cedar Circle Farm & Education Center
225 Pavillion Road
East Thetford, VT 05043
E-mail: Alison@cedarcirclefarm.org
Telephone: 802-785-4737
Web site: www.cedarcirclefarm.org
Butternut Apple Crisp
Tomato Coconut Soup
Wheat Berry Salad with Fresh Herbs

City Market, Onion River Cooperative
82 South Winooski Avenue
Burlington, VT 05401
E-mail: info@citymarket.coop
Telephone: 802-861-9700
Web site: www.citymarket.coop
Massaged Kale Salad with Asian Peanut Dressing
Vegan Chili

Clear Brook Farm
Route 7 A and Hidden Valley Road
Shaftsbury, VT 05262
E-mail: Andrew@clearbrookfarm.com
Telephone: 802-442-4273
Web site: www.clearbrookfarm.com
Arugula, Fig, and Goat Cheese Salad with Orange
Vinaigrette

Cleary Family Farm
137 Gray Road
Plainfield, VT 05667
E-mail: info@clearyfamilyfarm.com
Telephone: 802-454-8614

Web site: www.clearyfamilyfarm.com
Dutch Baby

Cloudland Farm
1101 Cloudland Road
Woodstock, VT 05091
E-mail: vtangus@sover.net
Telephone: 802-457-2599
Web site: www.cloudlandfarm.com
Chicken Breast Stuffed with Chevre and Sautéed
Ramps Served with Pickled Ramps and a Rhubarb
Gastrique

Conant's Riverside Farm
2258 West Main Street
Richmond, VT 05477
E-mail: riverside@gmavt.net
Telephone: 802-434-2588
Web site: www.conantsweetcorn.com
Fresh Corn Quiche
Caribbean Cornbread

Pamela Cohan
213 Hidden Pasture Road
Hinesburg, VT 05461
E-mails: pcohan@gmail.com; tiger0413@aol.com
Telephone: 802-482-7717 or 201-280-7069
Maple Cornbread
Caesar Salad Dressing

Consider Bardwell Farm
1333 Vermont 153
West Pawlet, VT 05775
E-mail: angela@considerbardwellfarm.net
Telephone: 802-645-0932
Web site: www.considerbardwellfarm.com
No-Bake Vanilla Bean Cheesecake
Pawletti

Courtney Contos
14 Grandview Avenue
Essex Junction, VT 05452
E-mail: thegoldencarrot@yahoo.com
Telephone: 802-318-7328
Web site: www.chefcontos.com
Braised Red Cabbage

D
Dana Forest Farm
P.O. Box 991

Waitsfield, VT 05673
E-mail: danaforestfarm@gmail.com
Telephone: 802-595-0522
Web site: www.facebook.com/danaforestfarm
Shiitake Bits

Daily Chocolate
7 Green Street
Vergennes, VT 05491-1363
E-mail: dailychocolatevt@yahoo.com
Telephone: 802-877-0087
Web site: www.dailychocolate.net
Daily Chocolate's Hot Cocoa

Darby Farm
54 North Main Street
Alburgh, VT 05440
E-mail: darbyfarm@faripoint.net
Telephone: 802-796-3105
Web site: www.darbyfarm.com
Honey Ice Cream Topped with Fresh Strawberries

Dunc's Mill
P.O. Box 150
Passumpsic, VT 05861
E-mail: duncsmill@gmail.com
Telephone: 802-745-9486
Web site: www.duncsmill.com
Dunc's Backwoods Rum Cake

E
Earth Sky Time Community Farm
1547 Main Street
Manchester Center, VT 05255
E-mail: earthskytime@gmail.com
Telephone: 802-384-1400
Web site: www.earthskytime.com
Red Cabbage and Carrot Slaw with Cilantro
Vinaigrette

Eden Ice Cider Company
P.O Box 71/1023 Sanderson Hill Road
West Charleston, VT 05872
E-mail: contact@edenicecider.com
Telephone: 802-895-2838
Web site: www.edenicecider.com
Pan Roasted Berkshire Pork Chops with Vermont
Ice Cider

Essex Vermont Culinary Resort
70 Essex Way
Essex Junction, VT 05452
E-mail: shawnc@vtculinaryresort.com
Telephone: 802-324-7013
Web site: www.vtculinaryresort.com
Turkey Waldorf Salad

F

Farmer Sue
343 Lawyer Road
East Fairfield, VT 05448
E-mail: farmersue@myfairpoint.net
Telephone: 802-827-3815
Pickled Cucumber and Sweet Onion Salad
Zucchini Spread

Fiddlehead Brewing Company
6305 Shelburne Road
Shelburne, VT 05482
E-mail: matt@fiddleheadbrewing.com
Telephone: 802-399-2994
Web site: www.fiddleheadbrewing.com
Beer Battered Fiddleheads
Orange-Basil Dipping Sauce

Five Corners Farmers' Market
Lincoln Place
Essex Junction Village, VT 05452
E-mail: www.5cornersfarmersmarket@gmail.com
Web site: www.5cornersfarmersmarket.com
Braised Red Cabbage
Rolled Stuffed Beef (Rouladen)

FlowerPower Farm
991 Middlebrook Road
Ferrisburgh, VT 05456
E-mail: flowerpowervt@comcast.net
Telephone: 802-877-3476
Web site: www.flowerpowervt.com
Farm Quiche

Food Works
64 Main Street
Montpelier, VT 05602
E-mail: joseph@foodworksvermont.org or Marcia@
foodworksvermont.org
Telephone: 802-223-1515
Fax: 802-229-5277

Web site: www.foodworksvermont.org
Winter Root Pancakes

Foote Brook Farm
641 VT Route 15 W
Johnson, VT 05656
E-mail: joie@footbrookfarm.com
Telephone: 802-635-1775
Fax: 802-635-7337
Web site: www.footebrookfarm.com
Grilled Coconut Delicata Squash
Stuffed Collard Greens

Fowl Mountain Farm & Rabbitry
P.O. Box 83
West Dummerston, VT 05357
E-mail: fowlmt@gmail.com
Telephone: 802-254-3601
Roasted Pheasant with Thyme Roasted
Sweet Potatoes and Sherry Cream

From The Ground Up, LLC
106 Rose Street
Unit #5
Burlington, VT 05401
E-mail: abby@fromthegroundupbakery.com
Telephone: 802-540-0871
Web site: www.fromthegroundupbakery.com
Whole-Grain Waffles

Full Moon Farm, Inc.
2083 Gilman Road
Hinesburg, VT 05461
E-mail: nevittrac@gmail.com
Telephone: 802-598-2036
Web site: www.fullmoonfarminc.com
Rachel's Caprese Sandwich with Heirloom Tomatoes,
Extra-Sharp Cheddar Cheese, and Basil

G

The Gleanery
P.O. Box 535
Putney, VT 05346
E-mail: itsme@ismailthechef.com
Telephone: 802-380-4651
Web site: www.thegleaney.com
Roasted Pheasant with Thyme Roasted Sweet
Potatoes and Sherry Cream

Graze
2 Heron Lake Lane
Westport, CT 06880
E-mail: Christy.colasurdo@grazedelivered.com
Telephone: Toll-free: 1-888-WEGRA7F
Web site: www.grazedelivered.com
Individual Holiday Beef Wellingtons

Greenfield Highland Beef, LLC
487 Gray Road
Plainfield, VT 05667
E-mail: info@greenfieldhighlandbeef.com
Telephone: 802-454-7384
Web site: www.greenfieldhighlandbeef.com
Amber Ale–Braised Highland Beef Chuck Roast

Green Mountain Garlic
780 Kneeland Flats Road
Waterbury, VT 05676
E-mail: info@greenmountaingarlic.com
Telephone: 802-882-8263
Web site: www.greenmountaingarlic.com
Winter Squash with Roasted Garlic

H

Hermit's Gold Wild Edibles
P.O Box 58
963 Rte 214
East Montpelier, VT 05651
E-mail: colin@colinmccaffrey.com
Telephone: 802-454-1007
Web site: www.colinmccaffrey.com/hermitsgold.html
Spaghetti and Porcini Mushroom Meatballs

High Ridge Meadows Farm
1800 Chelsea Mountain Road
East Randolph, VT 05041-0125
E-mail: info@highridgemeadowsfarm.com
Telephone: 802-728-9768
Web site: info@highridgemeadowsfarm.com
Musquée de Provence Pumpkin Bisque
Nana's Caraway Seed Biscuits
Panko-Encrusted Minute Steaks

J

Patsy Jamieson
Food Writer, Stylist, and Consultant
pinot@together.net
www.kitchenties.org

Jasper Hill Farm
P.O. Box 272
Greensboro, VT 05841
E-mail: mateo@juasperhillfarm.com
Telephone: 802-533-2566
Fax: 802-533-7431
Web site: www.cellarsatjasperhill.com
Caramelized Onion and Bayley Hazen Blue Galette

Jericho Settlers' Farm
22 Barber Farm Road
Jericho, VT 05465
E mail: jsfarmvt@gmail.com
Telephone: 802-899-4000
Web site: www.jerichosettlersfarm.com
Cider-Braised Pork Chops with Apples and Onions

K

Kimball Brook Farm, LLC
128 Bayview Road
North Ferrisburgh, VT 05473
E-mail: kbfvermont@gmail.com
Telephone: 802-734-6346
Web site: www.kimballbrookfarm.com
Cheryl's Organic Oatmeal and Chocolate Chip Cookies
Corn Chowder
Organic Milk Biscuits

King Arthur Flour Company
135 Route 5 South
Norwich, VT 05055
E-mail: Jeffrey.hamelman@kingarthurflour.com
Telephone: 802-526-1870
Fax: 802-649-3365
Web site: www.kingarthurflour.com
Currant Scones

Kingsbury Market Garden
284 Route 100
Warren, VT 05674
Telephone: 802-496-6815
Web site: www.kingsburymarketgarden.com
Kingsbury Slaw

Knoll Farm
700 Bragg Hill Road
Fayston, VT 05673
E-mail: helen.whybrow@gmail.com
Telephone: 802-496-5685
Web site: www.knollfarm.org

Blueberry Goat Cheese Pizza with Caramelized
Onions and Rosemary

L

L'Amante Ristorante
126 College Street
Burlington, VT 05401
E-mail: kevin@vermontwineschool.com
Telephone: 802-863-5200
Web site: www.lamante.com
Orecchiette with Caramelized Turnips, Tuscan Kale,
and Cracked Pepper
Squash Blossom Fritters with Taleggio, Truffle Oil,
and Honey

Lazy Lady Farm
973 Snyderbrook Road
Westfield, VT 05874
Telephone: 802-744-6365
E-mail: laini@lazyladyfarm.com
Telephone: 802-744-6365
Web site: www.lazyladyfarm.net
Lazy Lady Farm Three-Cheese au Gratin Potatoes

Ledgenear Farm
2342 Andersonville Road
West Glover, VT 05875
E-mail: info@ledgenearfarm.com
Telephone: 802-525-9881
Web site: www.ledgenearfarm.com
Maple Apple Pie

Longview Farm
141 Roizin Road
Bennington, VT 05201
E-mail: longviewlambs@gmail.com
Telephone: 802-442-4998
Web site: www.longviewlambs.com
Roast Grass-Fed Leg of Lamb
Leftover Roast Leg of Lamb Tacos

M

The Mad Taco
72 Main Street
Waitsfield, VT 05673
E-mail: joey@themadtaco.com
Telephone: 802-839-9658
Web site: www.themadtaco.com
Habanero Carrot Hot Sauce

Manchester Farmers' Market
P.O. Box 982
Manchester Center, VT 05255
E-mail: mfmvt@yahoo.com
Telephone: 802-353-3539
Web site: www.manchestermarket.org
Patriotic Potato Salad
Simple Mayonnaise

Maplebrook Farm
453 East Road
Bennington, VT 05201
E-mail: johann@mountainmozzarella.com
Telephone: 802-440-9950
Fax: 802-440-9956
Web site: www.maplebrookvt.com
Polenta Bites Stuffed with Smoked Mozzarella

Peter McLyman
717 Levesque Drive
Hyde Pak, VT 05655
E-mail: peter@countryclubvt.com
Telephone: 802-888-6123
Grilled Shrimp with Smugglers' Notch Vodka and
Mango Cocktail Sauce
New York Strip Steaks with WhistlePig Whiskey
Demi-glace Sauce
Penne with Creamy Smugglers' Notch Vodka Sauce
WhistlePig Whiskey and Molasses–Marinated
Salmon Filet

Misery Loves Co.
64 Hickok Street
Winooski, VT 05404
E-mail: aaron@miserylovescovt.com
Telephone: 802-825-1910
Web site: www.miserylovescovt.com
Nettle Soup with Brioche Croutons
Korean Reuben

Misty Knoll Farm
1685 Main Street
New Haven, VT 05472
E-mail: mistyknollfarm@gmavt.net
Telephone: 802-453-4748
Fax: 802-453-5193
Web site: www.mistyknollfarms.com
Coq au Vin

Mt. Mansfield Creamery
730 Bliss Hill Road
Morrisville, VT 05661
E-mail: cheese@mtmansfieldcreamery@gmail.com
Telephone: 802-888-7686
Web site: www.mtmansfieldcreamery.com
Creamy Camembert Cheese and Potato Soup
with Black Pepper Croutons

N

Newhall Farm
P.O. Box 128
Redding, VT 05062
E-mail: tedcnewhallfarmvt.com
Telephone: 802-342-1513
Web site: www.facebook.com/newhallfarm
Newhall Farm Berkshire Pork Loin with Poached
Apples
Newhall Farm Pumpkin Custard

New Leaf Organics
45 Mountain Terrace
Bristol, VT 05443
E-mail: newleaf@gmavt.net
Telephone: 802-453-4300
Web site: www.newleaforganics.org
Spring Frittata
Fresh "Springy" Spring Rolls

O

The Original General Store
3963 Route 100
Pittsfield, VT 05762
E-mail: leeann@riversidefarmvermont.com
Telephone: 802-746-8934
Fax: 802-746-9093
Web site: www.originalgeneralstore.com
Original General Store Blue Cheese Dressing

Osborne Family Maple
23 Westphal Road
Lake Elmore, VT 05657
jon@osbornemaple.com
Telephone: 802-888-9468
Website: www.osbornemaple.com
Maple Bars
Maple Crème Brûlée

P

Pebble Brook Farm
24 Cram Hill Road
West Brookfield, VT 05060
Telephone: 802-595-0656
Roasted Chicken withChilled Heirloom Tomato Purée,
and Scallion Rice Cakes Topped with Crispy Kale
Turnip Greens and Red Leaf Lettuce with Roasted
Onions, Toasted Corn Kernels and Basil Vinaigrette

Pistou Restaurant
61 Main Street
Burlington, VT 05401
Telephone: 802-540-1783
E-mail: maxmack13@gmail.com
Telephone: 802-540-1783
Web site: www.pistou-vt.com
Butter Poached Halibut with Forbidden Black Rice,
Beet Dashi, and Fennel Salad
Seared Day Boat Scallops, Braised Endive, Confit
Potato, and Shaved Prosciutto with Orange
Beurre Blanc

The Pitcher Inn
275 Main Street
Warren, VT 05674
Telephone: 802-496-6350
Web site: www.pitcherinn.com
Hush Puppies
Spicy Mayo
Turnip-Potato Gratin

Pitchfork Farm
26 Rose Street
Burlington, VT 05401
E-mail: pitchforkfarmvt@gmail.com
Telephone: 802-233-6445
Web site: www.pitchforkfarmvt.com
Chicken Paprika
Hungarian Nokedli (Dumplings)

Pomykala Farm
197 East Shore Road N
Grand Isle, VT 05458
E-mail: pomykala@surfglobal.net
Telephone: 802-372-5157
Web site: www.pomykalafarm.com
Asparagus and Brown Rice
Chocolate Zucchini Cake

Poorhouse Pies
23 Park Street
Underhill, VT 05489
Telephone: 802-899-1346
Web site: www.poorhousepies.com
Raisin Hell Pie
Maple Pecan Pie

R
Red Clover Inn
54 Red Clover Lane
Killington, VT 05701
E-mail: jeff@tylerplace.com
Telephone: 802-868-4000
Fax: 802-868-5621
Web site: www.redcloverinn.com
Back Home–Style Portuguese Steamed Middleneck
Clams

The Reluctant Panther Inn and Restaurant
P.O. Box 678 West Road
Manchester Village, VT 05254
E-mail: jcox@reluctantpanther.com
Telephone: 802-362-2568
Web site: www.reluctantpanther.com
Autumn Spice Crème Anglaise
Buttermilk Doughnuts
Pork Two Ways
Spiced Cider Semifreddo
Apple Cider Caramel Sauce

River Berry Farm
191 Goose Pond Road
Fairfax, VT 05454
E-mail: riverberryfarm@comcast.net
Telephone: 802-849-6853
Web site: www.riverberryfarm.com
Berry Good Smoothies

S
Saxton's River Distillery
940 Saxtons River Road
Saxtons River, VT 05154
E-mail: sapling@saplingliqueur.com
Telephone: 802-246-1128
Web site: www.saplingliqueur.com
Sapling Tiramisu

Scott Farm
2463 Sunset Lake Road
Dummerston, VT 05301
E-mail: ckelly@sover.net
Telephone: 802-251-0947
Website: www.scottfarmvermont.com
Country Apple Cake
Applesauce Cake

Screamin' Ridge Farm, Inc.
170 Dillon Road
Montpelier, VT 05602
E-mail: jbuleyjr@comcast.net
Telephone: 802-461-5371
Web site: www.screaminridgefarm.com
Lemon Ginger Roast Chicken with Brown Rice Soup

Silver Fork Restaurant
P.O. Box 1122
Manchester Center, VT 05255
E-mail: thesilverfork@yahoo.com
Telephone: 802-768-8444
Web site: www.thesilveforkvt.com
Bread Pudding Soufflés with Coconut Vanilla
Crème Anglaise

Simon Pearce Restaurant
The Mill
1760 Quechee Main Street
Quechee, VT 05059
Telephone: 802-295-2711
Web site: www.simonpearce.com
Rory's Irish Scones
Vermont Cheddar Soup
Warm Apple Crisp with Hazelnut Crumble

Smugglers' Notch Distillery
P.O. Box 69
Jeffersonville, VT 05464
E-mail: Jeremy@smugglersnotchdistillery.com
Telephone: 802-309-3077
Web site: www.smugglersnotchdistillery.com
Grilled Shrimp with Smugglers' Notch Vodka
and Mango Cocktail Sauce
Penne with Creamy Smugglers' Notch Vodka Sauce

Snug Valley Farm
824 Pumpkin Lane
East Hardwick, VT 05836
E-mail: info@snugvalleyfarm.com

Telephone: 802-472-6185
Web site: www.snugvalleyfarm.com
Rolled Stuffed Beef (Rouladen)

Stonewood Farm
105 Griswold Lane
Orwell, VT 05760
E-mail: stone@stonewoodfarm.com
Telephone: 802-948-2277
Web site: www.stonewoodfarm.com
Cranberry and Turkey Sausage Stuffing

Sterling College
P.O. Box 72
Craftsbury Common, VT 05827
E-mail: aobelnicki@sterlingcollege.edu
Telephone: 802-586-7711
Web site: www.sterlingcollege.edu
Green Chicken
Late Summer Quinoa Salad
Roasted Beet Salad with Cilantro and Lime

Stowe Mountain Lodge
7412 Mountain Road
Stowe, VT 05672
E-mail: jberry@destinationhotels.com
Telephone: 802-760-4745
Web site: www.stowemountainlodge.com
Pecan and Caramel French Toast
Pork Tenderloin Medallions Stuffed with Dried
Fruit and Cheddar Cheese, Cranberry Braised Red
Cabbage, and Vanilla Whipped Sweet Potatoes

Sugarbush Resort/Timbers Restaurant
1840 Sugarbush Access Road
Warren, VT 05674
E-mail: gnooney@sugarbush.com
Telephone: 802-583-6311
Web site: www.sugarbush.com
Ski Vermont Farmhouse Potato Chowder

Sunshine Valley Berry Farm
129 Ranger Road
Rochester, VT 05767
E-mail: patricia@vermontberries.com
Telephone: 802-767-9385 (home/office) or 802-
767-3989 (farm)
Web site: www.vermontberries.com
Blackberry-Blueberry Jam
Sunshine Smoothies

Square Deal Farm
362 Woodward Road
Walden, VT 05843-7034
E-mail: mail@squaredealfarm.org
Telephone: 802-563-2441
Web site: www.squaredealfarm.org
Maple-Glazed Sweet Potatoes

T

Thistle Hill Farm
107 Clifford Road
North Pomfret, VT 05053
E-mail: info@thistlehillfarm.com
Telephone: 802-457-9349
Web site: www.thistlehillfarm.com
Alpen Macaroni

Bob Titterton
2367 Elmore Mountain Road
Morisville, VT 05661
E-mail: bob@how-to-food.com
Telephone: 802-888-5123
Web site: www.how-to-food.com
Polenta Bites Stuffed with Smoked Mozzarella

Twin Farms
P.O. Box 115
Barnard, VT 05031
Telephone: 802-234-9999; Toll Free: 800-894-
6327
Web site: www.twinfarms.com
Slow-Cooked Veal Shoulder with Savoy Cabbage
and Wild Rice
Twin Farms Red Polenta with Wildcrafted Oyster
Mushrooms Broth

Two Black Sheep Farm
142 Ferry Road
South Hero, VT 05486
E-mail: hello@twoblacksheepcsa.com
Telephone: 612-309-0896
Web site: www.twoblacksheepcsa.com
Zucchini Bread

The Tyler Place Family Resort
P.O. Box 254
Highgate Springs, VT 05460
E-mail: jeff@tylerplace.com
Telephone: 802-868-4000

Fax: 802-868-5621
Web site: www.tylerplace.com
Crème Brûlée French Toast
Tyler Place Maple Balsamic Vinaigrette

V

Valley Dream Farm, LLC
5901 Pleasant Valley Road
Cambridge, VT 05444
E-mail: valleydream@wildblue.net
Telephone: 802-644-6598
Web site: www.valleydreamfarm.com
Roasted Roots

Vermont Cranberry Company
2563 North Road
East Fairfield, VT 05448
E-mail: bob@vermontcranberry.com
Telephone: 802-849-6358
Web site: www.vermontcranberry.com
Vermont Cranberry Sauce

Vermont Peanut Butter Company, Inc.
125 Munson Avenue
Morrisville, VT 05661
E-mail: chris@vtpeanutbutter.com
Telephone: 802-244-5955
Fax: 802-735-1023
Web site: www.vtpeanutbutter.com
Chewy Peanut Butter Bars

Vermont Salumi
142 Cate Farm Road
Plainfield, VT 05667
E-mail: pete@vermontsalumi.com
Telephone: 802-454-8360
Web site: www.vermontsalumi.com
Lentils with Vermont Salumi's Daily Grind Sausage

Vermont Spirits
P.O. Box 443
Quechee, VT 05059
E-mail: steve@vermontspirits.com
Telephone: 802-295-7555
Fax: 203-621-3159
Web site: www.vermontspirits.com
Luxury Experience's Apple Pie with Tipsy Raisins
Vermont Spirited Apple Ice Cream
Panna Cotta with Maple Aspic
Maple Sauce

W

Warren Store
284 Main Street
Warren, VT 05674
E-mail: jack@warrenstore.com
Telephone: 802-496-3864
Web site: www.warrenstore.com
Harvest Hash
Vermont Maple Ice Cream

West Mountain Inn
144 West Mountain Inn Road
Arlington, VT 05250
E-mail: skinnychef67@yahoo.com
Telephone: 802-375-6516
Fax: 802-375-6545
Web site: www.westmountaininn.com
Bayley Hazen Blue Cheesecake with
Hazelnut Crust and Poached Pears
Pan-Seared Salmon with Crabmeat and
Sweet Potato Hash and Tomato Coulis
Sautéed Sea Scallops in a Smoked Bacon
and Maple Cream Sauce
Warm Chicken, Tomato, and Mozzarella Napoleon
with Basil Oil and Balsamic Glaze

WhistlePig Whiskey
WhistlePig Farm
1030 Palmer Road
Shoreham, VT 05770
E-mail: rpb@goamericago.com
Telephone: 802-897-7700
Fax: 802-897-5516
Web site: www.whistlepigwhiskey.com
New York Strip Steaks with WhistlePig Whiskey
Demi-glace Sauce
WhistlePig Whiskey and Molasses–Marinated
Salmon Filet

Wildflower Inn and Juniper's Restaurant
2059 Darling Hill Road
Lyndonville, VT 05851
E-mail: jim@wildflowerinn.com
Telephone: 802-626-8310
Fax: 802-626-3039
Web site: www.wildflowerinn.com
Apple Stuffed Chicken Breasts
Lazy Lady Farm Three-Cheese au Gratin Potatoes

Woodstock Farmers' Market
979 West Woodstock Road
Woodstock, VT 05091
E-mail: patrick@woodstockfarmersmarket.com
Telephone: 802-457 3658 ext. 228
Fax: 802-457-1981
Web site: www.woodstockfarmersmarket.com
Bow Thai Pasta Salad

Y

Your Farm
2340 Route 5 North
Fairlee, VT 05045
E-mail: info@yourfarmonline.com
Telephone: 802-291-2282
Web site: www.yourfarmonline.com
Summer Stuffed Heirloom Tomatoes

Recipes and Ingredients

Note: Page numbers in *italics* refer to recipe photographs.

People and Places

Note: Page numbers in **bold** refer to first page of contributed recipes.